Courtney Johnson is a career content creator, personal brand educator, entrepreneur, and creator of the viral Problematic Career Cheat Codes series. Her unfiltered, "no-BS" advice has garnered a loyal following of half a million career-focused individuals across social media platforms. With a background in navigating the complexities of corporate culture and building a personal brand that stands out in an over-crowded market, Johnson knows firsthand the limitations of traditional career advice. Johnson has alchemized her wealth of real-world corporate experience into her personal mission: to teach others how to thrive by un-gatekeeping traditionally gatekept advice.

Career Cheat Codes
Courtney Johnson

PIATKUS

PIATKUS

First published in the United States of America in 2026 by Ten Speed Press,
an imprint of the Crown Publishing Group, a division of Penguin Random House LLC

First published in Great Britain in 2026 by Piatkus

1 3 5 7 9 10 8 6 4 2

Copyright © Courtney Johnson, 2026

The moral right of the author has been asserted.

All rights reserved.
Penguin Random House values and supports copyright. Copyright fuels creativity, encourages diverse voices, promotes free speech, and creates a vibrant culture. Thank you for buying an authorized edition of this book and for complying with copyright laws by not reproducing, scanning, or distributing any part of it in any form without permission. You are supporting writers and allowing Penguin Random House to continue to publish books for every reader. Please note that no part of this book may be used or reproduced in any manner for the purpose of training artificial intelligence technologies or systems.

A CIP catalogue record for this book
is available from the British Library.

ISBN: 978-0-34944-765-0

Compositor: North Market Street Graphics

Printed and bound in Great Britain by Clays Ltd, Elcograf S.p.A.

Papers used by Piatkus are from well-managed forests and other responsible sources.

Piatkus
An imprint of
Little, Brown Book Group
Carmelite House
50 Victoria Embankment
London EC4Y 0DZ

The authorised representative
in the EEA is
Hachette Ireland
8 Castlecourt Centre, Dublin 15,
D15 XTP3, Ireland
(email: info@hbgi.ie)

An Hachette UK Company
www.hachette.co.uk

www.littlebrown.co.uk

To the little girl who wanted to be an author.

Look—we made it!

Contents

Introduction
Welcome to Career Cheat Codes ... ix
    How to Use This Book ... x
    F*ck the Gatekeepers ... xi
    A Note on Bias, Privilege, and the Limits of My Experience ... xiii
    Play the Game to Win the Game to Change the Game ... xiv

Part 1
Getting the Role ... 1
  1. The Résumé Refresh ... 5
  2. Impostor Syndrome? We Don't Know Her ... 20
  3. Mastering Job Apps ... 36
  4. Acing the Interview ... 49
  5. Get Your Bag: How to Get Paid What You're Actually Worth ... 66

Part 2
Office Politics ... 79
  6. IRL Survival Guide ... 81
  7. WFH Survival Guide ... 90
  8. Playing the Social Game ... 98
  9. Winning Over Your Boss ... 112

Part 3
## Personal Brand	127

10. Working LOUDLY!	129
11. Mastering Your Digital Identity	143
12. Becoming a Thought Leader	161

Part 4
## Staying Sane	179

13. Working Your Calendar	181
14. Time Management and Boundaries	188
15. Your Mental Health Matters	199
16. When Work Gets Messy: Toxic Work Environments	208

Part 5
## Leveling Up	225

17. Promotions: Climbing the Career Ladder	227
18. Delegate Like a Pro	250
19. Skills That Pay the Bills	255
20. Sneaky Networking	269

Part 6
## The Ultimate, Game-Winning Cheat Code	277

Conclusion: An Invitation to Break the Rules	289
Acknowledgments	295
Notes	297

Introduction

Welcome to Career Cheat Codes

Here's a stat that will ruin your day: The average person spends 90,000 hours of their life at work. That's 37 percent of your entire adult existence. And here's the kicker—research shows that 70 percent of people actively hate their jobs, while companies waste billions annually on "career development" programs that statistically change nothing about your actual career trajectory.[1,2]

You're here because you've finally caught on to the corporate lie: "Put your head down, work hard, and everything will work out for you."

Right?

WRONG. Put your head down, work hard—and you're destined for a career that's mediocre at best.

The problem is, this advice comes from an idealistic perspective. If you want to make an impact, you must approach your career strategy from a realistic perspective—and that's uncomfortable AF.

I get it, you're not looking for another "lean in" pep talk or "networking tips" listicle. You want the real playbook that the people at the top don't want you to have. This book isn't for people who are happy with 3 percent annual raises and pizza party rewards. This is for the ones who are done playing small; those who are ready to play to win.

When I walked into the corporate world, I didn't have the same playbook that everyone else seemed to be holding. I didn't have the family connections, the fancy degrees, or the perfect résumé. I was figuring things out as I went along—like trying to solve a puzzle while everyone else already had the picture on the box.

I quickly realized the traditional path was a trap designed to keep me small. It wasn't going to get me the life I wanted or the career I was meant to have. So I burned the rulebook and wrote my own. I turned a viral Problematic Career Cheat Codes TikTok series into a full-blown rebellion that's awakened millions of people from their corporate comas. I went from being a *nobody* to having Google beg me to speak to their teams; to commanding five-figure brand deals, six-figure salaries, and a seven-figure business; and now to writing the manual they don't want you to read—the real cheat codes that expose how the game actually works.

I'm here because the real game is invisible to everyone except the people who are winning it. So I'm making it visible. And I'm not some salesman selling you pretty lies from an ivory tower. Every strategy in this book has battle scars on it. Every piece of advice comes with receipts.

You already know the system is rigged. The question is, are you going to keep playing their losing game, or are you ready to flip the table and play by rules that actually work?

How to Use This Book

I invite you to read straight through or navigate to a chapter that resonates with your current situation.

This book is an invitation, not a prescription. There may be times when you think *That doesn't work for me* or *That's a bit too problematic*. Well, duh—that's OKAY. Take what resonates, leave what doesn't. No one's keeping score here. Each cheat code hits different depending on your industry and culture, so just implement what feels right for you.

And let's get something straight: This isn't another "hustle harder" manifesto trying to squeeze more hours out of your already burned-out soul. The system is rigged, period. You're already doing the work, so why not be strategic about it? Some of these tactics might look like pointless corporate theater, but they're actually your secret weapons in a game where nobody gave you the rulebook.

Think of me as your career big sis who's seen some shit and lived to tell about it. I'm not here to hold your hand or tell you everything's going to be fine. I'm here to give you the unfiltered truth that might make you roll your eyes but will absolutely put you in control of your career in the long run. Not because I'm trying to be a know-it-all, but because I genuinely want you to win at a game that wasn't designed for you to succeed.

F*ck the Gatekeepers

Pretty quickly in my career, I noticed two groups of my peers: the A Players, who knew how to play the corporate game, and the B Players, who didn't.

The A Players mostly came from privileged families who understood the unspoken rules of the workplace, who passed down that information to their kids, giving them a leg up. These were the kids whose parents had corner offices, who grew up hearing dinner-table conversations about strategic positioning, office politics, and how to leverage relationships. They learned from childhood that work wasn't just about doing the job—it was about being *seen* doing the job, by the right people, at the right time.

Their parents taught them that confidence was a skill, not a personality trait. That asking for what you want wasn't rude—it was essential. That networking wasn't sleazy—it was survival. That your personal brand mattered more than your work quality. That promotions weren't earned through merit alone—they were negotiated, strategized, and sometimes even orchestrated.

The B Players came from lower- or middle-class families, where they were taught to shut up, work hard, don't ask for what you want, and don't make too much of a fuss. These were the kids whose parents clocked in, kept their heads down, and believed that good work would eventually be rewarded. They were raised on values like "don't be pushy," "wait your turn," and "let your work speak for itself."

And some B Players came from even further outside the system—first-generation Americans, or the children of janitors, nannies, or day laborers. People whose families never worked in offices, never spoke the corporate language, maybe never even spoke English at home. Folks who didn't grow up in the United States or who were raised in cultures where "respect" meant deference—not negotiation. For them, the entire concept of "office politics" is a foreign language.

They learned that asking for raises was greedy. That self-promotion was bragging. That office politics were beneath them. That if they just worked harder and longer than everyone else, someone would eventually notice and reward them accordingly. They were taught to be grateful for any opportunity and never to rock the boat.

The A Players walked into meetings like they belonged there. The B Players waited to be invited. The A Players negotiated their starting salaries. The B Players accepted whatever was offered. The A Players built strategic relationships before they needed them. The B Players only networked when they were desperate.

The cheat codes in this book aren't unique—they're actually quite common sense to the A Players, a.k.a. the information-privileged few. But they are gatekept from the general public—until now.

If you grew up with ultrasuccessful parents, these cheat codes will be painfully obvious to you. But if you grew up like me, having to learn them the hard way, these cheat codes might seem uncomfortable, crazy, or even immoral. But the more you reflect on the cheat codes, the more you'll observe the stark difference between the A Players and B Players who surround you.

The same strategies that seem "natural" to people born into privilege are treated like trade secrets when it comes to everyone else. Research shows that 53 percent of those in management roles are from a high socioeconomic background, compared to 38 percent from a low socioeconomic background. Socioeconomic background is a major factor in career progression, and employees from lower socioeconomic backgrounds take, on average, 19 percent longer to progress to the next career level compared to their counterparts from higher socioeconomic backgrounds.[3,4]

And unfortunately, the stats get even scarier. In higher managerial and professional occupations, people from privileged backgrounds earn, on average, 16 percent more than colleagues from working-class backgrounds, even when they're doing the exact same job.[5]

It's not that B Players are less capable or less intelligent—they're just trying to crack a code that everyone else inherited. This book is about claiming the cheat codes that have been passed down by generations of corporate families and putting them in your hands where they rightfully belong.

A Note on Bias, Privilege, and the Limits of My Experience

Let's get one thing straight: This book is full of cheat codes. And they work. But they won't always work equally for everyone.

I'm not here to gaslight you into thinking that we all start from the same place. I don't know what it's like to be a person of color navigating corporate America. I don't know what it's like to job hunt with a disability, to be a first-gen kid trying to explain "networking" to your parents, or to show up as your full self in an office that wasn't built with you in mind. I haven't lived that. And my goal is never to speak on behalf of people who have.

Discrimination exists—racial, gendered, ableist, class-based, and more. Bias exists. Systemic exclusion exists. You don't need me to explain that to you. And no amount of "leaning in" or "optimizing your LinkedIn" can erase that. Some of the cheat codes in this book will absolutely help you level up—even in rooms that weren't designed for you. Others might feel out of touch with your reality. That's real. My hope is to validate your experience, while also sharing some of the tools that could pave the way for a more equitable future for everyone.

This book is for ambitious people of all backgrounds who want to get ahead—but it's written from *my* lens, and because my lived experience is different than yours, some of these cheat codes might not feel totally applicable to your life. A lot of the strategies in here reflect a goal of understanding the unspoken rules of power and playing the game better than the people who built it. But if the game itself is rigged against you? That's not your fault. And I'm never going to tell you that you're imagining it.

But just because the system is rigged doesn't mean you're powerless.

The very fact that you're reading this book tells me you have big dreams for yourself, and you want to make the game work for you. You're here to outsmart the rules, disrupt the ladder, and build your own table if there aren't any seats left at the old one. These cheat codes are meant to give you language, leverage, and strategy—but you bring the magic. You bring the lived experience, the resilience, the fire.

Some of the cheat codes in this book will work like a charm. Others might need some massaging before they fit your unique reality and goals. That's not because you're doing something wrong. It's because power in this world isn't distributed fairly—and success doesn't always follow effort the way it should. This book is a toolkit—not a one-size-fits-all uniform. Suggestions, not prescriptions. Use what fits, adapt what doesn't, and trust yourself to know the difference.

I'm rooting for you. I *want* you to win. So take what serves you, remix the rest, and don't let anyone convince you that you're not cut out for it. You are.

Play the Game to Win the Game to Change the Game

"Courtney, why can't we play nice?"

First of all, trying to be "nice" is a people-pleasing load of BS. Please. #EyeRoll

You're here because you want

- more equitable organizations;
- to be treated better at work;

- to make more money and make a bigger impact;
- to follow your creative passions, rather than being weighed down by soul-sucking work;
- to make an impact and to inspire and improve the lives of people around you and of those who come after you;
- change.

But change doesn't happen on its own or just because people want it to. Change takes people with vision and skills to implement it.

- If you want to make significant changes, you must become a leader.
- If you want to make significant changes, you must make money and gain resources.
- If you want to make significant changes, you must build impact and authority.
- You can't accomplish *any* change by sitting on the sidelines.

Class mobility is possible only through information equity—and that's exactly what I'm here for. The same unspoken rules that A Players learned at their parents' dinner tables—the networking strategies, the negotiation tactics, the political maneuvering—these aren't just career tips. They're the keys to the kingdom. And when only the privileged few have access to these keys, guess who stays in charge of making all the decisions?

I intend to cut straight through the flowery corporate bullshit and give you the *real* shit. I've made it my mission to say *fuck you* to the gatekeepers and share this information with the masses. When more good-hearted people gain leadership positions, when more B Players can learn to play like A Players, that's when we can change the systems from the inside out.

You don't like the corporate game; I get it. But the ONLY way to change the game is to win the game. And the ONLY way to win the game is to get really, really, really fucking good at playing it.

Luckily, you've just been handed the cheat codes.

Part 1

Getting the Role

Okay, so you want a job. Maybe you even have an idea of which job you want. Let's make it happen.

Whether you're trying to land your first "real" job, making a career pivot, or climbing to the next level, the hiring process is basically a game rigged against the B Players. You're competing against people who went to the "right" schools, have connections you don't, or simply understand the unspoken dynamics of how hiring actually works.

The good news? Once you learn the cheat codes, you can level the playing field. The hiring process doesn't reward the most qualified person—it rewards whoever knows how to play the game. That's going to be you.

Let's get something straight before we dive in. Where are you actually at right now? Take a minute—seriously, I'll wait—and be honest with yourself. Are you frantically applying to anything with a pulse and a paycheck? Or do you have some dreamy vision board of the perfect career hung somewhere between your student loan statements and that plant you're definitely neglecting?

There's no wrong answer here. We've all been in both those places, sometimes simultaneously. Maybe you're fresh out of school with a degree that suddenly feels about as useful as a LinkedIn endorsement from your mom.

Without direction, a career can start bouncing between "I'll take literally any job" and "I have a very specific dream that I can't quite articulate but will definitely know it when I see it." Your relationship with work is complicated—it's like dating someone who has all your financial information and controls your health insurance. The stakes are high, and the power dynamic is . . . not great.

So before we get to the tactical stuff, get clear on what you're actually chasing right now. Is it just survival money? A stepping stone? The beginning of something bigger? Or are you genuinely trying to land that dream role that makes Sunday evenings feel less like a slow-motion panic attack? Your answer changes the game plan—not dramatically, but enough that it matters.

Let's address the obvious elephant in the room: Getting your dream job may feel about as achievable as navigating through a hurricane with nothing but a cocktail umbrella and sheer willpower. The whole process is like a twisted game show where you're competing against hundreds of other people, except no one told you the rules, and the prize is getting to spend forty-plus hours a week in a place that hopefully won't make you cry in the bathroom.

But here's the thing: Landing the job you want isn't actually a game of chance. It's not about hoping the hiring gods smile upon your LinkedIn profile or praying that your résumé somehow catches someone's eye in the black hole of online applications.

The job search is a game. Those people who seem to land amazing jobs without breaking a sweat? They're not luckier than you. They're not even necessarily more qualified. They just know how to play the game.

And like any game, this one has cheat codes.

In the next five chapters, we're going to crack the code together. We'll transform your résumé from "meh" to "must-hire" (chapter 1), tackle the voice in your head that keeps saying you're not qualified (chapter 2), master the art of job applications that actually get responses (chapter 3), turn interviews into job offers (chapter 4), and finally, get paid what you actually deserve (chapter 5).

GETTING THE ROLE

Forget *following* the rules—we're mastering the game well enough to bend the rules in your favor. While everyone else is playing checkers with their career, you're about to learn chess.

The best part? Once you understand these cheat codes, they work forever. These cheat codes help you take control of your ENTIRE career trajectory. Whether you're fresh out of college or a seasoned pro, these cheat codes will give you a serious advantage and take you from B Player to A Player faster than your "five-minute TikTok break" turns into two hours of scrolling.

Grab your coffee (or wine—no judgment), get comfy, and let's turn you into the kind of candidate that makes recruiters slide into your DMs. By the time you finish this section, you won't be asking *Will I get the job?* You'll be asking *Which offer should I take?*

Time to level up, bestie. Let's get to it.

1

The Résumé Refresh

Whether you're about to graduate, just finished college, or are making a career pivot without a traditional degree path, you're probably staring at a blank document, wondering how the hell to make yourself sound hirable. Maybe you've got a decent GPA but zero real-world experience. Maybe you went the community college route, did online school, or skipped college altogether and taught yourself everything through YouTube and trial by fire. Either way, you're competing against people who seem to have perfect internships and fancy connections, and your experience feels . . . thin.

Let's start with the basics: A résumé is a one- to two-page snapshot of your professional experience designed to get you an interview. In some cultures (such as the UK), a résumé and a CV (curriculum vitae) are the same thing. In other cultures (such as the US), the two are different and a CV is a more comprehensive academic document that lists every conference, publication, and research project. If you're unsure what kind of document you need, do a bit of research into the country and industry you're applying for a job in beforehand.

Your résumé is not a historical document of everything you've ever done; rather, it's a marketing brochure designed to get you the right job for you. Yet most people treat it like a boring autobiography instead of the strategic weapon it should be.

If you're getting zero bites on your applications, your résumé probably isn't selling your story effectively. You might be undervaluing your experience, using the wrong keywords, or letting internal job titles misrepresent what you've actually accomplished.

Time to stop hoping HR will read between the lines and start making your value impossible to ignore.

"My résumé just isn't getting any bites," Dev sighed, slumping in his chair during our first session together. "I've applied to like fifty AI engineering roles, and it's just . . . crickets."

When he finally showed me his résumé, I nearly spit out my cold brew. This man had been building AI apps in his spare time, creating custom ChatGPT plug-ins, and teaching his friends how to use AI tools . . . but his résumé just said "AI Enthusiast."

Enthusiast?

Sir, you're literally doing the job already—you're just calling it the wrong thing. You're out there building full-stack AI applications and calling yourself an enthusiast while companies out there are desperate for exactly these skills.

Here's what most people don't know about résumés: They're not really about listing your experience—they're about translating your experience into language that gets you hired.

Most people are sitting on years of valuable experience they're not even counting—even those of you just finishing out your college years. That summer job? Those volunteer gigs? That side project you do "just for fun"? It *all* counts if you know how to frame it.

Time to stop selling yourself short and start selling yourself smart. Let's get into these cheat codes and transform your résumé from "meh" to "must-hire."

Cheat Code #1
Frame Your Internship as Real Experience—
Because It Is

Internships are *real* job experience. You showed up. You worked. You (hopefully) got paid. If you were a "marketing intern" but took on the responsibilities of a "marketing coordinator," then that's exactly what you should put on your résumé.

Companies don't hire you based on your title; they hire you based on what you can do. So, own it. Frame your experience for what it really was, not just what it was called.

That internship where you were "just helping out"? That summer gig where you were "just learning"? That's real work experience. Full stop.

I was coaching a client, Maya, who did a three-month internship at a tech startup. When I asked about her responsibilities, she rattled off: "Oh, you know, I just managed their product launch timeline, coordinated with the dev team, wrote the release notes, and handled customer feedback . . ."

JUST??

Maya, bestie, you weren't "just" doing anything. You were a full-on product manager. But on her résumé? "Product Management Intern—Helped with product launch."

This is the biggest mistake I see with internships. You diminish your role because you were "just" an intern, when in reality you were doing the exact same work as full-time employees.

Again, companies don't hire you based on your title; they hire you based on what you can do. If you had the responsibilities, you earned the title. Period.

The Internship Translation Guide

What They Called You	What You Actually Did	What to Put on Your Résumé
"Social Media Intern"	Created content strategy, grew followers by 50%	"Social Media Strategist"

What They Called You	What You Actually Did	What to Put on Your Résumé
"Marketing Intern"	Managed email campaigns, wrote blog posts	"Digital Marketing Specialist"
"Research Intern"	Conducted market analysis, created reports	"Market Research Analyst"
"Admin Intern"	Coordinated team schedules, managed projects	"Project Coordinator"
"Software Engineering Intern"	Built features, fixed bugs, wrote documentation	"Software Engineer"
"UX Design Intern"	Created wireframes, conducted user research	"UX Designer"
"Business Analyst Intern"	Analyzed data, made recommendations, built reports	"Business Analyst"

"But Courtney, that's lying!" Look . . . you're not lying or exaggerating. You're giving yourself credit for work you *actually* did. If you showed up, did the work, and delivered results, you've earned the right to claim that experience.

How to Upgrade Your Internship Experience

Don't Write This	Instead, Write This
Product Management Intern • Helped with product launch • Assisted team with tasks • Learned about product development	Product Manager • Led cross-functional team of eight through successful product launch • Developed and maintained product timeline using Agile methodology • Created and presented weekly status reports to senior stakeholders • Gathered and analyzed customer feedback to inform product iterations

But What If I Was "Just" an Intern?

Even if you really were "just" an intern who did basic tasks, you still gained valuable experience. Here's how an A Player would frame it:

Task	A-Player Framing
Supported team operations	Streamlined team workflow by managing key administrative processes
Helped with data entry	Maintained data integrity for company's client database of 1,000+ accounts
Took meeting notes	Documented key decisions and action items for executive team meetings

The key is to focus on the impact of your work, not your title. What problems did you solve? What processes did you improve? What results did you help achieve?

Pro Tip: Every job title on your résumé is a keyword that recruiters search for. Don't let "intern" be the thing that filters you out when you have the actual experience they're looking for.

Cheat Code #2
Don't Let Internal Titles Undersell Your Experience

If your internship or company gave you some weird made-up title that nobody outside the building understands, change it. Your résumé isn't a loyalty contract to your company's internal lingo; it's a tool to show recruiters what you actually did.

Internal Title	What You Actually Do	Better Résumé Title
"Customer Happiness Ninja"	Handle customer service and support	"Customer Success Manager"
"Growth Hacker"	Marketing and user acquisition	"Digital Marketing Manager"
"Chief of Stuff"	Office management and operations	"Operations Manager"
"Data Wizard"	Data analysis and reporting	"Data Analytics Specialist"

Pro Tip: Did your role involve more responsibility than the title suggests? Look up job descriptions for full-time roles with similar responsibilities. If you were doing 70 percent or more of those tasks, you can claim that title.

Cheat Code #3
Flip Your Service Job into Corporate-Speak

I really don't care if you were folding clothes, flipping burgers, or working the pole—if you worked in the service industry, reframe it. People love to throw unconscious bias at retail, restaurant, or unconventional jobs, but guess what? Skills are skills.

A few years ago, I was working with a client, Maria. While many of her college classmates were out racking up internships, Maria spent three years as a server at Cheesecake Factory, because she was paying her own way through school (go Maria!). She was so nervous about the edge her fellow students would have on her when entering the job market after graduation—but that's because she was discounting all of her real-world experience. When she first showed me her résumé, this was all it said:

Server, The Cheesecake Factory

- Took orders
- Served food
- Cleaned tables

To give Maria her due credit, we transformed it into this:

Customer Experience, The Cheesecake Factory

- Managed customer relationships and resolved concerns for 100+ daily guests
- Coordinated with cross-functional teams to ensure seamless service delivery

- Consistently exceeded upsell targets, generating additional $500+ in sales per shift
- Trained and mentored 5 new team members on service protocols and procedures
- Maintained detailed knowledge of 200+ menu items and daily specials
- Mastered multitasking in high-stress scenarios while maintaining customer satisfaction

Same experience, completely different impact.

The Service Job Translation Matrix

If You Did This...	On Your Résumé, That's...	Corporate Would Call It...
Dealt with angry customers	"Developed solutions for high-stakes client concerns"	Conflict Resolution
Trained new employees	"Facilitated onboarding and skills development"	Team Leadership
Covered others' shifts	"Demonstrated adaptability in dynamic staffing environment"	Resource Management
Handled the register	"Managed financial transactions and balanced accounts"	Cash Flow Management
Restocked shelves	"Optimized inventory systems and supply chain"	Operations Management
Upsold menu items	"Drove revenue through strategic product recommendations"	Sales Strategy
Made drink/food specials	"Innovated new product offerings"	Product Development
Organized stock room	"Implemented organizational systems"	Process Improvement
Helped during rush hours	"Thrived in high-pressure, time-sensitive environment"	Crisis Management
Made schedule requests	"Coordinated cross-functional team availability"	Staff Management

Cheat Code #4
Play the Name Game

Okay, this one's controversial, but we *need* to talk about it: If you were given a super feminine name like Ashley or Kayla (or Courtney . . . eep!), or if your name carries a cultural or racial identifier, you might be facing an unfair disadvantage from the get-go.

And before you say "Well, I don't want to work somewhere that would discriminate against my name anyway"—let me stop you right there. We're not talking about conscious discrimination. We're talking about unconscious bias. And that's a whole different ball game. In fact, a landmark study by economists at the University of Chicago and MIT found that identical resumes with "white-sounding" names like Emily and Greg got 50 percent more callbacks than those with names like Lakisha and Jamal.[6] That's not an opinion. That's data. Unconscious bias doesn't need to be malicious to be real—it just needs to be baked into the system. And it is.

When a recruiter or hiring manager looks at your résumé, they're not sitting there thinking *Oh, with this name, she's female; let's put it aside.* They're not an evil villain twirling their mustache and plotting discrimination.

What's actually happening is much sneakier. They're scanning your résumé for like 0.5 seconds. That's not enough time for conscious thought. It's just enough time for their unconscious patterns and biases to kick in—biases they might not even know they have.

Even HR professionals, who are usually the most trained in diversity and inclusion, still carry unconscious bias. It's not because they're bad people—it's because they're human. Our brains are wired to make snap judgments based on patterns, even when we don't want them to.

This isn't just speculation—the data is overwhelming. Studies have shown that identical résumés receive different ratings depending on whether the applicant's name signals a man or woman, and both male and female recruiters are twice as likely to hire a male candidate over an equally qualified female candidate.[7]

If you feel like you are being discriminated against, one quick fix is to use your first initial on your résumé for just a few weeks, then evaluate how it went. (Example: C. Johnson.) That's it. That's the hack. You're not necessarily hiding who you are—you're just getting past that initial half-second scan where unconscious bias can kick in before your actual qualifications get a chance to shine. Revisit your experiment after the two weeks. Did anything change? Did you get more interviews, or fewer?

When you play the game strategically, you can get in the door and show them exactly why they'd be idiots not to hire you.

And once you're in that position of power? That's when you can start making real change from the inside. That's when you can start challenging these biases head-on and making space for others who come after you.

Because you can't change the system if you can't get in the door. And sometimes, getting in the door means playing a well-timed cheat code to outmaneuver that sneaky unconscious bias.

 Pro Tip: The name change is just to get past the initial résumé screen. Keep your full name on your LinkedIn profile, and use your full name once you're in the interview process. If you get pushback about the difference, just say you go by both professionally.

Cheat Code #5
Keyword-Load Your Résumé

We're about to hack the matrix. That résumé you worked so hard on? It's probably getting rejected by a bot before a human even sees it. But don't worry—I'm about to teach you how to speak robot.

Most companies use AI to screen résumés before they ever reach a human. If your résumé doesn't speak their language, you're getting ghosted faster than a bad Hinge date.

Your Sneaky Keyword Strategy

Job Description Says	Your Résumé Says	Your Résumé Should Say
Project management	Organized events	Led project management for key initiatives
Cross-functional teams	Worked with others	Collaborated with cross-functional teams
Data-driven decisions	Made improvements	Implemented data-driven strategies
Client relationship management	Talked to customers	Managed key client relationships

Crafting the perfect résumé descriptions can feel like a special kind of torture. You know what you did on the job, but translating your everyday work into that corporate-speak that recruiters eat up? Not everyone's gifted with that skill. That's where AI comes in.

Try this prompt in your favorite AI tool: "Transform these basic job descriptions into professional, keyword-rich résumé bullets that would impress a recruiter. Use action verbs, quantify results where possible, and incorporate industry terminology. Here's the job listing I'm applying for: [PASTE JOB DESCRIPTION HERE]"

Basic	Keyword-Rich
I helped customers	Provided comprehensive client solutions through strategic relationship management
I wrote some code	Developed and implemented full-stack solutions utilizing [exact technologies from the job description]
I made a dashboard	Engineered data visualization solutions that drove strategic decision-making

Now, head back to your résumé and swap out that boring language for those bot-bypassers!

Cheat Code #6
Turn Hobbies into Hustle

"I have zero marketing experience," my client Sadie sighed.

I didn't buy it.

"Tell me about your last weekend," I said.

Her eyebrows scrunched in confusion. "What does that have to do with—"

"Just humor me."

She rolled her eyes. "Fine. Well, I took some photos at Karina's engagement party. Nothing fancy, just candids. Oh, and I made a highlight reel for my church's kickball tournament. The team loves when I add those slow-mo effects and music drops . . ." She trailed off, seeing my growing smile.

"Keep going," I prompted.

"I mean, I posted some of the engagement photos on Instagram. Karina's friends kept asking for the filter preset I used, so I shared my settings and told her how to set it up. And the kickball video got shared so much that other church leagues are asking if I can film their games too . . ."

I held up my hand. "Let me get this straight. You're telling me you have zero marketing experience, but you actually do all of the following things!"

- create viral social media content
- build engaged audiences
- design video content
- create tutorials
- demonstrate how to use preset filters and editing software

- understand what makes content shareable
- can provide actual case studies of your work driving results

"But that's just stuff I do for fun," she protested. "It's easy!"

"Sadie, honey, that's called a portfolio. Most wannabe marketers are out there trying to manufacture fake projects to show their skills. You're living them. You're not starting from zero—you're already halfway there."

She sat back, coffee forgotten. "But it's just church kickball and friend photos..."

"No! It's content creation and community engagement. It's understanding your audience and delivering what they want. It's building a personal brand so strong that people seek you out. The fact that you did it with kickball instead of corporate products just proves you can make anything interesting."

We spent the next hour rewriting her résumé, transforming "takes photos for friends" into "Creates engaging visual content driving organic social media growth" and "makes kickball videos" into "Produces viral video content resulting in multiple client referrals."

Three weeks later, she texted me from her new job at a digital marketing agency. Turns out they were more impressed by her kickball highlight reels than by any corporate case study they'd seen.

Sadie's story isn't unique. Most of us are sitting on years of valuable experience we're not counting because we think it doesn't count if we enjoyed it or if we did it for free.

Skills are skills. Whether you learned them in a boardroom or a church basement, whether you got paid or did it for the love of the game—it all counts.

You just have to learn how to tell the story.

The Side Project Upgrade

Gaming → Professional Skills	Crafting → Business Skills	Social Media → Marketing Skills
Raid leading = Project management	Etsy shop = E-commerce	Hashtag strategy = SEO
Guild management = Team leadership	Supply buying = Vendor management	Building followers = Growth hacking
Strategy guides = Content creation	Product photos = Visual marketing	Post planning = Content strategy
Mod creation = Product development	Customer service = Client relations	Engagement = Community management
Streaming = Digital marketing	Pricing strategy = Financial planning	Analytics tracking = Data analysis

Remember: Your hobbies aren't "just for fun"—they're proof you can take initiative, learn new skills, build something from scratch, manage projects, create content, grow community, analyze results, and more. That's not a hobby; that's a whole-ass portfolio.

Cheat Code #7
Work for Your Friends and Family, and Add It to Your Résumé

If you need to *sprinkle* in some specific skills on your résumé ASAP, find a friend, family member, peer, or friend of your family who runs a small business or has a side hustle. Can't find *anyone*? Try local nonprofits and volunteer committees. Don't just cheer them on—work *with* them. Offer to help with tasks that match your career goals or build up the specific new skills you're trying to learn.

When writing about the specific new skills on your résumé, don't be basic. You could say: "Helped my friend with her business," or you could really sell your new skills with interesting, specific details, such as the following example.

E-Commerce Consultant, Beauty by Sarah

- Optimized product listings and SEO, increasing conversion rate by 32 percent
- Streamlined checkout process, reducing cart abandonment by 40 percent
- Implemented automated email sequences for abandoned carts and post-purchase follow-up
- Set up cross-sell/upsell funnels that boosted average order value by 25 percent
- Integrated inventory management system to prevent stockouts and overselling
- Analyzed customer journey data to identify and remove friction points
- Coordinated with suppliers to optimize product bundling and pricing strategy

 Pro Tip: I give you full permission to exaggerate the time you were working together. They may even offer to be a reference (wink, wink).

✱ Your Résumé Refresh Action Plan

Your résumé isn't just a list of jobs—it's your career story. And like any good story, it needs to be told in a way that keeps your audience (a.k.a. potential employers) interested and engaged. So *stop* downplaying your experience, dismissing your skills, and letting impostor syndrome tell you that your experience "doesn't count" just because it wasn't traditional.

Everything counts if you frame it right.

Now take these cheat codes and transform your résumé from a boring list of jobs into a compelling argument for why you're the obvious choice. Because you *are*. You just need to prove it on paper.

Think about your résumé design. Do some research (your go-to AI platform might be able to help you with this, or do a Google search) about what résumés look like in the field you'd like to work in. Medical résumés tend to be bare bones, just the facts, whereas a personalized design might give you an edge in marketing or creative fields. Keep in mind the *type* of organization you're applying to as well: You can have a little more fun and break some rules when applying to startups, whereas a Bank of America might want to see a traditional layout. You can find templates in Google Docs, Canva, Microsoft Word, or Notion.

Next Steps
1. Pull up your current résumé or create a new one using a template.
2. Go through each cheat code and apply it to your experience.
3. Create your keyword bank from target job descriptions.
4. Reframe at least one hobby or side project.
5. Run your résumé through a keyword matching tool.

Now go get that job, bestie. You've got this.

2

Impostor Syndrome? We Don't Know Her

Before you can convince anyone else you're qualified, you need to convince yourself. And right now, that voice in your head is probably running a highlight reel of all the reasons you're not ready, not experienced enough, or not smart enough for the roles you want. But that résumé you just crafted? I hope it gave you a perspective that your future employer will share: You've got unique skills and a strong work ethic, and they're going to be lucky to have you.

Confidence is a skill, not a personality trait—and it's a skill that directly impacts your earning potential. The most successful people aren't the smartest or most qualified; they're the ones who learned to quiet their inner critic long enough to take strategic risks.

You know that voice in your head that keeps saying you're not good enough, not qualified enough, or not ready enough? It's like having a mean kid from high school living rent-free in your brain, but instead of critiquing your handbag, they're coming for your career. For those of us who weren't handed the cheat codes, it can be especially loud.

But that voice? She's a *liar*.

Before you even start applying to jobs, we need to beef up your confidence. It doesn't matter if you have five minutes of corporate experience or fifty years, you (yes, YOU!) have incredible skills and qualities that are completely unique (and completely monetizable, too). You've been conditioned to downplay your achievements and second-guess your worth, even though you're completely qualified.

Every time you catch yourself thinking *I'm not ready* or *I'm not quali-*

fied, I want you to remember this: That mediocre dude who just got promoted? He wasn't ready either. He just didn't let that stop him. He had audacity. Or that coworker who seems to get every opportunity? They're not more qualified—they're just better at recognizing their own value and sharing it with others.

It's time to reprogram that voice in your head. And I've got the cheat codes to help you do it.

My client Simone had just graduated from university and was convinced she had absolutely zero career skills because she hadn't secured a single internship throughout college. Girl was spiraling, telling me she had nothing to offer and no experience worth mentioning.

"Okay, tell me what you actually do," I pressed her. "Like, what do you spend your time on?"

Turns out, she ran a Taylor Swift fan Instagram account with over fifty thousand followers. She also loved sports, had lived in Canada most of her life, spoke French, and like many Gen Zers, was ultra-tapped into pop culture.

While looking through job listings, we spotted a consulting gig from an American advertising agency. They were running a campaign to increase the number of NFL fans in Canada. Their ideal candidate would have a strong understanding of Canadian culture, speak French, understand sports, and have their finger on the pulse of social media and pop culture.

For Simone, this was a slam dunk in a kiddie hoop. She spoke French, deeply understood Canadian culture, got sports, and had a proven case study (her TS fan page) showing she could build and engage an audience. She secured the job and launched her career, even with "zero corporate experience."

This wasn't a fluke or blind luck. Once Simone stopped dismissing her skills as "just for fun" or "not real experience" and started seeing them as valuable assets, everything shifted. She wasn't suddenly more qualified—she just finally recognized the qualifications she already had.

You have *way* more skills than you realize. You've got talents you're taking for granted, experience you're downplaying, and knowledge you think is "just basic stuff everyone knows." (Spoiler: It's not.)

Cheat Code #8
Your Irrelevant Skills *Are* Relevant

Think you don't have any valuable skills? *Think again.* Every single thing you've done, learned, or experienced has given you skills that companies need—you just need to learn how to translate them. Yes, Every. Single. Thing.

Simone thought running a fan page was just a hobby. But when we break it down, you can see how this hobby was really a hustle:

- Growing an audience of 50K? That's community building.
- Creating visuals for followers? That's content strategy.
- Keeping fans engaged? That's audience retention.
- Overseeing comments and DMs? That's community management.
- Tracking what posts performed best? That's analytics.

She wasn't "just running a fan page"—she was developing a full suite of digital marketing skills.

✳ The Hidden Skills Inventory

Time to uncover your "irrelevant" expertise. Grab a pen and answer these questions:

What do you do "just for fun"?
Activity: _____
Skills involved: _____
Business value: _____

What do your friends always ask you for help with?
Topic: _____
Why they ask you: _____
How this translates to work: _____

What seems obvious to you but confuses others?
Knowledge area: _____
Why it's easy for you: _____
How this could help a company: _____

Cheat Code #9
Recognize That Winners Aren't Any Smarter Than You

I spent most of my early career running a very lucrative side hustle—ghostwriting LinkedIn posts for CEOs, founders, and executives. When I landed my first client (a tech startup founder who raised over a hundred million dollars), I was shocked. This guy was just . . . a regular person. Not any smarter than me, just *delusional*.

Then came the second client—same thing. Ultrasuccessful CEO, but average intelligence, nothing special, just delusional and willing to work hard.

By the time I'd written for my third, fourth, and fifth executive, it hit me like a ton of bricks: The only real difference between me and these (mostly) men was the audacity to believe in their own hype.

It reminded me of a conversation I once heard between Oprah and Michelle Obama. Oprah asked Michelle how she managed to hold her own at those big tables filled with powerful men. Michelle's response? "You realize pretty quickly that a lot of them aren't that smart."

I promise you, you are capable of great things. Don't ruin your chances before you even start by convincing yourself you're not smart enough.

Let's test this theory for yourself. The following activity will show you, in black and white, how small the actual gap is between you and the A Players you've been putting on a pedestal.

✳ The Confidence Gap Reality Check

Rate yourself on these qualities (1 = low, 5 = high):

Technical skills: _____
Problem-solving ability: _____
Communication skills: _____
Leadership potential: _____
Industry knowledge: _____

Now think of a peer in your industry who's "crushing it." Rate them on the same scale.

Technical skills: _____
Problem-solving ability: _____
Communication skills: _____
Leadership potential: _____
Industry knowledge: _____

Surprise: The gap probably isn't as big as you think. The main difference? That A Player believes they deserve to be there.

You're not going to level up in life until you accept that most of what we treat as "real"—jobs, corporations, social structures, power hierarchies—is a construction. They only work because enough of us agree to buy in. I'm dead serious. Our jobs, our systems, our corporations, our social structures, our power hierarchies—all of it is just a collective hallucination we've bought into. It's a shared agreement that has power only because we keep nodding along with it. Even your precious career is fake. Yep, that thing you stress about is just a performance you've agreed to put on.

Once you really grasp this truth? Everything becomes way less intimidating. When you realize everything is just a social construct that humans made up, it stops having this weird power over you—and suddenly *you* have power over *it*.

I used to look at corporate ladders and office politics like they were these massive, immovable forces hovering above me. Until I realized we're all just making this shit up as we go along.

If you want to dive deeper into this mind-bending reality check, *The Four Agreements* by Don Miguel Ruiz is a solid place to start. It's a cult-favorite self-help book that shows how every "rule" we live by is really just an agreement—one we can choose to rewrite.

Cheat Code #10
You Are a Cyborg, So Act like It

Imagine having all of the world's information at your fingertips. You would become some sort of crazy robot-human-genius hybrid. Well, congrats, you did it! That black box you're addicted to is the biggest career asset in all of human history.

You can find answers to virtually any problem in seconds. Sure, you may not know the answer to a question, but ChatGPT probably does.

A Players know that they're not expected to *know* all of the answers in their job; they're only expected to be able to *find* the answers. Our brains are so fucked from the school system—memorize, memorize, memorize—we don't realize that tracking down an answer is an even more important skill than memorizing information is.

Don't let an information gap keep you from doing the work you're capable of doing. Yes, qualifications are important, but so is trusting in your ability to find the answers to the things you haven't learned yet.

Cheat Code #11
Call Out Your Inner Critic's BS

Remember that annoying voice we've talked about? You know, the one that's always trying to convince you you're not good enough, that your ideas aren't worth bringing up in all-team, that someone else would probably do a better job heading that new project anyways? My own internal voice is loud AF. *Who do you think you are? Who are you to be leading this meeting? Are you even qualified to do this?* It's time to give that voice a reality check.

Think of your inner critic as a computer running Windows 95 in 2025. It's operating on seriously outdated software, programmed during those early years when you were learning to protect yourself from life's disappointments, rejections, and failures. It turns out the standardized schooling we received works *reeeeally* hard to tell you you're not good enough. The good news is that the real world operates a bit differently: There's so much more space for you to turn your specific strengths into a career. Yeah, having an eye for color probably didn't help you ace calculus—but it absolutely is the foundation for a stellar career in product design.

Your inner critic was originally designed as a protection mechanism. Like an overzealous antivirus program, it flags everything as a potential threat. That promotion opportunity? Dangerous. That bold business move? Risky. That dream project? Too ambitious.

But safe doesn't get you promoted. Safe doesn't get you paid. Safe gets you stuck.

Your Inner Critic Translation Guide

When Your Inner Critic Says...	Call Out the BS Like...	And Remember What's Actually True
"You're not qualified for this job."	"Bestie, the job description is a wish list, not a requirement."	The ordinary white guy with half your qualifications already applied.

When Your Inner Critic Says ...	Call Out the BS Like ...	And Remember What's Actually True
"Everyone here is smarter than you."	"Bold of you to assume anyone knows what they're doing."	Everyone is googling the same stuff you are.
"You're going to fail."	"And? What's the worst that could happen?"	Failure is just spicy feedback.
"They're going to realize you're a fraud."	"A fraud who keeps getting results? Make it make sense."	You've been getting stuff done—that's the opposite of fraud.
"You don't belong here."	"Neither does this impostor syndrome, but here we are."	If you were truly unqualified, you wouldn't even recognize what you don't know.
"You just got lucky."	"Damn right, *and* I worked hard. We love a combo."	Success = preparation + opportunity. You did both.
"What if they ask something you don't know?"	"Then I'll do what everyone else does—google it."	Not knowing something just means you get to learn something new.
"You're not ready for this promotion."	"Ready is a myth made up by people who want you to wait."	You'll figure it out like everyone else did.

The good news? Once you understand where these thoughts come from, they lose their power. Typically, your inner critic is loudest right before your biggest wins.

Your Action Plan
1. Next time that voice pipes up, acknowledge it: *I hear you trying to protect me, but I've got this.*
2. Notice when the criticism gets louder—it often means you're on the verge of something big.
3. Ask yourself: *Is this genuine concern, or just my old programming acting up?*

Cheat Code #12
There's Always Someone Ahead of (and Behind) You

You're doomscrolling LinkedIn, watching that one poster dropping her "How I Made Six Figures at Twenty-Three" story, or that guy who's apparently becoming a VP while you're still trying to figure out how to get a job that covers your rent. And suddenly you're in your feels about being "behind."

Picture your career as an infinite ladder stretching endlessly upward. No matter how high you climb, there's always another rung above you. Always someone with more experience, bigger achievements, or a fancier title. And here's the liberating truth: That's exactly how it should be.

While you're over here stressing about not being at the top, you're literally LIVING someone else's goals right now. That college senior is stalking your LinkedIn. The career-switcher is taking notes on your journey. The intern is trying to manifest your current position.

You're basically running a master class just by existing in your role.

While you're looking up at that tech executive or industry veteran, someone else is looking up at you. That fresh graduate is wondering how you landed your current role. The career switcher is studying your journey for clues. The intern is hoping to learn from your experience.

You're simultaneously a student and a teacher on this ladder. Every position you occupy is someone else's goal.

The Three Universal Truths of Career Growth

1. **There Is No "Ready."** If you're waiting to feel completely prepared before taking that next step, you'll be waiting forever. Every person you admire took roles they weren't "ready" for. They grew into them. That's not impostor syndrome—that's how growth works.
2. **The Ladder Never Ends.** The most successful people in any field are still climbing. They're still learning, still stretching, still failing sometimes. There's no final destination, no point

where you've "made it." Understanding this removes the pressure of trying to reach some imaginary finish line.
3. **Your Real Competition Is Yesterday's You.** Stop measuring your progress against others. The only meaningful comparison is between who you are today and who you were yesterday. Are you learning? Are you trying? Are you slightly braver than you were last month? That's what matters.

Let's get real—where you're at right now isn't just some random checkpoint on your way to something better. You've got a whole-ass unique view of the game from right here. Think about it: You can drop knowledge on the people coming up behind you *and* ask the real questions to those ahead. That's literally your superpower—being able to connect both ways makes you valuable AF exactly where you are right now.

When I get those LinkedIn DMs asking for "just fifteen minutes of your valuable time," my first instinct is to ignore them like a text from an ex. But I actually make myself say yes to most of them. Why? Because every time I hop on one of those calls, I walk away with this weird clarity hit. Seeing someone exactly where I was four years ago is like a progress report I didn't know I needed.

Next time someone below you on the ladder slides into your DMs asking for advice, don't ghost them. Take the call. Or better yet, reach out to someone whose career makes you feel like an underachiever, and ask for twenty minutes of their time. Do it right now while you're feeling brave. The career ladder gets a lot less intimidating when you're actively connecting in both directions.

Cheat Code #13
Create a Brag Folder for Your Wins

Start keeping a folder—digital, physical, whatever works for you—where you stash every win, big or small. Got a shoutout from a client? Landed a big project? Even if it's just a thank-you email from a coworker—save it. You're going to collect receipts for every W you take. And I mean Every. Single. One.

What Counts as a Win? Everything, Actually

What should you save in your brag folder? Probably more than you think. Remember to drop any of the following into your own folder.

- thank-you messages
- project compliments
- performance reviews
- achievement metrics
- client testimonials
- team shoutouts
- encouraging DMs
- awards/recognition
- training certificates
- impact numbers

This folder will become your personal hype file. On the days when impostor syndrome kicks in, you're feeling like you haven't done enough, or your freelance prospect is asking for case studies, pull out that wins folder and remind yourself who TF you are.

Cheat Code #14
Write the Brag-Worthy Bio You Deserve

"I'm going to tell you something that's gonna hurt ... if you have trouble receiving a compliment, you'll have trouble receiving money throughout your career."

I nearly choked on my matcha. My mentor sat across from me, calm as ever, while I was having what felt like an out-of-body experience in this overpriced café.

She had just watched me awkwardly deflect a compliment from our server about my confidence and speaking skills (I was loudly practicing my upcoming talk while we met). My usual "Oh, it's nothing" and "I just got lucky" responses had tumbled out automatically.

"What does accepting compliments have to do with making money?" I asked, genuinely confused.

"Money is receiving energy. Success is receiving energy. When someone gives you a compliment, they're offering you positive energy. When you deflect it, when you minimize it, when you push it away—you're literally training yourself to reject receiving."

I sat there, feeling called out and uncomfortable. Like she had just read my bank account and my entire psychological profile in one go.

I started to protest. "But—"

"But nothing. Every time you say 'oh, it was nothing' or 'anyone could do it,' you're telling the world that you don't deserve recognition. And guess what? The world listens. Money listens.

"For the next month, I want you to do one thing. When someone compliments you, just say 'thank you.' That's it. No explanations, no deflections. Just receive it. Watch what happens."

I thought she was crazy. But I also knew she made more in a month than I did in a year, so I decided to try it.

The first few days were excruciating. Every "thank you" felt like it was being dragged out of me. My throat would get tight. My cheeks would burn. But I did it.

Then something weird started happening. The more I accepted compliments, the more I started noticing opportunities. A client doubled their budget. A speaking gig materialized. A promotion discussion suddenly appeared on my calendar. It didn't happen all at once, but the more my confidence improved, the more I was able to speak up, ask for what I want, and advocate for my worth.

Now, this can be especially hard to do if you haven't spent your entire life receiving praise, or if you're not used to things being handed to you. I get it. But confidence in yourself undoubtedly increases others' confidence in you. Coincidence? Maybe. Career-changing? Absolutely.

It's been years since that coffee-shop conversation, but I still think about it daily. I'd like to say it's because I mastered some complex business strategy. But really? I just learned to say "thank you" without following it up with an excuse. Turns out my mentor was right. The simple act of receiving a compliment was actually training for receiving everything else I wanted in my career.

You know what's even harder than receiving a compliment? Complimenting *yourself*—and owning it.

Let's try a little experiment. Think about your work bestie—the one who absolutely crushes it but still somehow thinks she's not doing enough. What would you say about her accomplishments?

You'd probably be like: *"OMG, she's literally amazing! She led that huge project last quarter, mentors three junior employees, AND somehow finds time to run the company book club. Plus, everyone comes to her when they need help with client presentations because she's just THAT good at PowerPoint. Honestly, they're lucky to have her."*

Now . . . try to brag about yourself.

I'll wait.

crickets

Yeah, that's what I thought. Suddenly you're all "Oh, I just help out with some projects . . ."

GIRL. STOP.

Before you roll your eyes and flip the page, trust me. Listen, I know what you're thinking. *Another self-promotion exercise? Ugh.* You're probably fighting the urge to turn the page right now. But here's the truth: Your reluctance to own your achievements isn't humility—it's hurting your career.

Think about it: How many opportunities have you missed because you couldn't articulate your value? How many raises have passed you by because you couldn't clearly communicate your impact? How many times have you watched someone less qualified get ahead simply because they were better at owning their achievements?

Let's take a pause to celebrate *you*. To brag about *you*. To practice receiving. Before you roll your eyes, trust me. Stick with me for two minutes. You can do ANYTHING for two minutes.

> ✳ **The Friend Test Exercise**
>
> 1. Grab your phone or journal.
> 2. Set a timer for two minutes.
> 3. Pretend you're texting your group chat about your amazingly talented friend... except that friend is you.
> 4. Write EVERYTHING you'd say about them (you).
> 5. Don't stop until the timer goes off.
>
> **Example:** OMG, y'all need to hear about my friend [your name]! She's literally the QUEEN of [your job/skill]. Last month she [specific achievement], and everyone was so excited. She's also so good at [specific skill] that [impact]. Plus she has this amazing way of [unique trait/ability] that just makes everyone feel [positive result]. Honestly, I don't know how she does it all!

How did that feel? Scary? Uncomfortable? Were you able to receive the compliments, or did you try to downplay or push them away?

You're not off the hook just yet. Let's jump into building you a brag bank.

> ✳ **Your Brag Bank Template**
>
> Fill this out (seriously, do it right now).
>
> **Skills I'm Known for:**
> The thing everyone asks for my help with: _____
> The problem I solve better than anyone: _____
> The task I make look easy: _____

Recent Wins:

That project I crushed: _____

That person I helped: _____

That process I improved: _____

Secret Talents:

Thing I do naturally that others find hard: _____

Compliment I regularly receive: _____

Value I uniquely bring: _____

Level Up Your Bragging

You may have an instinct to stay humble, but it's not doing you any favors. We're about to level up your brag. Use these upgraded versions when you're interviewing, updating your LinkedIn, crafting cover letters, or refreshing your résumé. The difference isn't just semantic—it's the gap between being overlooked and being unforgettable.

Basic Brag	Better Brag	Best Brag
"I help with projects."	"I manage key projects."	"I led the redesign of our client onboarding process, cutting setup time by 50%."
"I'm good with people."	"I build strong relationships."	"I've mentored five team members who all got promoted within a year."
"I know Excel."	"I'm an Excel expert."	"I created automated reporting systems that save our team ten hours every week."
"I support the team."	"I drive team success."	"I implemented new collaboration tools that increased team productivity by 30%."

See the difference? The B-Player Basic Brag is what you mumble when you're afraid of taking up space. With the Better Brag, you start to own your expertise. But the Best Brag? That's where A Players stop hiding behind vague language and start speaking in the currency that matters—*results*.

Stop with the self-deprecation bullshit. You're not "just" anything. You're not "helping" or "assisting" or "supporting" unless you're literally an assistant (and even then, you're probably running someone's entire life). You're *driving* and *creating* and *transforming*.

Own it. Quantify it. And for god's sake, brag about it—because if you don't tell your story, who will?

> ✱ **The Real Truth About Impostor Syndrome**
>
> Here's the thing about impostor syndrome: It's not a personal flaw; it's a systemic lie designed to keep you playing small. Every time you doubt your abilities or downplay your achievements, you're buying into a narrative that benefits everyone except for you.
>
> The world needs your talents, your perspective, and YOUR unique combination of skills (what's been called the "zone of genius"). Not someday when you're "ready," but right now. Because you're *not* an impostor. You're just someone who's been taught to doubt their own power.
>
> It's time to flip the script. Take these cheat codes and use them whenever that voice of self-doubt creeps in. Start collecting your wins, owning your achievements, and showing up as the badass you already are.

Remember: The only person who needs to believe in you is you. And once you do? Watch how quickly everyone else follows suit.

3

Mastering Job Apps

So you've figured out what you want, and you believe you deserve it. Now comes the part where you actually have to convince someone else to give it to you. You're no longer the desperate new grad who'll take any opportunity. You have standards now, and skills worth paying for. It's time your application strategy reflected that.

The A Players getting hired aren't necessarily more qualified than you. They just understand that getting noticed requires more than uploading a PDF and crossing their fingers.

While most people treat job applications like a numbers game—randomly uploading résumés across dozens of postings—the smart ones treat each application like a mini marketing campaign. They research the company, customize their approach, and find ways to stand out in a sea of identical submissions.

"I've applied to forty-seven jobs," Mia sighed, slumping back in her chair. "Not a single response. Not even a rejection. Just . . . silence."

I looked at her strategy: She was qualified. Her résumé was solid. She was applying to all the right roles. But she was doing exactly what everyone else was doing: hitting Quick Apply on LinkedIn and praying to the job search gods.

"Okay, let's try something different for job number forty-eight," I told her.

Instead of just hitting Apply, we found the hiring manager on LinkedIn, created a quick video explaining why she was perfect for the role, and attached a one-pager with ideas for her first thirty days.

Guess who got a response within two hours?

If you're doing what everyone else is doing, you're going to get what everyone else is getting—ignored, ghosted, and sad. The job market is noisy AF. You need to cut through that noise.

Think about it: Companies get hundreds of applications for every role. Most of those applicants are doing the bare minimum—sending the same generic résumé and hitting Apply as many times as possible. Good luck with that.

Time to learn how to stand out. Let's get into these cheat codes.

Cheat Code #15
Go One Step Further Than Everyone Else

Look, anyone can hit Apply and hope for the best. But if you want to stand out in a pile of hundreds of applications, you need to make yourself impossible to ignore. While everyone else is throwing résumés at the wall to see what sticks, you're going to show up with a game plan that proves you're already thinking about how to crush this role.

Enter the Extra Mile Method. It's exactly what it sounds like—you're going one extra mile above what the application is asking for. Only a bit of extra effort for what will be a ton of payoff.

✳ **The Extra Mile Inventory**

Before we dive into the tactics, let's check your current application game. Rate yourself on the following questions (1 = rarely, 5 = constantly):

- How much research do you do before applying? _____
- Do you customize every application? _____
- Do you follow up? _____
- Do you make connections at target companies? _____
- Do you go beyond the basic requirements? _____

> Total them up. If you scored below 20, don't worry—we're about to level up your entire application strategy.

So how can you go the extra mile? There isn't just one way to go about it, but the list below gives you some options. Find what option works for you.

1. Find (and Reach Out to) the Hiring Manager

Think of reaching out to the hiring manager as your first impression—you want to make it count without being too pushy. Start by doing some detective work on LinkedIn, the company website, or even the job posting itself to find the right person. Sometimes they're listed right there in the job description; other times you might need get a little stalk-y and search for terms like "hiring manager" or the department head title.

Once you've found them, craft a message that's short but impactful. The key is to make it personal and specific—something like *"Hi Shawn! Saw your role for Senior Marketing Manager, and it seems like a perfect fit. I just applied and wanted to share why I'm excited: I've led similar social media campaigns that increased engagement by 150 percent, and I've managed teams of five-plus marketers to deliver projects under budget. Looking forward to connecting!"*

If you're new to the workforce, try citing something relevant you've done outside of work, or mention a shared value or passion as the organization. *"Hi Wei! Saw the role for Junior Fundraising Coordinator, and it seems like a perfect fit. I just applied and wanted to share why I'm excited: After organizing three campus fundraisers that collected over $5,000 for local homeless shelters, I'm passionate about continuing this work with an organization that shares my commitment to housing justice. I admire how Hope Housing Initiative has created permanent solutions for over two hundred families last year alone. Looking forward to discussing how my experience can contribute to your mission!"*

2. Show You Did Your Homework

This is where you prove you're not just another lazy girlie spamming the Apply button. This is your moment to flex that you've done more research than an FBI agent with a crush.

First, you need to stalk, but make it professional. We're talking following their press releases, LinkedIn updates, and literally any crumb of news about what they're up to. Maybe they just launched something major, got some funding (*cha-ching!*), or pivoted their strategy. Whatever it is, you're going to casually drop that knowledge like you eat business news for breakfast.

Let's say they just announced a new AI platform. Don't just be like "congrats on the AI thing!" Instead, hit them with: "Your recent launch into predictive analytics caught my eye—especially your focus on small business accessibility. I actually led a similar initiative that brought AI tools to mom-and-pop shops, increasing their revenue by 30 percent." See how you're not just showing you read the news, but connecting it directly to your bad bitch energy?

And those projects they're humblebragging about on their company blog? Study them like you're getting paid for it (because hopefully you will be). When you write your cover letter or hop on that interview, casually mention: *"I noticed your team's recent overhaul of the customer onboarding process. The way you reduced friction points while maintaining security is exactly the kind of challenge I live for—in my current role, I orchestrated something similar that cut churn by 25 percent."*

Don't forget to slide into their social content too. If the CEO posted some thought leadership piece about the future of their industry, reference it: *"Your perspective on blockchain democratizing finance really resonated—especially the point about user adoption being the key blocker. I've actually been in the trenches solving that exact problem."*

And if you don't yet have experience? No problem. Share something you're learning about the topic. *"Your perspective on blockchain really resonated—especially the point about user adoption being the key blocker.*

I've been researching this problem, and it's exciting to see the application of democratizing finance!"

The key is to be calculated but not creepy. You want to give "I'm already operating at your level" vibes, not "I printed out all your tweets and made a vision board" energy. Show them you're not just prepared for the role—you're already living and breathing their industry, their challenges, and their vision.

3. Create a Video Pitch

While everyone else is regurgitating the same boring "Dear Hiring Manager" emails that put recruiters to sleep, you're going to slide into their inbox with a sixty-second video (or Loom!) that proves you're already thinking about crushing this role.

A video lets you showcase your personality, communication skills, and professional vibe in a way that a résumé never could—plus it shows you're innovative enough to break out of the typical application box. And let's be real: When they've got two hundred identical applications to review, they're going to remember that one candidate who had the confidence to put themselves out there with a killer video pitch that perfectly nailed why they're the solution to the company's problems.

Example Video

- **0–15s:** Hook ("Your job posting for [role] caught my eye because . . .")
- **15–45s:** Value ("Here are three ways I can help . . . ")
- **45–60s:** Ask ("I'd love to discuss how . . . ")

4. Create a Mini-Project

Creating a mini version of a project is almost a guarantee that you'll stand out. Instead of just saying you can handle their marketing campaigns, why not design a sample one that shows exactly how you'd crush their next product launch? Or if you're in tech, throw together a quick prototype that solves one of their actual problems—even if it's just a basic mockup, it shows you're already thinking about solutions.

My personal favorite move is creating a strategy document that breaks down their current market position and outlines exactly how you'd take them to the next level.

The key is to pick something small enough that you can execute it well, but meaningful enough to make them think *Wow, if they're doing this just to apply, imagine what they'll do when they're actually on the team.*

Some mini-project ideas include designing a sample campaign, building a quick prototype, or writing up a strategy doc.

5. Make Content About Them

Instead of just lurking on their company social pages, create content that puts you on their radar in the most strategic way possible. Write a thoughtful LinkedIn article analyzing their latest product launch or industry move—not just fluff, but actual insights that show you understand their business inside and out.

Or, get really spicy and create a video breaking down why their approach to a specific challenge is genius (and drop a few suggestions about how to make it even better).

The key is to position yourself as a thought leader in their space, not just another fangirl. Maybe create an infographic showing how they're disrupting their industry, or record a quick case study about how their product solved a real problem you've encountered. When you tag them and their team in this high-quality content, you instantly become someone who's already adding value to their brand conversation.

And trust me, when they're reviewing applications and recognize your name as "oh yeah, that person who did that brilliant analysis of our market strategy," you've already got one stiletto in the door.

6. Build Something Useful

Instead of just talking about what you *could* do, create something they can actually use. This will vary by industry, but consider these examples.

For Engineering Roles: Build a simple diagnostic tool that addresses a specific issue you noticed in their GitHub repositories. For example, if you see they're struggling with test coverage, create a custom script that identifies untested code sections and prioritizes them based on complexity.

For Healthcare Administration: Develop a patient flow visualization dashboard using Tableau or Google Data Studio that maps bottlenecks in their current process. Use publicly available data or industry benchmarks to show potential efficiency gains.

For Finance Positions: Create a custom funding analysis using their public fundraising data from Crunchbase and press releases to calculate their estimated burn rate and runway. Build a scenario model showing how different cost-reduction strategies could extend runway by six to twelve months with comparisons to other companies in their industry.

When you can identify the problem your role will solve for the organization, the options become endless. If you notice they're struggling with operations, build them a custom automation that solves that exact pain point. Or maybe map out a workflow that streamlines their customer onboarding process (bonus points if you've noticed them mentioning this as a challenge in their quarterly reports).

If you're really trying to show off your skills, develop a simple but powerful tool that addresses a specific need—think a Google Sheets template that automatically calculates their key metrics, or a basic Chrome extension that solves a common problem their customers face.

When you show up to the interview with not just ideas but actual solutions they could implement tomorrow, you're already proving your ROI before they even hire you.

7. Become Their Customer

Instead of just researching their product, actually become a power user—sign up for their platform, download their app, or buy their service. But don't just be a passive customer—be the one leaving thoughtful product reviews, sending in actually helpful feedback (not just "great product!"), and documenting exactly how you're using their solution to solve real problems.

The Golden Rule of Extra

Make every extra effort count by showing you understand you future employer's needs and can solve their problems. Quality over quantity, always. Be strategic AF.

If you're going to spend an extra hour on your application, create something that shows them exactly how you'll make their lives easier. Skip the longer cover letter—build something that proves you can deliver value from day one.

For each high-intent job application, choose at least one of these tactics, and watch your job offers pile higher than a crypto-trader's assets after his dad gifted him that nest egg.

Cheat Code #16
Tap into the Hidden Job Market

My mind was blown when I discovered this: Most of the best jobs *never* make it to the job boards. That means there's an entire hidden job market just waiting for you to tap into it. You just need to know where to look. Lucky for you, I'm here to help point you in the right direction.

LinkedIn Posts

- Stalk people posting "We're growing!" or "So excited about our funding!"
- Look for humble brags about company growth.
- Watch for those "My friend's company is hiring . . ." posts.

- Pay attention when people announce they got promoted (their old role needs filling!).
- Search the hashtag #hiring.

Industry-Specific Newsletters

- Subscribe to those niche "insider" newsletters.
- Look for the "Who's Making Moves" sections.
- Pay attention to funding announcements (they're about to hire like crazy).
- Watch acquisition news (merger = new roles).

Local Professional Groups

- Join your city's industry Slack channels.
- Look for professional meetup groups.
- Get into private Facebook groups.

Alumni Networks

- your college's alumni portal
- department-specific email lists
- alumni LinkedIn groups
- your school's career center job board (yes, even years after graduating)

Discord Servers

- industry-specific servers
- career development communities
- tech communities (they always know who's hiring)
- freelancer groups (contract-to-hire opportunities)

Conference Networks

- virtual conference Slack channels
- speaker networks

- conference sponsor lists (they're usually hiring)
- post-event networking groups

Substack/Medium Publications

- follow company leaders
- industry newsletters
- company blogs
- founder updates

"Backdoor" Channels

- Reddit industry subreddits
- X/Twitter circles of industry leaders
- Instagram stories of companies you like
- WhatsApp groups (yes, they exist for industries!)

Start by picking three of these channels that feel most natural to you and setting up your feeds—then make checking them part of your daily routine.

Cheat Code #17
Slide into DMs for Referrals

When you see a job you want, don't just sit around waiting for a response—message someone who works there and ask for a referral. Trust me: Employees have major incentive to refer candidates because of those sweet, sweet referral bonuses. We're talking a few hundred to a few thousand bucks just for recommending you.

When you reach out, you're not just asking for a favor; you're doing them a favor. You're literally giving them a chance to make easy money. They'll be rooting for you like their paycheck depends on it . . . because it kinda does. You could be funding their next vacation.

Your Referral Request Templates

For someone you know (work bestie level):	Hey [Name]! I saw [Company] is hiring for a [role], and I'm interested! Would you be open to referring me? I know your company has a referral program, and I'd love for you to get your bonus if it works out! I've already applied through the portal and can send you my résumé if that helps make it super easy for you. Let me know!
For someone you've met (LinkedIn connection level):	Hi [Name]! I hope you're crushing it at [Company]! I saw the [role] position, and I'm really excited about it. I've been [relevant experience] for [X] years and love what [Company] is doing with [specific project/product].
	I know many companies offer referral bonuses—would you be open to referring me? Happy to send more info about my background or jump on a quick call if you'd like to learn more first.
For someone you don't know (cold DM level):	Hi [Name]! I love following your posts about [Company/industry topic]. I noticed [Company] is hiring for [role], and I'm really interested. I've been [relevant experience] at [Current Company], and what caught my eye about this role was [specific detail from job posting].
	I know referring someone you don't know is a big ask, but I'd love to hop on a quick call to share my background and see if you think I'd be a good fit. Plus, if it works out, you get that referral bonus!
	Let me know if you'd be open to chatting!

 Pro Tip: Most companies give bigger referral bonuses for engineering and technical roles. If you're in tech, mention that—it might make them even more excited to refer you.

Cheat Code #18
Follow the Money (Literally)

Want to find companies that are hiring? Follow the money trail. When a company has just secured funding, you better believe they're about to go on a hiring spree.

The Money-Following Framework

If you want to know who's hiring, don't waste your time scrolling job boards—follow the money. When a company secures funding, especially rounds like Series A or B, it usually signals that they're about to enter a major growth phase. And growth means hiring. If a company just raised millions, you better believe they're going to need people to build, market, and sell whatever they're scaling. You can keep tabs on this by tracking funding announcements on sites like Crunchbase, TechCrunch, and PitchBook, or just paying closer attention to LinkedIn posts and industry newsletters. And it's not just the funding itself—watch for other signs too. If a company is acquiring another brand, announcing a big partnership, or even moving into a larger office space, that usually means they're hiring to meet demand. Most people wait for a job to be posted. But if you're smart, you'll get in *before* the listing goes live—because by then, it's already too late.

Reach Out Like This

> Subject: Congrats on the Series A + Quick Question
>
> Hi [Name],
>
> Saw the news about [Company]'s $[X]M funding round—congratulations!
>   The vision for [specific thing they mentioned in funding announcement] is really exciting.
>   I'm an experienced [your role] with a background in [relevant skill], and I'd love to be part of [Company]'s growth journey. I noticed you're building out the [department] team—would you be open to a quick chat about how I could add value during this exciting phase?
>
> Best,
> [Your name]

 Pro Tip: Companies that just got funded are often more flexible on salary and equity because they have fresh cash and big growth targets.

✴ Making It All Work Together

Stack these cheat codes for maximum impact:

1. Find companies that just got funded (cheat code #18)
2. Connect with their employees through hidden channels (cheat code #16)
3. Get a referral from someone inside (cheat code #17)
4. Go above and beyond in your application (cheat code #15)

Your job search is a strategic campaign. Position yourself where the opportunities are, and make it impossible for them to ignore you.

Your Mastering-the-Apps Action Plan

Before you apply to another job:

- Set up alerts for funding news in your industry.
- Join at least three industry-specific communities.
- Create your custom follow-up templates.
- Prepare your "go above and beyond" materials.
- Build a list of target companies and their employees.

The job search isn't about hoping or wishing that someone picks you—it's about strategically placing yourself where opportunities are and making it *obvious* that you're the solution to their problems. Every application is a chance to stand out. Don't waste it by doing the bare minimum.

Now go forth and get that job, bestie. You've got this.

4

Acing the Interview

You've made it past the résumé screening—congrats, you're in the top 3 percent of applicants![8] You've already demonstrated something powerful: You have what they're looking for. Now comes the part where most people psych themselves out: the interview.

Interviews are your chance to show them you're what they've been searching for—the answer to problems they might not even know how to articulate yet. You already have everything you need to succeed. You just need to learn how to package and present it strategically. Now it's time to let that authentic power shine through and claim what's already yours.

"I'm just bad at interviews," my client Freya said, shrugging, after bombing her third interview in a row. "Some people are naturally good at them, but I get nervous and freeze up."

I'm gonna stop you right there. No one is "naturally" good at interviews. Let me repeat that for the people in the back: NO ONE IS NATURALLY GOOD AT INTERVIEWS.

Interviewing is a learned skill. It's like learning to drive—at first, you're hyperaware of every little movement, overthinking every decision, and probably sweating way more than necessary. But with practice? It becomes second nature.

The problem is, most people interview only when they desperately need a job. That's like never driving except when you need to make a cross-country road trip. Of course you're going to be rusty.

Let's get into these cheat codes and turn you into an interview master.

Cheat Code #19
Always Be Interviewing

Quick story time: My client Raquel landed her dream job and a $50K salary bump because she took an interview . . . when she wasn't even looking. She had a good job, but when a recruiter reached out, she thought *why not?* With zero pressure to perform, she crushed it. When they offered her the role with a massive raise, she was ready.

The secret? She was relaxed because she didn't *need* the job. She interviewed like she was having a casual conversation, not *pleading for her life*.

Interviewing regularly helps you stay sharp. It keeps your skills fresh, your story polished, and your market value top of mind. It's a chance to build relationships with recruiters, explore what's out there, and get more comfortable with negotiation—so when the right opportunity shows up, you're not scrambling to get ready. You already are.

 Pro Tip: Aim for at least one interview every quarter, even if you love your current job. Think of it as career maintenance.

Cheat Code #20
Prep Your Interview Answers Ahead of Time

Most interview questions are as predictable as a shitty romcom. *"Tell me about yourself."* *"What's your biggest weakness?"* *"Why do you want to work here?"* Yawn. Like, did you really think they were gonna ask you to solve world hunger?

Let's get real for a second. These questions aren't some cosmic mystery. They're basically a choreographed corporate dance, and I'm here to teach you the moves to crush it.

Most people walk into interviews with about as much preparation as someone showing up to a marathon in flip-flops. But not you. You're going to be the one who has epic, ready-to-deploy stories that make interviewers sit up and take notice. Answers that demonstrate your skills, your hustle, and your confidence. Your competition is stumbling through generic responses, but you? You're about to walk in and own the room like an A Player.

The "Tell Me About Yourself" Interview Cheat Sheet

Question	"Tell me about yourself."
What they *really* mean	We're trying to judge your whole vibe.
Framework	Present → Past → Future → Why Them
Fill in the blank	"Right now I'm [current role] where I [biggest achievement]." "Before that, I [relevant past experience] which taught me [key skill they want]." "I'm looking to [career goal] and was really excited about this role because [specific thing about their company]."
Example	"Right now I'm a product manager at TechCorp, where I led our AI integration that increased user engagement by 40%." "Before that, I was creating custom AI tools for my startup projects, which taught me how to turn complex tech into user-friendly features." "I'm looking to scale my impact with a larger product team, and when I saw your company's focus on AI accessibility, I knew this was exactly the kind of challenge I'm looking for."

 Pro Tip: This is *not* your autobiography. Don't start with "Well, I was born in Ohio and always loved helping people..." Nobody cares about your childhood dreams or your college major unless it's directly relevant. Keep it tight, keep it professional, and keep it focused on why you're the solution to their problem.

The "Why Do You Want This Job?" Interview Cheat Sheet

Question	"Why do you want this job?"
What they *really* mean	We need proof you *actually* care and didn't just spam apply.
Framework	Their Growth + Your Skills + Specific Example
Fill in the blank	"I've been following [Company's] work on [specific project/product] and love how you're [unique approach]. "With my background in [relevant skill], I think I could help by [specific contribution]. "For example, [quick win you could deliver]."
Example	"I've been following Spotify's work on its AI-powered playlist curation and love how you're using machine learning to create hyper-personalized music experiences. "With my background in data science and recommendation algorithms, I think I could help by refining the predictive models that drive playlist recommendations. "For example, I developed a recommendation system at my previous role that increased user engagement by 27% by implementing more nuanced genre-blending techniques."

The "What's Your Biggest Weakness?" Interview Cheat Sheet

Question	"What's your biggest weakness?"
What they *really* mean	They want to know if your weakness will affect the role. And please, I'm begging you, don't say it's perfectionism. Instead, name a weakness unrelated to the role.
Framework	Real (unrelated) Weakness + Active Improvement
Fill in the blank	"I'm really strong with [strength related to the job], so I can sometimes struggle with [weakness unrelated to the job]. "However, I've been actively working on this by [specific action], and I've already seen improvement in [measurable way]."
Example	"I'm really strong with quantitative analysis and data, so I can sometimes struggle with high-level, abstract presentations. "However, I've been actively working on this by taking an improv comedy class to improve my storytelling and presentation skills, and I've already seen improvement in my ability to translate complex data into engaging narratives that resonate with nontechnical audiences."

ACING THE INTERVIEW | 53

The "Where Do You See Yourself in Five Years?" Interview Cheat Sheet

Question	"Where do you see yourself in five years?"
What they *really* mean	Will you quit as soon as we train you?
Framework	Growth Within Role + Company Impact + Industry Contribution
Fill in the blank	"I'm excited to [master current role], then grow into [logical next step] where I can [bigger impact]." "I'd love to become known for [industry contribution] while helping [Company] achieve [their goals]."
Example	"I'm excited to master my current role as a software engineer, then grow into a technical product management position where I can bridge engineering and strategic product development." "I'd love to become known for creating scalable, user-centric solutions while helping Airbnb achieve more seamless global travel experiences."

The "Tell Me About a Challenge You Faced" Interview Cheat Sheet

Question	"Tell me about a challenge you faced."
What they *really* mean	Prove to us you won't cry when things get hard.
Framework	Situation + Action + Result + Learning
Fill in the blank	"We were facing [specific problem] that risked [consequence]. "I [action you took] and [how you involved others], which resulted in [positive outcome]. "This taught me [lesson learned] which I've used since [similar situation]."
Example (experienced)	"We were facing a critical data integration bottleneck that risked delaying our quarterly product launch by several weeks. I developed a custom ETL script and collaborated with cross-functional teams to redesign our data pipeline, which resulted in reducing our data processing time by 65% and meeting our launch deadline. "This taught me the importance of proactive problem-solving and collaborative communication, which I've used since when addressing complex technical challenges in subsequent projects."

Question	"Tell me about a challenge you faced."
Example (new grad)	"We were facing declining attendance and member engagement in our newly launched campus book club that risked the entire initiative being discontinued after just one semester. "I implemented a member survey to identify interest gaps and collaborated with the English department to secure a small budget for refreshments and occasional guest speakers, which resulted in a 200% increase in regular attendance and recognition as the 'Most Improved Student Organization' that year. "This taught me the value of soliciting direct feedback and building strategic partnerships to solve resource challenges, which I've used since when organizing team-building activities and managing limited resources in my internship projects."

Cheat Code #21
Do Your Homework—Research the Company and Their Competitors

Walking into an interview without knowing the company's whole vibe is like showing up to a date without stalking their socials. Amateur hour.

Scrolling through a LinkedIn page for five seconds isn't going to cut it. You need to become a detective who knows more about the organization than some of their own employees. We're talking deep-dive mode into the actual heartbeat of how they operate.

Start with their website. Read between the lines. Look at their recent press releases, check out the leadership team's backgrounds, dig into their blog posts. What are they actually talking about? What problems are they trying to solve?

Social media is your secret weapon. And I'm not just talking about their corporate LinkedIn. Look at their TikTok, their Instagram; see how they actually communicate. Are they formal? Playful? Technical? Every company has a personality, and your job is to decode it. Check out their employees' posts, their company culture videos. You want to speak their language before you even sit down.

The goal is to show that you're genuinely interested, that you've done your homework, and that you're not looking for just any job—you're looking for *this* specific job. Because let's be real: Hiring managers can sniff out generic applications from a mile away.

Your Pre-Interview Research Checklist

Company Basics

- ☐ mission statement
- ☐ core products/services
- ☐ recent news/announcements
- ☐ major competitors
- ☐ company culture/values
- ☐ revenue model
- ☐ growth stage (startup, scaling, established)

People to Know

- ☐ CEO/Founder background
- ☐ your potential boss
- ☐ team structure
- ☐ recent key hires

Industry Intel

- ☐ market trends
- ☐ major challenges
- ☐ recent innovations
- ☐ regulatory changes
- ☐ competitive landscape

Pro Tip: If you want to take this even further, set up Google Alerts for the company and their competitors a few weeks before your interview. You'll walk in with the freshest intel.

Cheat Code #22
Leverage Biases for Your Own Gain

Remember how recruiters make decisions in half a second? That's not enough time for logical thinking. They're working off gut feelings and unconscious associations. Research consistently shows that people with certain names, features, or speech patterns are judged more harshly during interviews—even when qualifications are identical. It's called unconscious bias, and it disproportionately affects candidates of color, women, and other underrepresented groups. It's not fair—but it's real. None of us can eliminate systemic bias on our own, but we can learn how it operates—and make choices that tilt power back in our direction.

Luckily, just as there's negative bias, there's also positive bias. If you can tap into that positive bias—like the halo effect, similarity bias, or confirmation bias—why wouldn't you?

The Halo Effect: Good Looks Create an Illusion of Competence

The halo effect is basically when one positive trait creates a glow around everything else about you. Unfair? Maybe. Exploitable? Absolutely.

So how can you work the halo effect to your advantage?

Take care of your physical appearance. Let's be blunt—attractive people get hired more often and make more money. But "attractive" doesn't just mean conventional hotness. It means "polished but not trying too hard." It means being well-groomed (yes, even for remote interviews) and wearing clothes slightly nicer than the job requires. Interviewing at a casual startup? Business casual. Corporate gig? Full business attire. You get the idea.

Wearing glasses is one of the easiest "halo effects" in action—where one positive trait (in this case, perceived intelligence) creates a positive impression that extends to other unrelated qualities about the person.

Studies have shown that people wearing glasses are often perceived as more intelligent and knowledgeable, more serious and professional. Glasses make you look more focused and detail-oriented, more hardworking and dedicated—even more trustworthy and honest!

Is it fair that wearing glasses might give you this multifaceted advantage? No. But neither is getting passed over because you didn't understand the psychological shortcuts happening in every interview. Play to win. We live in a world of visual shortcuts. People literally judge books by covers, candidates by first glances, and yes, apparently, intelligence by eyewear. No actual prescription needed—we're talking about those blue light blockers or classic frames that scream "I read academic journals for fun."

Pro Tip: For video interviews, curate your background with subtle "smart person" props—organized bookshelves, minimalist desk setup, a plant (says you can keep things alive).

Similarity Bias: People Hire Their Reflection

Humans naturally gravitate toward people who remind them of themselves—it's called similarity bias. Before your interview, take a few minutes to research your interviewer on LinkedIn and look for subtle ways to build connection. Mirror elements of their professional style, highlight any genuine common ground you share—like similar schools, past companies, or overlapping interests—and adapt your language to match the company's culture. Whether the vibe is formal or casual, technical or plainspoken, matching their tone helps you build rapport and makes you feel like "one of us."

Confirmation Bias: Give Them What They Want to See

People look for evidence that confirms their initial impression. So research the role extensively and drop specific knowledge within the first five minutes. You should also use industry terminology naturally (but don't overdo it) and reference company values or recent news to show you're already aligned.

Confirmation bias exists whether you use it or not. Your competition is either intentionally leveraging it or accidentally benefiting from it. Either way, you're playing a game with unwritten rules—might as well know what they are.

Cheat Code #23
Stalk Your Interviewer (in a Noncreepy Way)

Not even googling the interviewer? Rookie move. Find something—ANYTHING—you have in common. Maybe you went to the same college, shared a previous employer, follow the same thought leaders, have similar career paths, or care about the same causes.

Why Affinity Bias Works

Affinity bias is our natural tendency to prefer people who remind us of ourselves. Humans are tribal by nature—we instinctively trust people who share our background, experiences, and values. Think of this as the "you're just like me!" effect.

But please, please, PLEASE keep it casual and natural. Don't be like "I saw on your LinkedIn that your dog's name is Buddy and you had sushi for lunch yesterday." That's creepy.

Natural	Creepy
"Oh, I noticed you also worked at [Company]. How was your experience there?"	"I saw you worked at [Company] from 2019 to 2021 under Kim Souza in the marketing department on the social media team . . ."
"I saw you attended Northwestern; so did my sister. Were you in Greek life?"	"I found a college picture of you in Foster Hall; my sister used to complain about how small the rooms were too!"

Likability Bias: Being Qualified Isn't Enough

People hire people they like. Period. The "most qualified candidate" is almost always the most qualified candidate *that they enjoyed talking to.*

That said, let's be honest—what's considered "likable" is deeply influenced by unconscious bias, especially around gender and race. You shouldn't have to contort yourself to meet someone else's biased expectations—but understanding the dynamics at play helps you navigate them strategically, without losing yourself in the process.

Studies show that likability often overrides competence in hiring decisions. Why? Because we spend more time with our coworkers than with our families. No one wants to hire someone who makes their day worse, no matter how talented they are.

To leverage likability bias, practice the following tips during your interview:

- Mirror their energy level—match their pace and tone (if they're high-energy and enthusiastic, don't be flat; if they're calm and methodical, don't be bouncing off the walls).
- Use their name (but don't overdo it)—"That's a great point, Micah."
- Show genuine curiosity—ask thoughtful questions about their experience at the company.
- Find appropriate moments to smile—likability is often just warmth plus competence.

 Pro Tip: Practice your "interested face" in the mirror. Nothing kills likability faster than a resting bitch face.

Cheat Code #24
Hit 'Em with a Fun Fact That's Too Wild to Forget

When an interviewer asks for a fun fact, don't waste it on something bland. This is your moment to be unforgettable. You want to be "the one who trained dolphins," not "I think they said they like hiking?"

So how do you come up with a fun fact that actually sticks?

Think beyond your résumé. Think hobbies, weird childhood phases, random side quests, family traditions, classes you've taken, volunteer gigs, startup flops, niche obsessions. What's something only a handful of people in your life know about you? What's something that makes your friends say, "Wait, what?"

The more specific and vivid, the better. "I love to travel" or "I like reading" are completely forgettable—every third candidate says the same thing. But if you say, "I gave a TED Talk about pasta," or "I built a generative AI that writes dad jokes," now you've got their attention. That's a detail that will actually survive the debrief.

Cheat Code #25
Ask the Right Questions—
You're Interviewing Them Too

When your interviewer asks, "Do you have any questions for us?" and you sit there looking blank, you're basically throwing away your professional leverage (and the job opportunity along with it). Do not, I repeat, DO NOT say no. You absolutely must have questions prepared if you want to be taken seriously.

You're not just there to impress them—they need to impress you too, no matter how excited about the job you are. This is a two-way street, and you're the one driving. They need to prove they're worthy of *your* talent, not the other way around.

Come prepared with questions that show you're strategic, curious, and absolutely *not* desperate. Ask about team culture, growth opportunities, how they support professional development.

Dig into their actual challenges—what keeps their leadership up at night? What are the real problems they're trying to solve?

Questions That Show You Mean Business

About the Role

- "What does success look like in this role after six months?"
- "How is performance measured and evaluated?"
- "What are the biggest challenges facing this role right now?"
- "Can you walk me through a typical day or week?"

About the Team

- "How would you describe the team's working style?"
- "What is your management style like?"
- "What's the mix of junior and senior team members?"
- "How does the team handle disagreements?"
- "What's the most successful person in this role doing differently?"

About Growth

- "What learning opportunities are available?"
- "How do you support professional development?"
- "Can you tell me about someone who got promoted from this role?"
- "What skills should I focus on developing to grow here?"
- "How will this role impact the organization's goals?"

About the Company

- "What's the biggest challenge the company is facing this year?"

- "How does this team contribute to the company's main goals?"
- "What changes do you see coming in the next one to two years?"
- "How would you describe the company culture to a friend?"

Cheat Code #26
Keep It Professional (and Private)

In the interview world, some personal details are like obstacles that could derail your career momentum. You might think you're building rapport, but you're actually opening the door to unconscious bias that can totally tank your chances before you even get started.

I'm talking about those seemingly innocent conversations that can unconsciously trigger an interviewer's hidden prejudices—even if they consider themselves totally open-minded.

An interview is your professional highlight reel, not a therapy session or a tell-all podcast.

Your family planning? Not their business. Your health challenges? Keep it professional. Political rants, financial struggles, religious deep dives—these are absolute no-go zones. Age, citizenship status, personal drama? Hard pass. Every extra personal detail is just static that can mess with your signal.

Topics to Avoid

- family planning/pregnancy
- health issues
- political views
- financial struggles
- religious beliefs
- age-related comments
- visa/citizenship status
- personal drama

If they try to fish for this info (which they shouldn't, but they might), redirect like a pro:

Their Question	Your Redirect
"Do you have kids?"	"I'm fully committed to my career goals and this role."
"How old are you?"	"I have [X] years of relevant experience in this field."
"Are you married?"	"I'm excited to discuss how my skills align with this role."
"Where are you from originally?"	"I've been working in [City/industry] for [X] years."

Remember: They can't legally ask about these things, but some still try to get the info indirectly. Stay professional and keep the focus on your qualifications. Bottom line: Protect your professional brand, control the narrative, and remember that some tea is best left unspilled. Your career will thank you. If they keep pressing you on personal details, it might be a sign of a poor or invasive company culture, and an indication it's not the right company for you.

Your Action Plan

Prepare the following items before every interview:

- ☐ research done
- ☐ stories prepared
- ☐ questions ready
- ☐ outfit planned (glasses optional but recommended)
- ☐ portfolio/examples ready
- ☐ virtual background tested (if remote)
- ☐ arrival time confirmed, link located and tested
- ☐ fun fact locked and loaded

Cheat Code #27
Follow Up After Every Interview

Let's talk about what *actually* happens after you nail that interview, do your little victory dance, and then . . . wait.

The interview isn't over when you leave the building (or close Zoom). That post-interview phase is not just dead space while you refresh your inbox and spiral about that one awkward answer. It's a crucial part of the game that too many people completely sleep on.

Even if you crushed every question, the hiring manager is talking to multiple candidates who are equally qualified. Your follow-up is your chance to stay at the top of their mental inbox when decision time comes.

After Every Interview
- ☐ Send a thank-you note within twenty-four hours.
- ☐ Connect on LinkedIn.
- ☐ Follow up if you don't hear back in a week.
- ☐ Note what worked or didn't work for next time.

Every interview is practice for your next interview. Even if you don't get this job, you're building skills for the one you really want.

The equation is simple but effective:

The more you interview ➜ The more comfortable you get

The more comfortable you get ➜ The better you perform

The better you perform ➜ The more offers you'll receive

Now go crush that interview, bestie. You've got this.

✱ Your Interview Action Plan

You now have the complete playbook to dominate any interview—time to put it into action.

1. Schedule a practice interview this month.
2. Write out your stories, using the frameworks.
3. Create your company research template.
4. Build your question bank.
5. Pick your memorable fun fact.

 Remember: Interviewing is a skill, not a talent. The more you practice, the better you'll get. Start practicing before you need it.

5

Get Your Bag

How to Get Paid What You're Actually Worth

At this point, you've survived the interview gauntlet and they want to hire you. Congratulations! This is huge—you've proven your worth, and now they're ready to bring you onto the team. Take a moment to look back at how far you've come! When you started this book, you were wondering whether you even had any marketable skills. That's insane progress—and while A Players are coasting in on insider networks, no one made that happen for you but you!

The most important conversation of the entire process is about to happen. We're about to talk about *money*. And not in that weird corporate way where everyone acts like wanting more of it is somehow dirty or ungrateful. Like?? Sorry I want to afford both rent *and* coffee??

If you're not negotiating your salary, you're literally leaving thousands of dollars on the table. And not just for this job—we're talking about money that compounds over your entire career. It's like compound interest, but for your bag.

Let me tell you a story that still makes me want to scream into a pillow:

When I got my first "real" job offer at twenty, I almost accepted $32K without negotiating, because I was just so grateful anyone would hire my fresh-out-of-college ass. But right before I hit "accept," my friend who worked in HR casually mentioned that the guy who had the role before me made $55K.

Same role. Same responsibilities. $23K difference. Why? Because he negotiated and I was about to accept their first offer, like a CLOWN.

I ended up negotiating up to $40K—not quite $55K, but that's

$8,000 I almost left on the table because I was too scared to ask. That's a lot of money! That's like . . . 1,300 oat milk lattes! Or two vintage bags! (Okay, maybe not the best examples, but YOU GET IT.)

Let's Talk About Your Money Mindset

You're sitting in a coffee shop, staring at your laptop screen. The job offer letter is right there in your inbox, but something doesn't feel right. The salary they're offering is . . . fine. Not terrible, not amazing—just fine. And you know you should negotiate, but your inner voice is spiraling.

Before we dive into the cheat codes, we need to deal with that voice in your head that's probably saying stuff like *What if they rescind the offer? What if they think I'm greedy? What if I'm not worth more? What if they laugh at me?*

First, they're not going to rescind the offer. They spent time and money recruiting you. They're invested. The worst they can say is no.

Second, wanting to be paid fairly isn't greedy. You know what's actually greedy? Companies underpaying people while their CEOs make 940 times more than their average worker. *That's* greedy.

Third, you *are* worth more. And even if you're not totally there yet, guess what? The mediocre frat guy who applied for this job definitely thinks he's worth more, and he's negotiating. So why aren't you?

> ✱ **Value Reality Check**
>
> Grab your phone or journal and write down:
>
> Three times you didn't speak up about money and regretted it
> Three skills you have that your company needs
> The salary you actually want (not what you think you "should" ask for)
>
> Be honest. No one's going to see this except you and your FBI agent.

Cheat Code #28
Inflate Your Previous Pay—It's Part of the Game

When you're negotiating for a new job, don't be afraid to . . . *inflate* your previous salary. Why? Because companies will use your past pay as a benchmark for what they think you're worth—and we're not about to let them lowball you.

Let's be real—companies play this game too. They advertise a position at $55K but only offer $32K when you show up. They keep everyone's salaries secret and actively discourage salary discussions among employees. You're not the only one massaging numbers in this equation.

If you were making $60K, say you were making $75K. If you're jumping from $80K, bump it up to $100K. Employers *expect* you to negotiate, and most of them are already padding their offers anyway. You're just leveling the playing field.

When a recruiter asks about your current salary, they're *trying* to lowball you based on what you made before. Don't fall for it. Instead, practice salary, ahem . . . *enhancement*.

Take your current salary and add 10 to 15 percent. That's your new "total compensation."

It's not *technically* lying if you're including your "total compensation package" (wink wink). You're just counting ALL the things—your base salary, that sad excuse for a bonus, the $50 monthly wellness stipend you never use, those stock options that might be worth something in 2045—you get the idea.

Your Sneaky Script Arsenal

"My total compensation package comes to approximately [current salary + 10 to 15 percent] . . ."

"My current compensation structure, with everything factored in, puts me around [current salary + 10 to 15 percent] . . ."

"Including benefits, bonuses, and other incentives, I'm at about [current salary + 10 to 15 percent] . . ."

 Pro Tip: Never give an exact number—always use words like "approximately," "about," or "around." It gives you wiggle room and sounds more natural.

Cheat Code #29
Negotiate, Negotiate, Negotiate

Look, I get it. Talking about money makes you want to crawl under a table and die. You'd rather explain your search history to your parents than ask for more cash from a potential employer.

But here's the thing. Every time you don't negotiate, you're basically setting a pile of money on fire. Like, actual thousands of dollars that could've been in your bank account, funding your vacation, paying off your loans, or buying those ridiculously priced designer shoes you've been eyeing.

The truth? Companies EXPECT you to negotiate. When they don't hear a peep after making their offer, they're not thinking *Wow, what a team player!* They're thinking *Cool! We just saved $15K a year because this person didn't know their worth.*

The Actual Negotiation: Your Step-by-Step Guide

You've made it to the offer stage. Congrats! But this isn't the finish line—it's the *starting line* of the negotiation. Most people fumble here because they're either too afraid to ask for more or they don't know how to ask in a way that lands. Not you. You're about to negotiate like an A Player.

Step 1: Do Your Homework
Before you negotiate, you need receipts. Here's your research checklist:

- ☐ Stalk Glassdoor and LinkedIn.
- ☐ Slide into the DMs of three to five people in similar roles.
- ☐ Creep on the company's funding (if it's a startup) or stock price (if public).
- ☐ Find out what people at roughly your career level make in your city.
- ☐ Write down your wins (times you killed it at work).

A Players never skip this step. Say "I want more money" with zero backup, and you've killed the negotiation.

When I was interviewing at a fintech startup, I messaged three people who had my target role on LinkedIn. Two ignored me (fair), but one told me the salary range was $15K higher than what they initially offered me. Armed with that info, I walked in ready to fight for every dollar.

Step 2: Know Your Numbers

You need three numbers:

1. **Dream number:** The salary that would make you screenshot the offer letter for the group chat.
2. **Target number:** The realistic number that would still make you feel like THAT girl.
3. **Walk-away number:** The minimum you need to keep you from walking on to the next offer.

Write these down somewhere private (not on a Post-it on your forehead during the negotiation call). These are your guideposts when things get intense and you start to panic.

Step 3: The Initial Response

When you get an offer, here's your script:

Thank you so much! I'm really excited about [Company] and can't wait to [specific project they mentioned]. I'd love to take some time to review all the details. When do you need my response by?

Step 4: The Negotiation Email

Here's your template (but make it sound like you):

> Subject: [Role] Offer—Quick Questions
>
> Hi [Name],
>
> Thanks again for the offer! I'm very excited about the possibility of joining [Company] and working on [specific thing they mentioned].
>
> I've had a chance to review the details, and I'd love to discuss the compensation package. Based on my research and experience with [brag about something specific you've done], I am hoping we can discuss a base salary of [your target number].
>
> I know I can bring a lot of value to the team, especially with [mention something they seemed excited about in the interviews].
>
> Would you be open to discussing this?
>
> Best,
> [Your name]

The key here is to keep it short, sweet, and confident. No apologizing. No "I hate to ask, but . . ." No justifying why you need more money for rent or whatever. This is business, not a GoFundMe.

Pro Tip: Don't accept the offer right away (yes, even if the offer is amazing). Take at least twenty-four hours to "think about it." Trust. This is where most B Players mess up. They get so excited someone actually wants to hire them that they blurt out "YES, I ACCEPT" before they even have a second to think. Give yourself time to process. The offer won't vanish if you sleep on it.

Your Emergency Confidence Boost

Keep this list handy for when impostor syndrome hits during negotiations:

- They chose you out of all candidates.
- The worst they can say is no.
- Most companies expect negotiation.
- Your skills have real market value.
- If you don't ask, the answer will always be no.

Cheat Code #30
Apply Where Money Is a Delusion

Want to make the big bucks? You need to go where people have absolutely DELUSIONAL ideas about money. I'm talking about places and industries where throwing around huge salaries is just . . . normal. Where can you find these money delusion zones? Read on.

Cities That Think Money Grows on Trees

- New York (where a studio apartment costs your whole soul)
- San Francisco (where *so* many orgs are remote-friendly!)
- Boston (where they think $100K is entry-level)

Industries Living in La-La Land

- tech (especially startups that just got funding)
- finance (where bonuses are bigger than your salary)

- consulting (where they charge clients your yearly salary for two weeks of work)

The secret? These places have such a warped sense of money that what seems outrageous elsewhere is just Tuesday to them. Use that delusion to your advantage, bestie.

Cheat Code #31
Look Older Than You Are

Time for some tough love: That cute graduation photo on your LinkedIn? The one with you in the cap and gown, holding your diploma like it's a newborn baby? DELETE IT.

Why? Because that photo is screaming "Please give me an entry-level salary! I just learned what Excel is!"

When companies are deciding how much to offer you, age bias is real, whether they admit it or not. They're absolutely scrolling your profile to assess your experience level and how much they think you'll accept.

Your Age Optimization Checklist

- ☐ Remove graduation dates from your résumé if they're in the last five years (LinkedIn is okay).
- ☐ Never mention being "new" or "recent" anything.
- ☐ Use a professional headshot that says "I've seen some shit."
- ☐ Consider changing your social media settings to private if there's even a hint of anything NSFW.

Think about it: When was the last time someone got extra money for looking young and inexperienced? Never. That's when. Let them *assume* you're older than you are. Your youth is an asset in many ways, but not when it comes to salary negotiations. Save the graduation celebration photos for Instagram. On LinkedIn, you're not a fresh grad—you're a professional who knows their worth and expects to be compensated accordingly.

We're not *lying* about our age—we're just not giving them reasons to lowball us based on it.

Cheat Code #32
Talk About Your Salary (and Make It Normal AF)

The whole "don't discuss your salary" thing? That's just corporate propaganda to keep us underpaid. It's *literally* how they maintain pay gaps. Every time you share your salary info with peers, you're like a tiny Robin Hood, but instead of stealing from the rich, you're just exposing their BS.

Silence around salary serves *only* your employer, not you. When you don't know what others are making, it's a lot easier for companies to get away with paying you less than you're worth. Start having real conversations about money—with coworkers, industry friends, or even that person you met at the last networking event.

The only way we're going to close the pay gap and get everyone paid what they deserve is by sharing the numbers. The more we talk, the more power we have to demand fair pay.

How to Bring It Up (Without Making It Weird)

The Same-Level Coworker	"I'm looking at some job postings and trying to figure out what's realistic. Would you be open to sharing salary ranges for our level? Happy to share mine too!"
The Mentor Vibe	"I really admire your career path! Would you be comfortable sharing how your salary has grown? I'm trying to understand what's possible."
The Direct Method (for your work bestie)	"Hey, I'm trying to negotiate, and I need a reality check. Can we talk numbers? I'll show you mine if you show me yours 😏"

Cheat Code #33
Know Your Value When Negotiating a Raise— Show Them the Money

When it's time to talk raises, don't just walk in saying you *deserve one*—bring the receipts from your brag folder! Understand the monetary impact you have on the company and use it to your advantage. This means knowing both your direct and indirect contributions.

A Players have always known this game. They've been passing around the secret playbook for generations while the rest of us were told to "work hard and wait your turn." But I'm spilling all the tea today. By the time you finish this cheat code, you'll be stepping into A-Player mode with strategies they don't want you to know.

If you're in sales or revenue-generating roles, this is easy—show them how much money you've brought in, deals you've closed, or transactions you've upsold. That's your direct impact. But even if you're not in a role that directly makes money, you can still make a strong case. Think about your indirect impact—are you improving employee retention, streamlining processes, or reducing turnover? All of these things save the company money, and that's *just* as valuable as bringing in revenue.

Direct Versus Indirect Impact

Direct Impact	Indirect Impact
When you can literally point to dollars you've brought in:	When you saved them time, money, or headaches:
• Sales numbers ("Closed $500K in new deals") • Revenue growth ("Grew accounts by 127%") • Client upsells ("Added $200K in upgrades") • New accounts ("Landed five major clients")	• Process improvements ("I cut this weekly meeting from one hour to thirty minutes, saving the team twenty-six hours annually") • Employee retention ("Started mentoring program, reduced team turnover by 25%") • Time savings ("Automated this thing that used to take five hours") • Cost reductions ("Found a new vendor, saved $20K/year")

Direct Impact	Indirect Impact
Think of this as the "look at all this cash I made you" flex.	Think of this as the "look at all the money I stopped you from wasting" flex.

Companies care about *both*. Making them money? Hot. Saving them money? Just as hot. They're not giving you a raise because you're cute—they're giving you a raise because you're impacting their bottom line. So bring those receipts, whether they're direct or indirect.

> ✱ **Your "Get That Bag" Action Plan**
>
> Here are five things you can do now to prepare for your raise conversation:
>
> - ☐ Research salaries for your role (yes, right now; I'll wait).
> - ☐ Write down your three numbers (Dream/Target/Walk-away).
> - ☐ Practice saying your target number without apologizing.
> - ☐ Draft your negotiation email.
> - ☐ Text your work bestie and ask about their salary.
>
> These are negotiation openers that communicate confidence, curiosity, and collaboration:
>
> - "Based on my research..."
> - "Given my experience with..."
> - "I'm really excited about..."
> - "Could we discuss..."
> - "I'd be more comfortable with..."
> - "What kind of flexibility do we have here?"

It's a red flag when they....
- 🚩 want an answer right TF now.
- 🚩 won't put anything in writing.
- 🚩 are weird about discussing future raises.
- 🚩 won't budge on literally anything.
- 🚩 act offended that you're negotiating.

Your negotiation isn't just about you. It's about every person who comes after you, especially other women and marginalized folks who might use your salary as their benchmark. Negotiating is truly a revolutionary act. You're creating a new standard that makes it harder for companies to underpay the next person. Make it count.

This book exists because nobody handed us the playbook. The rules of success have been gatekept for too long, passed down through old boys' clubs and family connections. But not anymore. Every time you use these cheat codes, you're not just winning the game—you're changing it.

Now go get that money, bestie. Make your bank account as thick as your boundaries.

 Remember: If you're still stepping into your power—still figuring this out, still learning to ask—you're not behind. You're a B Player turning into an A Player. The A Players? They've been doing this forever. Quietly. Strategically. And they've already helped one another climb. Now it's your turn. Normalize asking for what you're worth—and watch how fast the ceiling starts to crack.

Part 2

Office Politics

Congratulations—you're no longer the person fetching coffee or asking where the bathroom is. You've got some tenure under your belt, maybe even a few wins to your name. But you've also started to notice something: The people getting promoted aren't always the ones doing the best work.

Welcome to office politics, the unspoken game that determines who gets the good projects, the corner offices, and the fast-track promotions. You can pretend it doesn't exist—while watching less qualified colleagues zoom past you—or you can learn the rules and start playing to win.

This is the corporate jungle, where your performance review has less to do with your actual performance and more to do with whose birthday you remembered. I know, I know—you thought those days of playground politics ended with high school, but surprise! The adult world just wrapped those same dynamics in blazers and taught them to say "circle back" instead of "whatever."

In this part, we're going deep into the unspoken rules of workplace social dynamics—the stuff they definitely don't teach you in orientation but somehow expect you to know anyway. Consider this your unofficial employee handbook, the one HR would have a collective aneurysm over if they found it in the copy room.

Whether you're the person who eats lunch alone with your headphones and a spreadsheet (been there) or you're already decent at the small-talk game but want to level up your influence, I've got you.

6

IRL Survival Guide

You spend more time with your coworkers than your family, so you might as well make it work for you. The relationships you build at work aren't just about having someone to complain to about the cafeteria food—they're your professional lifeline for opportunities, information, and advancement.

But there's a difference between being genuinely liked and being strategically networked. Time to upgrade from friendly coworker to workplace power player.

"I just don't understand," my coworker Mateo sighed. "I do great work, but somehow Kate from marketing gets every opportunity. It seems like all she does is . . . hang out in the kitchen making coffee?"

Oh honey. Kate figured out something you haven't: Those kitchen conversations are where she learns whose budget got cut, who's about to quit, which VP hates which director. You're working. She's mapping the terrain.

Here's the thing about being good at your job: It's like having a smartphone without WiFi. Sure, you've got a powerful tool, but you're missing the network that makes it actually useful. Those "nothing" moments—the kitchen coffee runs, the elevator small talk, the pre-meeting banter? That's where the real downloads happen.

I can hear you now: "Ugh, Courtney, that's so fake! I just want to do my work and let it speak for itself." I used to be Team No Small Talk too. But here's the memo I wish I'd received on day one: Humans are pack animals, even in their natural corporate habitat. The most successful people aren't just technically skilled—they're relationship alchemists, mixing just the right amount of competence with connection.

Let me serve you some truth tea I wish I'd sipped earlier in my career: Stop fighting the game and learn to play it. I spent years rolling my eyes so hard I could see my own brain, thinking *This is all such BS*. But you know what was actually BS? Thinking I could single-handedly revolutionize corporate culture by refusing to play. Instead of wasting energy being the workplace rebel, I should have been studying the strategy guide and mastering the power moves.

Cheat Code #34
Keep a Candy Bowl at Your Desk

I'm about to share the most underrated power move in IRL corporate history: strategic candy placement. And no, this isn't some cutesy "be the office mom" garbage. We're creating your own gravity well of influence.

Psychologists call it a "social anchor," but I call it the Chocolate Gambit. That premium candy bowl on your desk? It's basically a corporate bug zapper for humans, except instead of zapping them, you're collecting intel, building allies, and becoming the hub of office information flow while Susan from accounting thinks she's just being sneaky about her daily 3 p.m. sugar fix. (We see you, Susan. We all see you.)

While everyone thinks you're just being the office sweetie, you're actually building your own intelligence network that would make Miranda Priestly proud. Need to know what went down in that closed-door meeting? Someone's sure to swing by for a Ghirardelli square and spill faster than an intern after their first espresso. Wondering about that upcoming reorg? The answers are probably worth exactly two Ferrero Rochers to the right person (it's Susan, and you both know she'll be back for more).

With great candy comes great responsibility. You're orchestrating a complex web of sugar-coated influence that would have Machiavelli clapping. Keep it classy, keep it premium, and for heaven's sake, keep those wrappers full. Nothing kills the girlboss vibe quite like a bowl of loose, linty chocolates looking like they survived three corporate wars and a hostile takeover.

Go forth and build your A-Player candy empire. May the office politics be ever in your favor.

 Pro Tip: Want to go a step further? Keep some spare chargers (iPhone, Android, perhaps an extra USB or HDMI cable) at your desk. Watch how quickly half the office owes you a favor.

Cheat Code #35
Bring in Fresh Coffee or Snacks Occasionally

The secret here is intermittent reinforcement—the same psychology that makes slot machines so damn addictive. Like, have you ever noticed how the person who brings donuts every Monday becomes as exciting as watching paint dry? Sure, everyone appreciates the sugar rush, but your aunt's Facebook updates are more memorable.

But that person who randomly rolls in with coffee and bagels like some kind of breakfast ninja? LEGENDARY. It's the workplace equivalent of that one friend who shows up at your door with pizza exactly when you're having the world's worst day. You never forget that friend.

Let me break down why this hits different: Our brains are basically overexcited puppies when it comes to unexpected treats. That predictable Monday donut? Your brain's like "yeah, whatever, scheduled serotonin." But random Tuesday breakfast tacos? Your neural pathways are doing backflips of joy.

Think about it—when was the last time you got genuinely excited about something you could set your watch to? The magic happens in the maybe. It's why your favorite coffee shop's "surprise cookie Wednesday" keeps you coming back like a caffeinated goldfish. You never know if today's the day you'll score that red velvet masterpiece.

And let's talk about that (manipulative—sorry!) association boost. When *you* are the source of random joy, people's brains start playing a fun little game called "what will they do next?" Suddenly, every time you walk into a room, there's this tiny hit of dopamine in everyone's brain. Are you carrying coffee? Cookies? The secret to eternal youth? Who knows! But they're excited to find out.

So yeah, while Janet from accounting is still getting polite smiles for her clockwork contribution of Monday morning muffins, you'll be out here creating literal psychological obsession with y-o-u. Think of it as being the human equivalent of finding money in your jacket pocket. Nobody remembers the wallet they use every day, but everyone remembers the surprise twenty they found in their winter coat. Be the surprise twenty.

The Surprise Snack Strategy

Do	Don't
Use random timing.	Create a schedule.
Opt for quality items.	Go too cheap.
Mix it up.	Set expectations.
Remember dietary restrictions.	Make it about recognition.

Cheat Code #36
Find a Buddy in Each Department

There seems to be no avoiding it: the diabolical torment of drowning in corporate bureaucracy. You want to get your project or idea across the finish line, but first you need to fill out three forms, get two approvals, draft three project plans and two budget proposals, and probably sacrifice your firstborn to the gods of middle management. Like, seriously? I just want to update our client onboarding process, not launch a mission to Mars.

And don't even get me started on the approval chain. It's like a game of corporate hot potato where everyone's afraid to make a decision. Your proposal bounces from Janet (who needs to "loop in some key stakeholders"), to Mark (who wants to "align on strategic priorities"), to Sarah (who needs to "pressure test the assumptions"), until finally landing in some mythical committee that apparently meets only when Mercury is in retrograde.

I swear, sometimes it feels like we've built a system specifically designed to turn three-day tasks into three-month odysseys. By the time you finally get all the approvals, your innovative idea has aged like milk, and you're too exhausted to even care anymore. But hey, at least we followed the process, right?

Luckily, there *is* a way to circumvent this chaos: the department buddy system. Your mission is to identify and build a relationship with at least one person from each department. While everyone else is drowning in red tape and waiting three weeks for Sally in accounting to process their expense report, you've got Amy giving you the "Hey, slide that over to me, I'll handle it" treatment.

Start with the holy trinity: IT, HR, and Finance. These are your power players, the ones who can either make your work life flow like melted butter or feel like you're swimming through concrete. Find your people here first. That IT person who actually explained things without making you feel like a tech dinosaur? That's your new best friend. The HR rep who gave you straight answers about benefits without the corporate word salad? Golden ticket, right there.

You've got to give before you can get. Maybe you're the one person who remembers that Dante in finance is training for a marathon and actually asks about his progress. Or you're the rare soul who notices when Anjali in legal posts about her kid's art show and sends a genuine "How did it go?" message. Small deposits in the relationship bank that pay major dividends later.

And when they do help you out? Don't just say thanks—make it memorable. Be specific: "Sarah, you literally saved my presentation by fast-tracking that trademark review. The client loved it, and my boss actually smiled. Like, with teeth showing and everything." That kind of acknowledgment sticks.

Once you've got your department buddy network set up, you become everyone else's secret weapon too. Suddenly you're the person people come to when they need to know "who to talk to" about something. And that, my friend, is corporate currency you can't earn any other way.

 Pro Tip: Keep a Notes app entry with key details about your department buddies—work anniversaries, big projects they're proud of, that time they mentioned their kid got into college. Not in a creepy way, but in an "I actually care enough to remember" way.

Cheat Code #37
Create Collision Opportunities

With a little intention, you can actually manufacture serendipity. "Right place, right time" is actually a science, not just dumb luck.

People don't get promoted just because they're good at their jobs. They get promoted because the right people know they're good at their jobs.

That's what "creating collisions" is about—putting yourself in situations where quick, casual interactions with decision-makers can actually happen. Not in a forced, networking-event kind of way. Just small, natural moments where people outside your department start to recognize your face, learn your name, and hear your ideas.

These are the hallway chats. The lunch line run-ins. The "Oh hey, we've met before" moments that make you stick in someone's mind.

You can totally manufacture these moments with just a little strategy—and when you do, they won't feel random. They'll feel like momentum.

> ### ✳ Your Office Collision Strategy Guide
>
> **First Up: Coffee Choreography**
> 8:30 a.m. is your power hour. That's when the C-suite emerges from their glass-walled habitats for their first caffeine hit. Sure, you could be answering emails at your desk, *or* you could be casually steaming oat milk while the CFO discusses quarterly targets three feet away from you. Just saying.
>
> **The Meeting Migrations**
> You know those fifteen minutes between hours when everyone's doing the conference room shuffle? That's your sweet spot. Need to print something? Funny how it's always when the product team is wrapping up their road-map session. Pure coincidence, obviously.
>
> **Lunch Logic**
> 12:00 p.m. isn't just lunchtime—it's intelligence-gathering happy hour. The senior leadership team doesn't just happen to get their overpriced salads at the same time every day. They're creatures of habit, and you're about to be their new favorite familiar face.
>
> **The Afternoon Power Plays**
> 3:00 p.m.: The post-meeting coffee rush. Perfect time to "refuel" while everyone's spilling tea about what just went down.
>
> 4:30 p.m.: When the decision-makers start wrapping up. Amazing how you always need to "grab something from your desk" right when they're having their end-of-day chats.

Please, for the love of corporate Jesus, don't make this obvious. Nothing screams "trying too hard" like sprinting to the coffee machine the second a VP walks in. Move with purpose, like you just happened to need that third coffee right when the CEO is giving their investor update prep talk. Weird coincidence, right?

Pro Tip: If your office has a gym, schedule your gym time around when the VPs do their workouts. Nothing builds rapport quite like suffering through burpees together. Plus, you can't avoid talking to someone when you're both waiting for the only working water fountain.

✷ Making It All Work Together

Look, I get it. All this might feel like you're being asked to play office politics instead of just doing your job. But you're already playing the game, whether you want to or not. The only question is whether you're playing it well.

Remember our friend Mateo from the beginning of this chapter? The one watching Kate from marketing seemingly coast by on coffee runs? Kate isn't playing a different game—she's just playing it smarter. She understands something crucial that took me years to learn: Skills and expertise might get you in the door, but it's relationships that get you the corner office.

Once you stop fighting these unwritten rules and start working with them, something magical happens: It stops feeling like a game at all. Those strategic moves become genuine connections. That candy bowl becomes a hub of real conversations. Those department buddies become actual allies in your corner.

So go forth, you beautiful corporate strategist. Stock that candy bowl, time those coffee runs, build those relationships, and remember: In the end, we're all just humans trying to make it through another workday. Might as well make it suck a little less for everyone involved.

Your Office Space Action Plan
1. Start small. Set up your basic supplies.
2. Map out office patterns.
3. Identify key connection points.
4. Create your collision opportunities calendar.
5. Build your support network.

 Remember: The office is an ecosystem. The more you contribute to making it function better, the more valuable you become to everyone in it.

7

WFH Survival Guide

Working from home was supposed to be the dream—no commute, no office politics, no pants required. But you've probably discovered that remote work comes with its own set of challenges: staying visible when you're not physically present, building relationships through a screen, and competing for attention in a world of endless Zoom fatigue.

The A-Player remote workers aren't just good at their jobs—they're strategic AF about their digital presence and intentional about their virtual relationships.

Last year, I worked at a Fortune 500 tech company with a VP named Ming. She had masterfully engineered a fully remote work life years before COVID made it mainstream. Five days a week, she was "working from home" while actually running her side consulting business from Bali (*shhhh*). Her productivity was off the charts, her team was thriving, and no one had a clue she was sipping mojitos on the beach between quarterly planning sessions.

Her secret? Ming had cracked the code of remote work asymmetry. While everyone else was trying to prove they were working by being constantly available, she was leveraging the invisible advantage—that is, the ability to define her own narrative without the performative demands of physical presence. In an office, people can see when you arrive early, stay late, or look stressed. Working remotely? That visibility is gone. Which means your colleagues' perception of you is yours to shape. When used strategically, that gap becomes power.

"Most people," she told me, "think remote work is about being seen. But that's amateur hour. Real power comes from controlling *when* and *how* you're seen."

Ming's strategy was brilliant in its simplicity. She maintained the *illusion* of constant presence through carefully orchestrated "visibility moments"—high-impact contributions at strategic times that made her seem omnipresent while actually working about 60 percent of the hours her peers did (mad respect).

When Ming's company announced a return-to-office mandate, Ming didn't fight it. Instead, she leveraged her perceived indispensability to negotiate a "special arrangement"—officially sanctioned full-time remote work with a 20 percent pay bump. Why? Because she had mastered the art of being valued for her impact, not her presence.

And if you're thinking *Must be nice,* pause right there. This playbook isn't just for seasoned execs—it's a mindset shift that anyone, at any level, can start building now.

Welcome to the advanced class in remote work manipulation, bestie. We're about to turn your home office into a power center that would have Olivia Pope raising an eyebrow.

Cheat Code #38
Keep Your Virtual Background On When You're Traveling

Freedom of location is a privilege you earn by never letting anyone know you're using it. The quickest way to lose your remote work freedom? Flaunting it on Zoom (even when your Instagram page looks like a travel influencer's humblebrag). Every time you dial in from what's clearly a new location, you're triggering something in your boss's lizard brain that whispers: *They're not committed.*

Is it fair? No. Is it real? Absolutely. Your boss might be consciously fine with remote work, but subconsciously counting every palm tree and hotel room headboard that shows up in your background.

When's the last time you saw a CEO taking calls from a beach? NEVER. Because they understand the power of controlled perception. You might be in Tahiti, but your background should be simple and consistent, every single time.

Virtual Background Power Moves

Do	Don't
If you're stationary, create an aspirational "office" setup that subtly signals success.	Show your poolside workspace (even if you're crushing it).
Use the same curated background consistently—make it your personal brand.	Broadcast from airport lounges.
Keep your background minimal but intentional. (Think organized bookshelf, subtle art, or clean lines.)	Let them see different hotel rooms.
Test your lighting to ensure you look powerful and present.	Change your setup more than once a quarter.

Your virtual background is a strategic AF tool for perception management. Choose something that could believably be your home office, even if you haven't seen your actual home office in months. Or show "company pride" by using the ugly marketing-issued branded background.

 Pro Tip: Keep a log of the background you used with each team. The day that account lead who saw you Zoom from your "home office" in Seattle last week sees your NYC apartment background, you can kiss your digital nomad dreams goodbye.

Cheat Code #39
Master the Art of Strategic Visibility

When you're remote, out of sight can definitely mean out of mind—and *not* in a good way. You don't need your boss wondering if you're actually working—or taking an extended lunch break (again). Pop up on Slack or Teams at least once a day. Drop a quick update, respond to a thread, or even just hit that emoji reaction to show you're on task.

Slack, Teams, or whatever other communications tool your company uses is more than just a communications tool—it's a stage for your personal brand. Every message, emoji reaction, and status update is a performance that shapes how people perceive you and your value.

The mistake most remote workers make? They treat Slack like a task, something to check off their list. "Posted in stand-up channel ✓ Done!" But the A Players? They treat Slack like a curated gallery, where every contribution is deliberately displayed to shape how others see their work.

Think about it: When people can't see you working, they create their own story about what you're doing (yikes!). Your job isn't to correct their story—it's to write it yourself.

Remote Visibility Choreography

- React to important announcements with the perfect emoji (quick way to show you're in the loop without looking like you have nothing better to do—the eyes 👀 emoji is your bestie here).
- Share a quick win or project update: "Just tried this feature that cut our load time by 30 percent. NBD, but thought someone might want it for the next sprint."
- Ask a thoughtful question that makes others look good: "Jen, that customer segmentation you presented was fire—mind sharing how you approached the demographic breakdown?"
- Respond to someone else's question (but wait a beat—being too quick looks like you're not busy enough).
- Share a funny meme or joke—not the cringe corporate humor your uncle posts on LinkedIn, but something that shows you get the culture.
- Ask strategic question: "Are we considering how this pricing structure might affect our enterprise clients during renewal

season?" Watch your SVP's eyes widen when they realize you're not just another task rabbit.

Cheat Code #40
Upgrade Your Internal Profiles

Visibility goes far beyond your chat messages. Make sure your Slack or Teams (and email!) profile photo is conveying organization, professionalism, and leadership. That tiny circle of pixels is representing *you*, 24/7. Your profile picture is your digital first impression on steroids. While Jessica's still rocking that blurry vacation snap from 2019 (we get it; you went to the Bahamas), you're about to level up your image game.

Rookie Moves	Power Plays
Cropped group photos	Professional headshot
Vacation shots	Clear face shot with genuine smile
The dreaded blank avatar	Solid or subtle background
Heavily filtered selfies	Good lighting (natural light is your bestie)

 Pro Tip: Update your photo every eighteen to twenty-four months. Not because you need to, but because it shows you're intentional about your presence. Plus, it gives people a reason to notice you again. "Oh, new photo? Looking sharp!" is free visibility points.

Cheat Code #41
Strategic Status

Your Slack status isn't just some cutesy toggle—it's literally free real estate for your internal personal brand jujitsu. When Jessica from Product sees you're "In client workshop" instead of boring old "Busy," she's picking up what you're putting down: that you're the queen who's driving revenue and crushing client relationships.

And when Brad notices your "Deep work: Q4 strategy planning" status, he's getting the memo that you're not just answering emails—you're the visionary who's thinking three steps ahead. Strategic status updates are your silent flex, and honey, in this economy, every flex counts.

Rookie Moves	Power Plays
Working on stuff	Deep focus: Finalizing Q4 strategy
Away	In client workshop until 2 p.m.
Busy	Head down on [specific project]

 Pro Tip: Create a swipe file of power status updates. When you're busy with actual work, you can quickly grab one that fits without breaking your flow.

Cheat Code #42
Get a Top-Quality External Camera and Microphone

Why do some people command attention on Zoom while others fade into the background? Your brain makes snap judgments about someone's authority, competence, and trustworthiness within 0.1 second of seeing them on video. Unfair? Absolutely. Real? One hundred percent.

Studies from *Harvard Business Review* show that video quality directly impacts perceived credibility. People with clear audio are rated 30 percent more trustworthy than those with poor sound quality, according to University of California research. High-definition video with good lighting makes you appear 25 percent more competent and a whopping 41 percent more likely to be considered for leadership roles. Additionally, research published in the *Journal of Applied*

Psychology found that individuals with higher video quality were rated approximately 17 percent more competent than those with low-quality video.[9,10]

Think about that: You could be saying the *exact same things*, but better equipment makes people literally perceive you as more important.

If you're still using your laptop's built-in camera and mic, it's time for an upgrade. Investing in a good-quality external camera and microphone can instantly level up your presence on video calls. It makes you look—and sound—like you've got your shit together, which low-key makes you seem more important. Crisp audio and a clear picture say "I take my work seriously," even if you're in (off-camera) sweatpants.

Cheat Code #43
Make the Effort to Meet Up with Remote Coworkers (or Clients)

When you're remote, you need to orchestrate the serendipitous encounters that office people get for free. When you've got a solid reason to be in a city—like a client meeting, conference, or team gathering—that's your golden ticket to stacking additional face time. Hit up every worthwhile contact in that zip code. "Hey, I'll be in NYC for a leadership summit—would love to grab coffee while I'm there!"

The dirty little secret? Sometimes you create the "anchor" meeting just to justify the trip. Maybe you "happen" to be in Chicago for a "planning session"—suddenly you can fill your schedule with valuable face-to-face connections.

When you start showing up as someone who "makes the effort" even when it's not required, your colleagues see you as someone who goes above and beyond to strengthen relationships. And honestly? Those dinners, coffees, and impromptu meetups are where the real bonds form and deals happen. One casual drink with a client can do more for your relationship than fifty Zoom calls.

The Psychology of Presence

Scarcity creates value (basic economics, baby): When you're not constantly available in the office, your physical presence becomes more valuable and noticeable. Just like limited-edition anything, people value what's rare.

Selective attendance signals power (you choose when to be there): This strategy works best once you've established some credibility and are no longer entry-level. When you're strategic about which in-person events you attend, it shows you're in control of your schedule and can prioritize what matters.

Quality face time outweighs quantity (make it memorable).

> **Pro Tip:** When you do show up in person, aim for a slightly more polished appearance than you expect to see in everyone else. The contrast between your "casual" remote presence and your in-person power looks creates an aspirational image.

✱ Virtual Relationship Building Template

Because you can't bump into people at the coffee machine anymore.

Monthly Connection Plan

Week 1: Schedule two virtual coffee chats: one peer and one person from another team.

Week 2: Engage in three nondepartment Slack channels: Share a meme, event, or something light or funny; ask a question; respond to someone else.

Week 3: Reach out to two "weak ties": someone you rarely work with, a former project colleague.

Week 4: Make three meaningful meeting contributions: share a win, highlight a teammate, build on someone else's idea.

8

Playing the Social Game

You're past the point where showing up and doing good work is enough to stand out. At this stage of your career, your technical skills are table stakes—everyone at your level can do the job. What separates the promoted from the passed over is emotional intelligence and social strategy.

"I don't do office politics," my client announced proudly during our first mentorship call. "I'm just here to work."

I muted myself so she wouldn't hear me cackling.

Three months later, she was back, absolutely fuming. She'd just found out the teammate she'd trained had been promoted over her. The teammate who was always chatting with the VP in the kitchen. The teammate who organized happy hours. The teammate who—you guessed it—played the game.

Saying you "don't do office politics" is like saying you don't believe in gravity. Cute, but gravity still exists, and you're still stuck to the earth whether you believe in it or not.

Office politics isn't some optional side quest in your career game. It's the main storyline. You can ignore it, but you're still playing—you're just playing to lose.

But Courtney, you're probably thinking, *isn't this all just fake and manipulative?* Bestie . . . is it manipulative to understand human psychology? Is it fake to build relationships? Is it evil to care about how people perceive you?

No. It's smart.

Let's get into the cheat codes that'll turn you from a social game rookie into a certified office politician (in the best way possible).

Cheat Code #44
Treat Higher-Ups Like They're Real People (Respectfully)

Executives exist outside of quarterly earnings calls and terrifying all-hands meetings. They have dogs that puke on carpets, they binge streaming shows, and some of them go to concerts alone (shocking, I know).

Most people treat VPs and above like corporate deities. In their presence, or at the mere mention of them, they get sweaty, talk in buzzwords, and stick to work topics only. This is why having an actual human conversation with these exalted beings is your secret advantage.

I learned this while working customer experience for a professional sports team. One day, I overheard our VP of Operations talking about seeing The National in concert. Instead of pretending I didn't hear, I jumped in: "You were at the Dallas show? I was there too!"

Her face lit up. "You like The National? Nobody here knows who they are!"

Just like that, we shared a passion that had nothing to do with ticket sales or fan complaints. Whenever we crossed paths after that, we'd trade concert stories and music recommendations. I had a better connection with her as a customer experience rep than directors who'd been there for years.

Why? Because everyone else tried to impress her with performance stats and technical questions. I just talked to her like a person with a life outside the arena. That made me stand out among people who only discussed attendance numbers and concession revenue.

So, how do you pull this off without being creepy?

The "They're Just People" Strategy

Notice the details. Spot the photos on their desk, their office decor, or what they mention casually. Marathon medals? Guitar collection? Dog photos? Those are your conversation starters.

Ask real questions. "Is that your Labrador in that photo? I just got one" beats "How's the weather?" Specific questions get actual conversations.

Share when it's genuine. If they're into rock climbing and you are too, mention it. Don't fake interests you don't have. People smell bullshit.

Follow up later. If they mention their kid's championship game, ask about it next time. "How did Tyler's game go?" shows you actually give a damn.

Know the boundaries. Stick to hobbies, interests, travel, and pets. Skip politics, religion, or personal drama. Friendly, not invasive.

These talks don't need to be long. A quick minute about their weekend hike or a new restaurant creates more connection than an hour of shoptalk.

The higher someone rises, the less people treat them normally. Being the person who sees beyond their title is surprisingly powerful.

Next time you're stuck in the elevator with the CFO, don't stare at your phone or babble about quarterly targets. Be the A Player who asks about their marathon training or comments on the book they're carrying. It shows confidence, builds real connection, and reminds both of you that behind all the org charts and titles, we're just people who sometimes rock out to indie bands alone.

Cheat Code #45
Play the Birthdays and Names Game

Want to instantly become everyone's favorite coworker? Keep track of their kids' and pets' names. I'm dead serious.

Here's some wild psychology for you: Your brain literally lights up like a Christmas tree when it hears your own name. Scientists have found that hearing your name triggers unique brain activity that doesn't happen with any other word. It's like a dopamine hit straight to your ego.

Why? Because from the time you were a tiny baby, your name has been the most important word in your world. And guess what? The same goes for people's kids and pets. When you remember little Timmy's name or ask about Princess Fluffles the cat, you're triggering that same feel-good brain response.

I have a Notes app entry that looks like this:

- Aliyah (VP): daughter Clara (soccer), son Xavier (guitar), golden retriever Luna

- Brianna (Marketing): cats Milo and Olive, studying for LSAT

- Dev team: John's new baby girl Zuri, Calvin's French bulldog Zeus

Is it extra? Yes. Creepy? Maybe. But does it work like magic? Absolutely.

When you ask, "How's Clara's soccer season going?" or "Did Zeus get used to the new apartment?" you're saying "I care enough to remember what matters to you."

 Pro Tip: Add life updates to your notes after conversations. It takes ten seconds and pays off forever.

* * *

Let's be honest—nobody actually remembers birthdays anymore unless Facebook tells them to care. Which is exactly why being that person who mysteriously never forgets is like having an A-Player superpower. It's giving "I have my shit together" energy while literally just using a calendar app like a functioning adult.

Here's the lazy girl's guide to looking thoughtful AF: Make a separate Google calendar, dump everyone's birthdays and work anniversaries in there, and set those notifications. Then keep a stack of blank cards in your desk drawer like you're someone's cool aunt. *Boom.* You're now the most emotionally intelligent person in your office for doing the bare minimum.

A Players know that this strategy works on literally everyone. Your boss? Secretly thrilled you remembered their work anniversary. That scary senior VP? Melts like butter when they get a "happy birthday" Slack message that isn't automated. Even that one weird guy from Sales Ops who never makes eye contact will remember that you were the only one who acknowledged his five years of turning things off and on again.

Birthday Homework for the Overachievers

1. Create your "I'm a thoughtful bitch" calendar right now.
2. Set those notifications for two days before each date (because showing up exactly on time is giving "I remembered only because of technology" energy).
3. Collect blank cards from local shops and artists (or order a pack from Amazon, if you must).
4. Write down one weird personal detail about each coworker when they mention it (their dog's name, their favorite coffee order, their hatred of Carol from accounting).
5. Use these details in your birthday messages to gaslight everyone into thinking you're actually paying attention to their lives.
6. Accept your Oscar for Best Performance in a Corporate Role.

Pro Tip: Bonus points if you start a shared spreadsheet of everyone's coffee orders "to be helpful" (but actually to have blackmail-level knowledge of everyone's high-maintenance Starbucks modifications so you can swoop into the office with a lil birthday treat that blows them away).¹

Cheat Code #46
The Strategic Gossip Pivot

Gossip isn't just petty drama—it's how humans have bonded since we were living in caves. Anthropologists have found that gossip has played a crucial role in our evolution as a species. It's how we figure out social norms and understand who we can actually trust. So really, when I'm binge-listening to three hours of celeb breakup drama on my favorite podcast, I'm not being shallow—I'm participating in an ancient human tradition that's practically anthropological research.

Think of gossip like social glue. If you completely opt out, you're essentially choosing to be an outsider. But if you dive in too deep, you'll get stuck and possibly drown in the drama. The key is to teeter right on that edge—present enough to build bonds, smart enough to stay clean.

People who say they "don't gossip" usually just aren't invited to hear the good stuff. Stay in the loop, keep your hands clean, and master the art of the strategic pivot.

The Tea-Spilling Strategy Guide

Office gossip is inevitable, but you don't have to choose between being a total asshole who shuts down someone trying to bond with you or getting dragged into the toxic swamp of workplace politics. These scripts help you gracefully redirect without burning bridges or becoming the office drama repository.

When Someone Spills Tea About...	You Should Say...
Work drama	"Oh wow, that's interesting! Did you see [celebrity drama] though?"
Someone's personal life	"That must be tough for them. Hey, have you tried that new lunch spot?"
Office relationships	"People are always speculating! Speaking of relationships, do you watch *Love Is Blind*?"
Company changes	"I guess we'll see how it plays out. BTW, what did you think about [safe topic]?"

The Gossip Pivot Formula

- Acknowledge ("Oh wow, that's interesting...").
- Validate the emotion ("I can see why that would be frustrating").
- Redirect to safer territory ("Speaking of drama, did you see the latest *House of Dragons*?").

Example Pivots

Them	You
"Did you hear about what happened in the marketing meeting?"	"No, but did you see that wild drama with [insert celebrity] on Twitter?"
"I heard Sarah's leaving because..."	"Speaking of career moves, have you been watching *Succession*?"

This little move works like magic because you're threading the needle perfectly. You're basically saying "I see you trying to connect with me" without becoming the office secret keeper. The person still feels heard (which is what they wanted in the first place), but you haven't thrown anyone under the bus or stored up potential ammunition for drama. The conversation keeps rolling instead of hitting that awkward oh-they're-no-fun wall, and you've given them somewhere else to direct their energy.

Best part? You've subtly branded yourself as someone cool enough to chat with but smart enough not to get messy. It's social genius disguised as casual conversation.

 Pro Tip: Being anti-gossip is like being anti-weather. It's going to happen whether you participate or not. Your job isn't to stop it—it's to navigate it strategically.

Cheat Code #47
Make Others Look Good (So You Look Even Better)

Want to know the fastest way to build allies? Make other people look good. While B Players work the same tired game of credit-hoarding and blame-dodging, A Players run a whole different playbook.

Look, I understand your competitive instincts, but the "haven't evolved past saber-toothed tiger times" vibe is not it. It's time to graduate from your Regina George era. The secret to becoming that bitch at work is by (spoiler alert!) not actually being a bitch at all.

Here's the move: Every time your coworker does something that doesn't completely suck, blast it everywhere like you're their personal PR team. Drop it in Slack, mention it in meetings, bring it up to your boss while you're doing that hallway small talk thing.

Why? Because while everyone else is still trying to girlboss-gatekeep-gaslight their way to the top, you're building your own little army of people who would die for you. Like, Kiara from marketing will LITERALLY jump in front of a bus for you (or even more heroic, take blame for a failed project) because you gave her credit for that good idea she had in 2023.

The best part? This strategy requires literally zero effort. You're just stating facts about other people's work, but somehow *you* end up looking like a confident queen who's secure enough to hype up the competition. You're basically doing the bare minimum of being a decent human and getting paid in workplace political capital. We love a strategic queen who works smarter, not harder.

Your Shout-out Strategy

Any time a coworker does something even mildly impressive, gas them up like you're their personal PR team. Drop a casual mention in Slack, shout them out in a meeting, reference their idea when your boss walks by. Say things like, "That actually reminds me of the deck Kai built last week," or "Aisha's suggestion totally set us up for this win." It takes zero effort and builds infinite goodwill. Over email? Slide in a quick "Thanks to Sasha's quick thinking . . ." or "Credit to the design team—especially Pat." On Slack, toss in a "👏 @Rowan coming in clutch," or "Can we talk about how @Taylor absolutely nailed this?" It's the bare minimum of decency and it pays you back in workplace political capital.

 Pro Tip: When you genuinely celebrate others, you come across as confident and secure. Only insecure people need to hog the spotlight.

Cheat Code #48
Strategic Helpfulness (or How to Build Your Office Karma Without Becoming Everyone's B*tch)

This is some advanced-level, A-Player workplace manipulation that *looks* like basic human decency. When you see someone drowning in work and stress-eating their third bag of M&M's Minis before noon, that's your cue to swoop in like a corporate guardian angel. But a smart one who doesn't get taken advantage of.

You want to be just helpful enough that people think you're a saint, but not so helpful that you become the office doormat. Think of it as micro-favors—quick tasks that take you five to ten minutes but save someone else an hour of stress. Proofread that email they're overthinking. Grab them a coffee when you're already going. Take notes in that one meeting they're running late to. It's practicing "I'm a team player" without the "please dump all your work on me" invite.

Keep your helping strategic AF. Save your generous moments for either (1) people with actual power to help your career or (2) the underappreciated superstars who secretly run the place (looking at you, executive assistants and IT wizards). And always, ALWAYS help in visible ways during high-stress times. Nothing says "promote me" like being the calm, collected queen who helps others during a crisis while everyone else is having a meltdown.

But here's the most important part: boundaries. The second you become known as the yes girl, you're done. Your helping should be like a surprise flash sale—unexpected, appreciated, and definitely not available 24/7. When someone starts expecting your help, hit them with the "So sorry, I'm slammed right now!" faster than you can say "quiet quitting."

The Not-a-Pushover Playbook

- Keep a mental list of quick, low-effort tasks you can easily do.
- Help visible people in visible ways (let someone else deal with Lisa's private printer crisis).
- Track your favors like you track your enemies.
- Master the art of saying "I wish I could help but [insert believable excuse here]."
- Never volunteer for anything that could become recurring.
- Perfect your "sympathetic but busy" face for when you need to say no.

 Pro Tip: You're going for "helpful queen who has her shit together," not "human TaskRabbit with no boundaries." Now go forth and selectively slay.

Cheat Code #49
Find a Common Enemy (but Keep It Light)

Fun fact: Our brains are wired to bond over shared hatred. It's some caveman psychology BS where hating the same thing made tribes stronger—except instead of bonding over our mutual fear of saber-toothed tigers, we're bonding over that one Microsoft Teams notification that sounds like it's judging you.

Nothing brings people together like shared frustration, so *find one*. It could be the never-ending email chain, the old printer that always jams, or even that one tedious monthly meeting. A little venting creates camaraderie—just don't go too negative.

The key to professional complaint bonding is picking safe targets. We're not here to get canceled—we're here to unite people faster than a pizza party in a conference room. The office thermostat that's clearly possessed by a demon? Fair game. Janet's aggressive reply-all habit? Too spicy; keep it moving. Instead of targeting actual humans (major rookie move), redirect that energy toward inanimate objects that can't file HR complaints. You want the kind of complaints that make people nod aggressively while saying "OH MY GOD, YES" but won't end up in a strongly worded email from leadership.

Become the person who complains hilariously, not annoyingly. When the video conference fails for the forty-seventh time, don't be the one sighing dramatically—be the one who says "I see our technology is participating in Throwback Thursday again, serving us that 1999 dial-up realness." Congratulations! You've just turned tech issues into a stand-up routine, and everyone's secretly hoping the video will fail just to hear your commentary.

Strategic complaining builds more bonds than those mandatory happy hours ever will. Just aim your wit at the malfunctioning tech, not the humans. You'll stay out of HR's crosshairs while becoming the person people actually want to grab lunch with. Office nemesis: identified. Office allies: multiplied.

Cheat Code #50
Find Out What Motivates People—and Mention It

Let's get manipulative for a good cause, besties. Everyone's got their own personal currency, and it's usually not what you think. Your boss might *seem* like she's all about the bottom line, but what she really craves is recognition (hello, youngest VP syndrome). Meanwhile, that scary HR manager isn't actually the fun police—they just need to feel in control because their home life is chaos. It's like everyone's wearing a sign saying "PLEASE VALIDATE THIS SPECIFIC THING ABOUT ME," but only the real ones can read it.

Start keeping track of what makes people light up. Build yourself a little black book of professional dreams and schemes. When someone mentions they're saving for a trip to Fiji, that's not just small talk—that's future conversation currency, baby.

The best part? This strategy works on literally everyone because people are basically just walking egos waiting to be stroked. Your boss wants recognition? CC them on their every win like you're their personal hype woman. That type A project manager? Show them how you're making their life easier. The office overachiever? Ask them about their side hustle podcast that definitely doesn't have any listeners yet.

If someone is working toward a goal, *any* goal—like a promotion, running a marathon, or a splurge vacation—mention it in conversations: "Hey, how's marathon training coming along?" It shows you remember and care about what's important to them.

Office Currency Tracker
Different things have value to different people. Track what matters to who.

Person	Their Currency	How to "Pay" Them
My boss (love her!)	Recognition	CC them on wins.
Sales Lead	Efficiency	Save them time.

Person	Their Currency	How to "Pay" Them
HR Manager (ugh)	Control	Keep them informed.
Work Bestie	Innovation	Bring new ideas.

> ✱ **Your Social Game Action Plan**
>
> We've covered a *lot* of ground here, so let's break down these power moves that'll take you from office wallflower to workplace puppet master (in the best way possible, obviously).
>
> **1. Create Your Power Tools**
> Set up that stalker-level Notes app system.
>
> Make your Strategic Calendar of important dates.
>
> Start your Motivation Currency tracker.
>
> Order those blank birthday cards (yes, really).
>
> **2. Your Thirty-Day Challenge**
> Week 1: Learn three new personal details about different coworkers.
>
> Week 2: Execute at least two strategic gossip pivots.
>
> Week 3: Make someone else look good in a meeting (and watch the karma roll in).
>
> Week 4: Help someone strategically (and keep the receipts).
>
> **3. Your New Morning Routine**
> Check your calendar for strategic opportunities.
>
> Review your notes before any important meetings.
>
> Practice your "wow, that's so interesting" face in your front-facing camera.

People will forget what you said and what you did, but they'll never forget how you made them feel seen. The difference between being forgettable and unforgettable isn't a grand gesture—it's just paying attention to what makes someone tick, then making sure they know you noticed. You're not being manipulative—you're being emotionally intelligent. And you're definitely not playing office politics—you're just finally learning the rules of a game you've been playing all along.

9

Winning Over Your Boss

Your relationship with your direct manager is the single most important factor in your day-to-day work satisfaction and long-term career trajectory. Think of your boss as the gatekeeper to everything you want in your career: They control your projects, your visibility to senior leadership, your performance reviews, and, ultimately, your upward mobility.

A good boss can accelerate your growth like rocket fuel, advocate for your advancement in rooms you'll never see, and shield you from the organizational chaos that could otherwise consume your sanity. They become your career champion, opening doors you didn't even know existed. A bad one? They can make your life absolutely miserable regardless of how much you love your actual work, turning even dream projects into daily torture sessions.

The good news? Managing up is a skill you can learn, regardless of what type of manager you're dealing with. Once you crack the code on managing up, you'll wonder how you ever navigated your career without it.

I'm in my favorite wine bar, nibbling on some crudité, when I overhear what has to be the most painful conversation ever. This girl is trauma-dumping to her friend at the next table about how her boss "hates her"—meanwhile, she's working seventy-hour weeks, taking on every project, and basically living at the office.

"*I just don't get it,*" she whispers. "*I'm doing EVERYTHING right.*"

I sigh into my hummus. Because honey . . . no. No, you're not.

Here's the thing about bosses: They're not teachers grading your homework. They're not keeping a secret scorecard of your overtime hours. They're just humans with egos and their own stress to deal with. And if you're trying to win them over by being the hardest worker, you're playing the wrong game entirely.

The people who have their bosses wrapped around their little finger aren't usually the ones grinding away until 9 p.m. They're the ones who've cracked the code of boss psychology. And bestie, I'm about to spill all the secrets.

Before we dive into the specific cheat codes, we need to understand what makes bosses tick. Most bosses? They're just like you—trying not to look bad in front of their boss. They want the win. They want to be seen as strong leaders. And deep down, they're just as scared of messing up as you are. They need to feel in control. They want to look good. Give them that, and you've already won.

Your job? Figure out how to make their life easier while making them look good. That's it. That's the game.

Cheat Code #51
Don't Outshine Your Boss (Don't Be Seen as a Threat)

I get it—you're a star, you're crushing it, you could probably do their job better than them on a bad day. But if you start outshining your boss too much, you're gonna end up in their crosshairs, and that's not the kind of attention you want.

This is a career truth that separates the A Players from the B Players: Understanding power dynamics is about perception. While you might be that girl who's revolutionizing workflows while your boss is still figuring out how to convert a Google Doc to a PDF, remember that the corporate game is played in the mind as much as in the spreadsheet.

Play it smart. Instead of trying to be the star of the show, make your boss the star and yourself the incredible supporting actor. When you nail a project, throw some credit their way, even if they contributed minimally. Make sure you're seen as a valuable asset, not a competitor.

The workplace dynamic is a delicate ecosystem. Every single action creates ripples of social capital. Your boss, regardless of their capabilities, holds positional leverage—a form of power that transcends pure merit. When you consistently outshine them, you might be triggering their primitive survival instincts, which could lead to a contentious working relationship—to be avoided at all costs. Instead, master the art of strategic attribution: "This insight came from building on [Boss's Name]'s framework" or "The foundation that [Boss's Name] laid made this possible."

The Not-So-Subtle Art of Boss Credit

Don't Say This	Instead, Say This
"I did this all by myself!"	"Your guidance really helped shape this project."
"I figured it out without any help."	"That strategy you mentioned really paid off."
"I actually came up with that idea."	"Following your lead on this made a huge difference."

A quick caveat: This cheat code is designed for a normal work environment with a (relatively) sane boss who can see past the end of their nose. Unfortunately, some of us work for bosses who like to go ahead and take that credit before we even offer it . . . or worse. Go ahead and peek at cheat code #87 if you think you might be in this scenario.

 Pro Tip: The goal isn't to minimize your contributions but to create a narrative where your boss feels like they played a meaningful role in your success. Think of it like adding a coproducer credit to your hit single—you're still the star, but you're not the only name in lights.

Cheat Code #52
If You Can Google It, Don't Ask It

If you can find the answer with a quick search, don't waste your boss's time asking about it. Nothing screams "I didn't bother to try" like asking questions that Google could've handled in literally two seconds. You want your boss to see you as resourceful and on top of things, not as someone who needs their hand held for every little detail.

Before you ask, take a sec to do your homework. Then, if you still need help, you'll be able to ask *better* questions that show you've actually put some effort in.

A Players understand that every question you ask is either a deposit to or a withdrawal from your professional reputation bank account. When you pop into your boss's office asking about the company's PTO policy (which is literally pinned in Slack), you're telling them a story about who you are. And honey, that story is giving "I expect others to do my thinking for me" energy, which is about as attractive as a guy who still has his mom do his laundry. Major B-Player energy.

A Players show up to conversations having already done the first three levels of research. Think of Google as your personal executive assistant: Let it handle the basic queries while you save your boss-directed questions for the kind of intellectual heavy lifting that actually requires more brainpower.

 Pro Tip: Stupid questions *do* exist, so filter them. The goal is to make every question you ask feel like it was worth your boss's time to answer. That's the difference between being seen as an energy drain or as an energy multiplier in your organization's ecosystem.

Cheat Code #53
Don't Just Bring Problems—Bring Three Solutions (and a Favorite)

My old coworker Isra had a habit that was slowly killing her career. Every time she had an issue, she'd go to our boss like: "The client is unhappy with our timeline . . . what should we do?"

Meanwhile, our other coworker Ali (who was otherwise a mediocre performer, tbh) would walk in with: "Hey, the client's concerned about the timeline. I've mapped out three ways we could handle this. My recommendation is solution 2, but I'm happy to discuss all three."

Guess who got promoted.

Your boss doesn't want to be your problem-solving fairy godmother. They want to be your strategic advisor. And the difference between those two roles is exactly three solutions.

If you're bringing a problem to your boss, don't just show up empty-handed and expect them to magically fix it. Come in with three possible solutions *and* highlight which one you think is the best option. This way, you're not just dumping your mess on them. You're showing you actually thought it through and took the time to figure out a game plan.

Bosses don't want to play "guess what I'm thinking" or come up with all the answers—they want people who make their lives easier. By presenting solutions and recommending one of them, you're making it a no-brainer for them to trust your judgment. Plus, it shows that you're ready to handle bigger decisions down the road.

✳ **The Three-Solutions Script**

Hey [Boss], wanted to discuss the client's timeline concerns. I've outlined three potential solutions:

1. Speed Up Current Plan
- Add two team members temporarily.
- Work some planned overtime.
- Deliver original scope faster.

Pros: Maintains full scope
Cons: Higher cost, team strain
Cost: ~$10K additional

2. Phased Delivery Approach [Recommended]
- Break into three priority-based phases.
- Deliver high-impact features first.
- Adjust later phases based on feedback.

Pros: Earlier value delivery; flexible
Cons: More complex coordination
Cost: Within current budget

3. Reduce Initial Scope
- Cut nonessential features.
- Focus only on core requirements.
- Add options to solution 2.

Pros: Fastest timeline, lowest risk
Cons: Less initial functionality
Cost: Potential loss of $20K in features

    I recommend solution 2 because it balances the client's timeline needs with our quality standards and budget constraints. It also gives us flexibility to adjust based on their feedback.
    Would you like to discuss the details of any of these solutions?

Pro Tip: Three is the magic number because it shows you've done your homework, thought through alternatives, still respect their input, and made it easy for them to decide.

Cheat Code #54
Help Your Boss with Selfish Goals

Every boss is quietly striving toward a selfish goal. That might be a promotion, securing a high-stakes deal, gaining recognition, or even something deeper, like feeling love or friendship.

Think of your boss's personal aspirations as a hidden leverage point in your professional ecosystem. Everyone at work is pursuing their own version of success—whether that's earning industry recognition, landing a prestigious promotion, or building their reputation. Your boss is no different; they just have more power to influence your trajectory.

Your move is to help your boss's dreams become just a bit more attainable. Take a micro-step to helping them get 1 percent closer to their goal. Find out what it is, and do whatever you can to help make it happen. When you're that person who's making their life easier and their goals more achievable, they'll be *obsessed* with you (in a good way).

It's human nature—people are naturally drawn to those who support their dreams. When you support their aspirations—subtly, with a strategic support framework—you become indispensable.

Level 1: Recognition and Research

- Notice patterns in what they emphasize in meetings.
- Track what initiatives they invest extra energy in.
- Observe whose success they admire or reference.

Level 2: Tactical Implementation

- Document small but impactful ways to advance their goals.
- Surface opportunities aligned with their interests.

- Connect them with valuable networks or resources.
- Highlight their contributions in ways that reach key stakeholders.
- Create platforms for them to demonstrate expertise.

Understand that when you actively contribute to someone's professional narrative, you become an essential part of their success story. By helping manifest their goals, you're building the kind of professional alliance that transcends typical employee-boss dynamics.

Pro Tip: Keep a strategic opportunity log. When your boss mentions aspirations or interests, note them down. Sneaky AF, sure, but you'll be able to map out the intersection between their goals and your potential value-add.

Cheat Code #55
Use the Monday, Friday, Daily Rule to Keep Your Boss off Your Back

If you're tired of your boss being *constantly* up your ass, here's how to make them chill out: Follow the Monday, Friday, daily rule. On Monday, send them a quick email with your top five goals for the week. On Friday, send an update on five things you actually accomplished. And every day, send them one small update about your progress.

Day	Action	Details
Monday	Weekly goals email	Send top five goals for the week
Tuesday through Thursday	Daily update	Send one small progress update
Friday	Accomplishments report	Send five things accomplished this week

When you're proactive with communicating progress, it keeps your boss in the loop and shows them you're on top of your game. Basically, you're giving them less reason to breathe down your neck. The more you keep them informed, the more likely they are to back off from micromanaging, which means *way* more freedom for you to do your thing without someone constantly looking over your shoulder.

Cheat Code #56
Learn to Manage Up

Don't wait for your boss to tell you what to do. If you know they have a recurring task or need help with a regular project, take the initiative and get it done before they ask. Learn to anticipate their needs and literally PULL things off their plate.

Your boss is probably buried under their own avalanche of nonsense—endless meetings about meetings, emails that should've been Teams messages, and deadlines that keep multiplying like rabbits.

Here's where you come in: Instead of being another task on their list, become the person who makes tasks vanish. Not by brownnosing or bringing them coffee (though caffeine never hurts), but by systematically absorbing their predictable headaches before they turn into migraines. When you master this, you transform from "helpful direct report" into "indispensable strategic partner who might be secretly running things." An A-Player move.

While B Players are polishing their performance review buzzwords and perfecting their "team player" smile, you're actually building real career capital. You'll become so fundamentally valuable that your boss starts wondering how they functioned before you showed up.

The catch? There's a fine line between being invaluable and being stuck. When you become too good at handling your boss's tasks, they might resist promoting you because "nobody else can do what you do." This is the assistant trap: becoming so good at supporting someone that they never let you grow beyond that role. (See cheat code #90 for how to avoid this pitfall.)

I learned this lesson at my internship in college. My boss, Marcus, was notoriously disorganized. One Monday, I watched him frantically searching for a quarterly report due for the executive meeting in an hour.

"Do you need the Q3 sales breakdown?" I asked, sliding a printed copy across his desk along with a summary of key points.

He looked at me like I'd performed magic. "How did you know?"

"You present these every quarter on the first Monday. I pulled the data Friday and formatted it the way you usually do."

He stared at the report. "This would have taken me three hours."

After that, I made it my mission to get ahead of his predictable crises. Monthly budget reconciliation? Done before he asked. Weekly client tracker? Updated every Friday morning.

Within two months, his stress visibly decreased. Within four months, I got assigned to a more visible client. Within six months, he was bringing me to leadership meetings I had no official business attending. I was even offered a role after graduation.

"You make me look good," he told me. "But more importantly, you make me better at my actual job because I'm not drowning in the small stuff."

The A-Player move: I didn't just silently absorb these tasks forever. For each one, I documented the process, created templates, and eventually trained others to do them too. This prevented me from becoming the indispensable assistant who can never move up because "no one else can do what you do."

The goal is to demonstrate your capacity to think ahead, solve problems proactively, and operate at a higher level than your current role suggests.

When you pull things off your boss's plate before they ask, you're showing them exactly what you're capable of, often before they would have thought to test those waters themselves.

The Low-Maintenance Checklist

- ☐ Solve problems independently when possible.
- ☐ Keep emails brief and to the point.
- ☐ Avoid being the person who needs constant validation.
- ☐ Meet deadlines without reminders.
- ☐ Handle team drama without involving them.

Your boss isn't your babysitter. If you want to stand out, show them you can handle things *on your own*. Solve problems. Make decisions. Skip the constant check-ins and hand-holding.

 Pro Tip: Being low-maintenance is about building *trust*. The less they have to worry about you, the more they'll see you as someone who can take on bigger projects, bigger responsibilities, and bigger opportunities.

Cheat Code #57
Learn and Mirror Their Communication Style

Your boss is the kind of person who sends emails with exactly three exclamation points and precisely one emoji (always the thumbs-up 👍), but you've been responding with novel-length messages decorated with enough emojis to crash an iPhone 4. Congratulations: You've just created the digital equivalent of showing up to a black-tie event in a bikini.

Workplace communication is a sensitive dance, but instead of not stepping on toes, you're trying to not step on egos. When your boss sends their typical staccato, bullet-point message at 7 a.m., replying at midnight with a magnificent stream-of-consciousness manifesto won't win you any awards. Unless those awards are for Most Likely to Make Their Boss Question Their Hiring Decisions.

Think of it as linguistic chameleon-ing (yes, I just made that term up, and I'm standing by it). If your boss treats email like a rare commodity, using each word as if they're paying per letter, then suddenly your ability to be concise becomes your superpower. On the flip side, if they're writing emails that read like Victorian literature, complete with elaborate salutations and postscripts, then by all means, channel your inner Charles Dickens.

> ✳ **Communications Pop Quiz**
>
> Your boss says: "Hey—need that report by EOD. Thx."
>   How would you respond?
>
> 1. Greetings and salutations! I shall endeavor to complete the aforementioned report by close of business today. Warmest regards, *etc.*
> 2. k will do
> 3. Got it—will have it to you by EOD.
>
>   If you chose anything but option 3, please go back through this cheat code until it's cemented deeper into your brain than your childhood trauma.

Matching your boss's communication style is a small adjustment, but it makes EVERYTHING smoother and shows you're paying attention. This is how you become the person they *want* to work with. If your boss is all about emails, stick to emails. If they're into quick updates, don't send them an essay. If they're formal, match their tone. If they joke around, you have full permission to joke around too (but keep it PG, por favor).

Cheat Code #58
Ask for Feedback (and Actually Implement It)

Every time I make dinner for my partner, instead of waiting until he's cleaned his plate to ask "So . . . how was it?" (while he awkwardly tries to hide that piece of criminally overcooked chicken under a lettuce leaf), I ask him to taste test *while* I'm cooking. That's what proactive feedback is like at work—catching things while they're still simmering, not after they've burned.

Most bosses are secretly thrilled when you ask for feedback. It's like when someone actually reads the instructions before assembling IKEA furniture instead of just assuming they know where that weird L-shaped piece goes. The key is to make it easy for them. Don't ambush them with a surprise "Tell me everything I'm doing wrong!" meeting. Instead, try catching them after project milestones or dropping a casual "Hey, I'd love your thoughts on how I handled that client presentation" in your next one-on-one.

Only B Players wait for their annual review to find out how they're doing. A Players check in regularly. A Players routinely ask, "Is there anything I could be doing better?" Then take that feedback and actually *use* it.

Here's where most B Players really fumble the ball—they get feedback and treat it like a book they'll read later. (Spoiler: They never do.) If your boss suggests you need to be more proactive in meetings, don't just nod sagely and continue your impression of a very well-dressed houseplant. Come back a week later and say "I've spoken up in the last three meetings—did you notice a difference?"

A Players know how to track their feedback journey. Keep a little document (I call it the "Career Feedback Log," but you can use a more fun title if you must) where you note down the feedback you get, what you did about it, and how it worked out. When review time comes around, you've got a ready-made highlight reel of your greatest hits in self-improvement.

Here's how to make this feedback loop your superpower:

- **Start small and specific:** "How could I make my weekly reports more useful?" beats "Am I doing okay?" (That's too vague—it's like asking "How's the weather?" when you really want to know if you need an umbrella.)
- **Time it right:** Ask after completing projects or handling big tasks, when the details are fresh. Not during lunch when your boss is trying to enjoy their sad desk salad.
- **Follow up like a pro:** "Last month you mentioned I should delegate more. I've started assigning smaller projects to the team—have you noticed any improvement?" (*Chef's kiss*—that's how it's done.)
- **Create feedback loops:** Make it a regular thing, like checking your phone notifications, but actually productive. Monthly quick checks > yearly anxiety-inducing feedback dumps.

✳ The "Three Angles" Feedback Gathering

1. Pick three people with different perspectives on your work (your boss, a peer, and maybe someone you work with regularly from another department).
2. Ask each of them: "What's one thing I'm doing well, and one thing I could improve?"
3. Look for patterns—if everyone's saying your project updates could be clearer, they might be on to something.
4. Create an action plan for the most common feedback.
5. Circle back in a month and ask specifically about the areas you've been working on.

Asking for feedback isn't admitting weakness. It's actually a major strength, like having a personal GPS for your career instead of just driving around hoping you'll eventually end up somewhere good. Those

A Players who seem to "naturally" excel at their jobs? They're usually the ones who've been quietly collecting and implementing feedback.

Look, I *know* it can feel scary as hell. That stomach-dropping moment when you're about to ask "How am I doing?"—yeah, I know that feeling. It's like your inner critic is having a field day screaming "DON'T DO IT!" But here's the real talk: *Your boss wants you to succeed.* Full stop. No asterisks. No fine print.

Trust me on this one: When your boss gives you feedback, they're not keeping some sadistic spreadsheet of your screw-ups. They're investing their time in you because they see something worth investing in. They are giving you feedback because THEY WANT YOU TO BE BETTER! It's that simple. Why? Because your growth makes their life easier, makes the team stronger, and proves they know talent when they see it. Feedback is good. Say it again: FEEDBACK IS GOOD!

Now go forth and ask for that feedback. Just maybe don't start on a Monday morning before your boss has had their coffee. There's being proactive, and then there's being foolish. And remember—embrace the feedback like an A Player! Every single piece of it, even the tough stuff that makes you want to hide under your desk, is just another step toward being that person who makes everyone else say "How do they make it look so easy?" (Spoiler: This is how.)

Part 3

Personal Brand

You've probably heard the term "personal brand" and immediately thought of LinkedIn influencers posting motivational quotes over sunset photos. But everyone has a personal brand, whether they've intentionally crafted it or not. Your brand is simply how you're perceived in your professional ecosystem.

At this stage of your career, you're no longer just trying to prove you can do the work—you're trying to establish yourself as someone worth paying attention to. Your personal brand is what opens doors before you even knock. Let's get to work on yours.

10

Working LOUDLY!

Congratulations! You've won over your boss. You're doing great work. Your projects are successful, your deliverables are on point, and you're consistently meeting (and exceeding) expectations. But the scope is bigger now—just like your aspirations are. You're not just riding your boss's coattails up the corporate ladder anymore. No, you're ready to arrive, in a way such that when you walk into that twenty-person conference room, you can claim that empty seat toward the head of the table without anyone batting an eye, because you belong there.

The question is, how do we get from being the reliable workhorse in the background to sitting at the leadership table? The stakes have changed, and so should your approach. A Players know it's no longer about deliverables; it's about *visibility*.

In a world of information overload and constant distractions, good work that isn't actively promoted becomes invisible work. If you're over in the corner just quietly executing, your less talented but more vocal colleagues will be building their reputations and snagging those promotions.

Your work ethic means jack shit if no one notices it. Harsh? Maybe. True? Absolutely.

I've watched too many brilliant people get passed over for promotions while mediocre colleagues with louder mouths climb the corporate ladder like it's their personal jungle gym. I'm tired of it. It's enough to make you want to rage quit your entire career.

I'm not here to sell you some LinkedIn-friendly "just be your authentic self" bullshit. The workplace isn't a meritocracy; it's a perception game. And if you're not playing it strategically, you're basically competing in the Olympics with your shoelaces tied together.

The beautiful thing about personal branding? **It works at *any* stage of your career journey.**

Precareer: Build your reputation before you even start by learning in public. Share what you're studying, create projects that showcase your skills, and engage with communities in your target industry.

Early career: Establish yourself as someone who's hungry to grow. Document your learning curve, ask thoughtful questions, and make your enthusiasm visible without being annoying about it.

Midcareer: You've got experience now—work in public. Share your process, your wins, *and* your challenges. Position yourself as someone who doesn't just do the work but thinks critically about the work.

Senior level: You're no longer hunting for opportunities; you're creating gravity that pulls them toward you. Build platforms (whether they're internal initiatives or external thought leadership) that showcase your strategic thinking.

Regardless of where you are in your journey, once you know the rules of the game, you can absolutely dominate it without working yourself into burnout oblivion.

In this chapter, I'm dropping cheat codes that have helped me and hundreds of others transform from "who?" to "absolutely essential" in their organizations. These tactical moves actually work in environments where politics and perception matter just as much as your actual output.

Will some of these strategies make you cringe a little? Maybe. But you know what's more cringe? Watching your less talented coworker get the promotion you deserved because they understood something fundamental that you didn't.

Time to level up your career game and work loudly. Let's go.

Cheat Code #59
Strategic Visibility: How A Players Get Noticed

Let's demolish the biggest lie in B-Player history: "Your work speaks for itself." No, it fucking doesn't.

Your work sits there silently while Chatty Cathy from marketing (who does half the amount of work that you do) gets all the recognition because she's mastered the art of broadcasting her every minor achievement like it's breaking news.

Your work does not speak for itself—you have to speak for it, and speak LOUDLY. I don't care if you're an introvert; you've got to make some noise. Make sure your boss and team know about your progress, your wins, and the value you're bringing. A Players know that work is 50 percent *doing* the task and 50 percent *bragging about* the task.

The corporate world isn't a meritocracy. It's a visibility contest. Here's why working quietly is career suicide:

- People are busy AF. Your boss has fifteen other employees and ninety-nine problems. They're not forensic investigators dedicated to discovering your hidden brilliance.
- Perception shapes reality. In most workplaces, people who are *perceived* as high performers get treated as high performers, whether or not the data backs it up (annoying, I know).
- Promotion decisions happen when you're not in the room. If no one can quickly recall your contributions during that meeting, guess who's not getting the promotion? You. Sorry.

- Someone else will take credit. Nature abhors a vacuum, and corporate America abhors unclaimed achievements. If you don't attach your name to your work, someone else eventually will.

Normalize Progress Updates. Start treating progress updates as part of the job, not a personality flaw. Working loudly equals strategically ensuring your work gets the visibility it deserves. It may feel like bragging, but it's all part of the A-Player game. Here's how to (sneakily!) get noticed like an A Player:

Make Your Work Shareable. Create visuals, one-pagers, or dashboards that make your accomplishments easy for others (especially your boss) to share upward. When you make your boss look good, you look good.

Ask Strategic Questions. One of the smartest ways to show your impact without sounding like you're bragging is to ask a question that happens to highlight your win. This is A-Player energy: You're not dumping a list of accomplishments into someone's inbox—you're inviting them into your process, showing initiative, and low-key reminding them how valuable you are. "I just finished optimizing that workflow we discussed—it's now running 30 percent faster. Would you like me to share the approach with the team in next week's meeting?"

Credit-Stack with Colleagues. "Sofia and I just wrapped up the project, and her marketing expertise, combined with my data analysis, resulted in a campaign that's performing 40 percent above benchmark."

Sharing credit doesn't diminish your contribution. It actually makes you look more collaborative and confident (and less intimidating to your coworkers—you'll need that street cred later).

Strategically Shout Out Others. "I want to highlight Alex's brilliant solution to that client problem in yesterday's meeting. His approach saved us at least twenty hours of work."

Publicly recognizing colleagues' contributions does three powerful things: (1) builds goodwill (which often gets reciprocated); (2) positions you as a confident team player who's not threatened by others' success;

and (3) lets you subtly signal your involvement without bragging about yourself. Plus, leaders notice people who lift others up—it's Executive Presence 101.

Your A-Player Brag Guide

In Meetings	"Just a quick update! I completed the client analysis and found three opportunities to increase retention by 20%."
On Slack	"Quick win to share! Just automated that report that used to take us five hours each month. Should save the team about sixty hours annually."
Via Email	Send your supervisor a brief weekly bullet-point list of what you accomplished. Frame it as "keeping them in the loop" rather than bragging. (See cheat code #59: Strategic Visibility!)

The Career Math

Working quietly × amazing quality = staying exactly where you are

Working loudly × good quality = career advancement

Don't just assume people are paying attention. *Make* them pay attention. Working loudly is the difference between blending into the background and getting noticed for your hard work.

 Remember: If a tree falls in the forest and no one's around to hear it, it doesn't get promoted. Make. Some. Noise.

Cheat Code #60
Attend Webinars or Events,
Then Hit Your Team with the TL;DR

In a corporate world full of overwhelming information, there's one career cheat code with a wild ROI: becoming the company's "insight curator."

Sign up for industry webinars, virtual events, or even local meetups; afterward, send your team a quick rundown of the key takeaways. You get to look like the plugged-in, always-learning MVP without doing a ton of extra work.

Why This Works So Damn Well

Sharing takeaways from external events can position you as someone who's plugged into the broader industry and thinking strategically about what matters to your team. It's low-effort, high-impact—and unlike talking about your own wins, it doesn't feel like bragging. It feels generous, smart, and valuable.

This requires minimal effort but yields maximum perception points. And unlike bragging about your own work (which can sometimes feel awkward), sharing industry knowledge feels completely natural and helpful.

The Perfect TL;DR Formula

The key to a perfect TL;DR summary is to keep it concise and actionable. Nobody wants to read your novel-length conference notes. Here's the formula for a share that gets noticed:

> Subject: Quick Insights from [Event Name]
>
> Hey team,
>
> I attended [specific event] yesterday about [topic]. Thought I'd share the three most relevant takeaways for our work:
>   1. [Specific insight] → What this could mean for us: [brief application]
>   2. [Specific insight] → What this could mean for us: [brief application]
>   3. [Specific insight] → What this could mean for us: [brief application]

Happy to chat more about any of these if they resonate!

[Your name]

That "what this could mean for us" part is crucial—it transforms you from someone who just attends events into a strategic thinker who connects external knowledge to internal priorities.

Not all events are created equal; you need to find the ones that won't waste your time. Here's where to look for quality learning opportunities that won't bore you to tears:

Industry newsletters. These often list upcoming webinars (bonus: subscribing to these also gives you content to share).

LinkedIn Events. You can filter these by your industry.

Professional association calendars in your field. Join the ones that matter most.

Your company's learning budget. Many people don't even realize their company will pay for event tickets.

Competitor websites. Their public events often reveal strategic directions.

 Pro Tip: Set a calendar reminder for one lunch hour every two weeks dedicated to attending a virtual event while you eat. That's zero extra time commitment for you, with a big potential payout.

> ✳ **Put It into Practice: Your First TL;DR Share**
>
> 1. Find a free webinar happening in the next two weeks in your industry.
> 2. Block out forty-five to sixty minutes on your calendar to attend (or watch the recording).
> 3. Take notes using the three-takeaway framework just laid out.
> 4. Draft your TL;DR email during the last ten minutes of your blocked time.
> 5. Send it within twenty-four hours of the event.

Cheat Code #61
Always Go Above and Beyond by Taking One *Micro*-Step

Let me tell you about my old coworker and work bestie Eli. Smart as hell, worked just as hard as I did, yet couldn't figure out why I kept getting praised in meetings while we were doing basically the same work.

When we both sent project updates, Eli's would read something like:

> "Project is on track. All deliverables complete."

Meanwhile, I would write:

> "Project is on track. All deliverables complete. Also attached a quick summary of next week's milestones and flagged two potential risks we should discuss."

Same basic update. One tiny extra step. COMPLETELY different impact.

The 10 Percent That Changes Everything

If you want to stand out without burning yourself out, don't do just what's asked—take it one tiny micro-step further. Don't worry, you don't have to double your workload or stay late every night. You'll just be adopting strategic minimalism: the smallest possible effort for the maximum possible perception boost.

The micro-step isn't about working harder. It's more like the career equivalent of compound interest. Those tiny additions compound over time until suddenly everyone sees you as the indispensable team member who consistently overdelivers.

If you want to stand out, don't do just what's asked—take it one tiny micro-step further. It doesn't have to be a huge gesture. It could be adding an extra slide to your presentation, finding one more resource for a project, or sending a quick follow-up after a meeting. That *one little thing* is what separates the B Players who just *get it done* from the A Players who *crush* it.

So, how do you pick your micro-step? Ask yourself *one* of these questions:

- What might they ask next?
- What would save them time?
- What small thing would add value?
- What could prevent future issues?

Basic Delivery	Delivery with Micro-Step
The report will be ready by Friday.	The report will be ready by Friday. I've also started a quick list of talking points you might want for the client meeting—happy to send those over too if helpful.
Homepage redesign complete per requirements.	Homepage redesign complete per requirements. While testing, I noticed our load time could be improved—added a quick note about that in the docs if we want to optimize later.

Basic Delivery	Delivery with Micro-Step
We hit all our Q3 targets.	We hit all our Q3 targets, and I noticed a pattern in our best-performing weeks—can provide my quick one-pager analyzing what worked, if anyone wants to review.
Customer issue has been resolved.	Customer issue has been resolved. I also documented the solution in our knowledge base, since I noticed we've had similar questions before.

When you consistently go that extra 1 percent, people *will* notice. Your boss will see you as the person who always adds value, and your coworkers will know they can count on you to deliver more than the bare minimum.

Cheat Code #62
Don't Focus on Doing the Most Work— Focus on Doing the Most Impactful Work

My former mentee Teresa, a high school English teacher, was drowning in school busywork hell. Committee for staff picnics? She ran it. Holiday decorations? Her problem. Projector broken? "Teresa will figure it out!"

And yet, the school board leadership position she wanted kept going to less qualified teachers. The feedback? "We need to see more academic leadership."

One day, during a mind-numbing meeting about cafeteria utensils (seriously), Teresa had her lightbulb moment. She was burning her limited energy on absolute BS tasks.

The very next day, she dropped three committees and hit up an education conference instead. When she got back, she fired off a quick email to all faculty describing three innovative teaching approaches and exactly how to implement them.

The principal forwarded her email to the superintendent. Within months, Teresa was attending more seminars and translating complex education theory into "here's what actually works" gems for her colleagues.

When the board position opened again, she didn't apply—she was recruited. As the superintendent put it, "We need someone who can cut through the noise and focus on what matters."

Some people attend events and keep the knowledge to themselves. Teresa weaponized it and got exactly what she wanted.

Bye-Bye, Busywork

The work world is filled with B-Player busywork bots—a.k.a. the people who are always busy, but accomplish absolutely nothing that gets them noticed.

These are the folks who send emails at 11 p.m., jump between seventeen different projects, and humblebrag about how they "haven't had lunch in weeks." Yet somehow they never seem to get ahead. Major B-Player move.

Meanwhile, there's always that one person who seems relatively chill and leaves at 5 p.m. most days, but still gets promoted faster than everyone else. What's their secret? They've figured out that career advancement isn't about the *volume* of work you do—it's about the *impact* of the work you choose.

Think about your work in these four quadrants:

Effort–Impact Matrix

	Low Impact	High Impact
High Effort	Exhausting busywork	Strategic investment
Low Effort	Mindless time filler	Career rocket fuel

Most people spend their days trapped in the top-left quadrant—putting tons of energy into tasks that nobody actually cares about. Meanwhile, A Players hunt for those bottom-right opportunities: low-effort wins that make a massive impact.

Effort–Impact Matrix Examples

	Low Impact	High Impact
High Effort	Manually formatting spreadsheets that few people look at Creating detailed reports that no one acts on Excessively documenting processes that aren't mission-critical Managing projects that don't align with company priorities	Developing a new product feature that increases customer retention Creating automation that eliminates significant manual work for the team Conducting research that informs critical business decisions Redesigning a core process that improves efficiency company-wide
Low Effort	Organizing your email folders Making minor updates to documents no one uses Creating to-do lists without prioritization Helping colleagues with tasks they could easily do themselves	Identifying a critical bug before it affects customers Creating a simple dashboard that visualizes key metrics Flagging a competitive threat or opportunity early Creating templates that the whole team can use repeatedly

If you want to get noticed, focus on the stuff that actually *moves the needle.* You could be doing a ton of little tasks all day, but if the tasks aren't making a real impact, you're just staying busy, not actually being productive.

Look for the projects and tasks that bring the most value, solve big problems, or directly contribute to the bottom line. That's where you should be putting your energy. Your boss will care way more about the *results* than the number of hours you clocked.

Not sure what moves the needle in your role? Ask yourself these questions:

- What does my boss get evaluated on? (These are automatically high-impact areas.)

- What problems keep executives up at night? (Hint: revenue, costs, growth, major risks)
- What gets highlighted in company-wide meetings? (This shows what leadership actually values.)
- What work gets people promoted in my organization? (Look at who moved up recently and what they accomplished.)
- What would make our customers/clients significantly happier? (External impact often creates internal recognition.)

The more your work connects directly to these areas, the more impact it will have on your career trajectory.

The Career-Changing Power of No

Saying no to tasks can feel scary, especially early in your career. But consider this: Every time you say yes to low-impact work, you're essentially saying no to potentially higher-impact opportunities.

Try these scripts:

When your plate is full	"I'd love to help with that. Right now I'm focused on [high-impact project]. I can take this on after that's complete, or I can help you find someone else who might have bandwidth."
When it's not in your wheelhouse	"I think [colleague] would actually be perfect for this since they've been looking to develop skills in this area. Want me to connect you?"
When you want to redirect	"This is an interesting project. To make sure I'm prioritizing correctly, can you help me understand how this connects to our team's main objectives this quarter?"

 Remember: If you become known as the person who does all the busywork that no one else wants to do, guess what your career will become? Yep, busywork!

> ✱ **From Busy to Impactful: Your Thirty-Day Action Plan**
>
> For the next month, before starting any task, ask yourself: *Is this high-impact work or am I just staying busy?* If it's just busyness, see if you can batch it with similar tasks, automate it, or transform it by connecting it to a larger impact. No such luck? Try delegating it—or eliminating it completely.
>
> Your goal isn't to do the most work—it's to do the work that matters most. Your boss will care way more about the *results* you generate than the number of hours you clocked or emails you sent.
>
> Busy people work hard. Strategic people work smart. But the real winners? They work *impactfully*.
>
> You'll never close the gap between where you are and where you want to be by grinding harder. That's some toxic hustle-culture nonsense. You close the gap when you redirect your existing energy toward the high-visibility, high-impact moves that actually get you noticed.
>
> Try just one of these strategies consistently for a month. I dare you. Watch how differently people start responding to your work. Master all of them, and you'll be the one they can't afford to lose when layoff season hits (and let's be real—it's always layoff season somewhere).
>
> The workplace isn't fair. Never has been, never will be. But now you know how to make noise that matters.

11

Mastering Your Digital Identity

Your digital footprint is your new first impression. Before you walk into that interview, attend that networking event, or pitch that client, they've already googled you. What they find in those search results shapes their expectations before you even open your mouth.

If you're not actively managing your online presence, you're letting the internet tell your professional story for you. And the internet has terrible judgment.

If you're someone who's used to existing out of the spotlight or having someone else get the credit, there might be one major problem holding you back from achieving your career goals: fear of self-promotion.

This fear hits different if you're a woman, a person of color, or anyone else who wasn't raised with the belief that the world owes you a platform. You've probably spent your whole career watching other people take credit for your ideas, get promoted over you, or speak up in meetings while you stayed quiet. Society has trained you to be humble, to wait your turn, to let your work speak for itself. But here's the brutal truth: Your work can't speak if no one knows it exists.

Recently, I was giving a client (let's call her Nia) some tips to improve her LinkedIn when I noticed something big missing from her profile—her PhD.

"Wait—you just got your doctorate, right? Why isn't that on your profile?" I asked.

"Well, I just . . . I don't want to brag."

"I'm sorry—brag? You spent the last six years obsessively working on your biochemistry research. And you think putting it on your LinkedIn profile is . . . bragging?"

Nia rattled off a million reasons why it wasn't a good idea. "Um, well . . . There's just so many problems in the world. I mean, there are crises right now! And, and . . . and there are people who can't afford an education, and I'm not that qualified, and . . ."

"If you were talking to your best friend, what would you tell them?"

Nia's face lit up. "Well, I'd tell her how much of a badass she is, and how smart she is, and how she really should put herself out there because she has so much value to gi—" Nia stopped abruptly. "Oh . . . I see what you mean."

Nia's story isn't unique. Every single person I've worked with has similar hesitations about *"putting themselves out there."* We make a million excuses, thinking we'll finally promote ourselves only when we've achieved X amount in revenue, or finally completed that advanced degree, or achieved whatever other arbitrary accolade that makes us "worthy" of a personal brand.

These are real, valid feelings that I've experienced myself too. But here's the secret: You don't develop a personal brand *when* you achieve those goals. A personal brand is *how* you achieve them. Through self-promotion, you stay top-of-mind with your audience. This means you're first in line for opportunities as they come up, and these compound over time.

Realize that when you hold back from building your digital presence and sharing your expertise online, you're robbing the world of *you*. You essentially become invisible to the opportunities that could change your career.

You have unique value to share online. Value that's filtered through your unique perspective—a combination of your own learnings and experiences—that no one but you can fulfill. Your boss chose *you* from a stack of résumés for a reason. They saw potential in you that beat out dozens of other candidates. Don't shy away from that now!

Everyone has self-doubts, but the best gift you can give the world is to move forward, regardless, *because it gives others the permission to show up as well.*

Nobody is coming to discover you. Nobody is going to stumble across your brilliance if you're digitally invisible. Not your boss, not your professor, not your mentor, not the head of your firm, and not that bigwig CEO you admire. There is no magic career fairy who plucks you out of the crowd and carries you off into Dream Job Land. If you don't promote yourself online, no one will. Whether you're publicly sharing expertise on social media, routinely reminding your boss of your (major!) business impact, or building your network of like-minded women, there's only one way to promote yourself—your personal brand.

Let me be clear: Self-promotion isn't optional. Self-promotion is *mandatory* for a fruitful career.

Here's the good news—you already *have* a personal brand. It already exists in our online (and IRL) ecosystem. And while you don't get to decide whether or not you have one, you can decide to take fate into your own hands and shape it yourself, or let others fill in the gaps for you.

Your digital identity is everything that makes up how you are perceived throughout your career. It's your digital footprint. It's your positioning, your storytelling, and your content, your online profiles, your résumé, your reputation. And crafting and maintaining your personal brand, like everything else in business, is a learned skill—a vital, valuable skill.

Cheat Code #63
Google Yourself

Open a new tab right now and google yourself. Go ahead, I'll wait.

Now, what popped up? Your cringey fanfic from 2009? That random quote in your college newspaper? Your high school track meet stats? If you're not actively managing your search results, you're letting the internet tell your professional story for you—and bestie, the internet has *no* taste.

I found this out the hard way when a potential client told me they almost didn't hire me because the first thing that came up in their search was my ancient Tumblr account where I exclusively posted about my unhealthy obsession with *Twilight*-era Taylor Lautner. Fanfic and all. I know. Embarrassing. Not exactly the "thought leader" vibe I was going for.

People are googling you before they interview you, before they hire you, before they decide whether to promote you, and definitely before they decide to slide into your LinkedIn DMs. Your digital footprint is the new first impression, and most people's first impressions are a goddamn dumpster fire.

But it doesn't have to be that way. With a little strategic effort, you can transform your search results from "random internet person" to "total professional badass" without needing a degree in computer science.

The Strategic SEO Playbook: Claim Your Name Everywhere, Then Create Power Pages

Even if you don't plan to use them all, grab your name on:

- LinkedIn (duh)
- X/Twitter
- Medium
- Substack
- GitHub
- personal domain (YourName.com)
- Instagram
- industry-specific marketplaces

These platforms have ridiculously high domain authority, which means they rank well in search results. Even if you never post a single thing, having these profiles set up creates digital real estate that *you* control.

You don't need to be active on all these platforms. My client Imani set up profiles on six different platforms with the same headshot and bio, and she never touched them again. Still worked. Within weeks, their LinkedIn, X/Twitter, and Medium profiles dominated his first page results, pushing that embarrassing local news interview about his failed startup to page two, where no one would ever find it.

These are the pages that *should* pop up when someone googles you—the ones that tell your professional story the way *you* want it told.

LinkedIn Profile

- custom URL with your name (linkedin.com/in/yourname, not linkedin.com/in/user48576)
- fully filled out experience section (no lazy gaps)
- skills endorsed by colleagues (ask your work bestie to hype you up)
- content posted regularly (even once a month helps)

Personal Website

- YourName.com (costs like $12/year, worth every penny)
- professional portfolio showcasing your best work
- work samples that highlight your expertise
- contact info that makes you accessible

Professional Profiles

- industry-specific platforms (like Behance for designers, GitHub for developers)
- speaker bios from events (even small local ones count)
- company pages where you're mentioned
- professional organizations you belong to

The secret SEO sauce is linking the pages to one another. Put your LinkedIn URL on your personal website. Link to your website from your LinkedIn. This creates a virtuous circle that tells Google "these pages are all about the same awesome person."

Pro Tip: Use the same professional headshot and bio everywhere. Consistency helps Google understand "this is the same person" and strengthens the connection between your profiles.

Remember: You can't control everything people find about you online, but you can absolutely control what shows up first. And in the attention economy, first is the only place that matters.

Cheat Code #64
Optimize Your LinkedIn Profile to Thought Leader, Not Just an Employee

I still cringe when I think about my client Mitch.

Mitch was an environmental scientist with fifteen years of experience, groundbreaking research, and the personality of a stale cracker—at least according to his LinkedIn profile. His headline literally just said "Environmental Scientist at EcoSolutions Inc." His About section was three sentences of scientific jargon that could've described literally any researcher. His profile picture looked like it was taken at a funeral.

When I asked him why his LinkedIn was so basic, he said, "That's what everyone's looks like."

EXACTLY. Nail on the head, my friend.

If your LinkedIn looks like everyone else's, you become background noise in a sea of "experienced professionals" and "strategic thinkers" who all blend together in recruiters' nightmares.

Six months after a LinkedIn makeover, Mitch was getting inbound speaking requests and consulting gigs, and he'd tripled his network growth rate. All from changes that took less than a day to implement.

The secret? He stopped presenting himself as just another employee and started positioning himself as a standout candidate.

The Three-Second Test

Here's a hard truth: Visitors to your LinkedIn profile spend an average of three seconds deciding whether it's worth their time. Three. Seconds.

Open your profile right now and look away. Then look back for just three seconds and look away again.

- What stood out?
- What impression did you get?
- What would someone assume about you from that glance?

When I did this exercise with my client Amara, her takeaway was "boring corporate drone who does something with marketing." What she *wanted* people to think was "innovative social media strategist who helps sustainable brands connect with Gen Z."

Those are two very different impressions, and the gap between them was costing her opportunities daily.

Try this three-second test with the profiles of a few thought leaders in your industry, then with those of a few random employees. See the difference? Thought leaders design their profiles to communicate their value proposition instantly. Employees just list their jobs.

Headline: Job Title Versus Value Statement

Your headline is prime real estate—it follows you everywhere on LinkedIn, showing up in search results, comment sections, and connection requests.

B-Player Headline	A-Player Headline
Environmental Scientist at EcoSolutions Inc.	I help organizations reduce their carbon footprint through data-driven sustainability strategies | Climate Speaker | Published Researcher

See the difference? One tells me where you work. The other tells me who you help, how you help them, your unique value proposition, and your credibility markers.

The Headline Formula

> "I help [specific audience] achieve [specific result] through [your unique approach] | [credibility markers]"

My client Elena changed her headline from "HR Director at Global Health Inc." to "Building human-first workplaces that outperform the competition | Speaker on workplace culture | HR leader with 2M+ employees impacted"

The result? Recruiting outreach tripled in two months, and she landed two paid speaking gigs from people who found her on LinkedIn.

Profile Photo: Corporate Headshot Versus Authority Positioning

Your profile photo isn't just about looking professional—it's about conveying authority and expertise in your field.

B-Player Photo	A-Player Photo
Boring corporate headshot against a white background	You speaking on stage, teaching a workshop, or being interviewed

Can't get a photo of yourself speaking? Then at least make sure your headshot communicates energy and approachability. Skip the stiff, formal pose and opt for something that shows personality while still looking professional.

And for fuck's sake, make it current. Using your headshot from 2010 isn't fooling anyone, Kevin.

Pro tip: Test your photos with PhotoFeeler.com to see which one generates the highest scores for competence, likability, and influence. My client Rashid increased his "influence" score by 43 percent just by changing his photo angle and adding a subtle smile.

About Section: Résumé Summary Versus Compelling Story

Your About section shouldn't read like the first paragraph of your résumé. It should tell a story that makes people want to connect with you.

B-Player About Section	A-Player Thought Leader About Section
Environmental scientist with 10+ years of experience in climate research, sustainability assessment, and team leadership. Skilled in GIS mapping, carbon footprint analysis, and environmental impact assessment.	I believe environmental science has lost its connection to real-world implementation. We've become so focused on collecting data that we've forgotten our purpose is to create actionable change. That's why, after watching a $2M climate resilience project fail spectacularly at my last organization, I developed the Community-First Sustainability Framework that's now helped over 50 municipalities implement green solutions that actually work with their existing infrastructure. I speak and write about: • Science-based climate adaptation strategies • Translating environmental data into policy • Building sustainability teams that prioritize measurable impact over activity Want to chat about making sustainability initiatives more effective? DM me or email jamie@email.com.

The difference? The B Player lists qualifications. The A Player communicates values, shares a personal story, establishes expertise, and invites connection.

My client Trevor rewrote his About section, transforming it from a boring list of skills to a story about how he got obsessed with conservation after discovering an endangered frog species in his backyard creek at age twelve and organizing a neighborhood protection effort. His profile views jumped 78 percent the next month.

Experience Section: Job Descriptions Versus Impact Statements

Even your work history can position you as a thought leader, not just a good employee.

B-Player Job Description	A-Player Job Description
Managed a team of 5 scientists, oversaw data collection protocols, implemented new environmental monitoring systems, increased data accuracy by 25%.	Led the complete reinvention of our approach to urban conservation, moving from isolated green-space projects to integrated ecosystem corridors. The methodology I developed: • Increased biodiversity metrics by 137% • Reduced project implementation costs by 42% • Has since been adopted by three other municipal governments I regularly share the lessons from this transformation at scientific conferences and community planning sessions.

Notice how the A Player emphasizes the innovative approach, along with specific, impressive results. They also highlight the broader impact beyond just the role and how they're sharing this knowledge with others.

This subtle shift shows you don't just do a basic job—you develop methodologies, create frameworks, and share insights.

Activity: Consumer Versus Creator

Look at your recent LinkedIn activity. Are you mostly liking and commenting on other people's content? Or are you regularly publishing your own ideas, perspectives, and insights?

Here's the brutal truth: No one becomes a thought leader by lurking. Thought leaders don't just consume content; they *create* it.

"But I don't have anything original to say!" You're wrong; you absolutely do. You have unique experiences, perspectives, and opinions formed by your specific journey.

Start with a simple formula:

1. Industry observation
2. Why it matters
3. What you think about it
4. One actionable takeaway

For example: "I've noticed most companies are rushing to implement AI without considering the human skills they'll need alongside it. This creates huge knowledge gaps that actually reduce efficiency. I believe we need to invest in upskilling specifically for AI collaboration, not just technical training. Start by identifying which decisions should stay human-led, then work backward."

Do this consistently—even just once a week—and you'll start building a following of people who value your perspective.

My client Damon went from zero original posts to posting twice a week. Within three months, he was approached to coauthor an industry white paper based solely on the insights he was sharing on LinkedIn.

Featured Section: The Credibility Showcase

If you're not using the Featured section of your profile, you're missing out on LinkedIn's most powerful thought leadership real estate.

This is where you showcase:

- articles you've written
- talks you've given
- podcasts you've been on
- projects you've led
- media mentions
- PDFs of one-pagers or frameworks you've created

Don't have any of these yet? Then *create* them. Write an article on Medium. Record a ten-minute video sharing your expertise. Create a one-page PDF of your approach to solving a common industry problem. Make a digital product (see cheat code #70).

The Featured section instantly elevates you from "person who does a job" to "person who contributes to the industry conversation."

Some of you may be thinking *But isn't this all just personal branding BS? I just want to do good work.*

In today's economy, being good at your job is the bare minimum. There are thousands of people who are good at what you do. The opportunities go to those who are good *and* visible. You don't have to become some fake LinkedIn influencer posting inspirational quotes over sunset pictures. But you DO need to intentionally shape how you're perceived professionally if you want access to the best opportunities.

✱ **Your Thirty-Minute LinkedIn Makeover**

Not ready for a complete overhaul? Start with these quick wins. These five changes take thirty minutes total but dramatically shift how people perceive you when they land on your profile.

- ☐ Rewrite your headline using the formula on page 150 (5 minutes).
- ☐ Add a clear call-to-action at the end of your About section (5 minutes).

- ☐ Choose three pieces of content for your Featured section (10 minutes).
- ☐ Update your profile photo to something with more energy (5 minutes).
- ☐ Create a simple Canva template for your future posts (5 minutes).

Your LinkedIn profile is more than a résumé; it's your living, breathing, evolving portfolio. It's a platform for positioning yourself as a contributor to your industry's conversation. Build it with intention, and watch how differently people respond to you.

The best time to optimize your LinkedIn profile was five years ago. The second-best time is right fucking now.

Cheat Code #65
Ask for LinkedIn Recommendations from Everyone, Not Just Bosses

I was scrolling through my client Jana's LinkedIn profile when I noticed something weird: She had *three* recommendations, all from former bosses, and all saying basically the same corporate-approved bullshit about her being "detail-oriented" and a "team player."

"This is a problem," I told her.

She looked confused. "But they're all positive. What's wrong with them?"

Everything. Absolutely everything.

Your LinkedIn recommendations aren't just nice-to-have digital compliments. They're strategic pieces of social proof that should paint a complete picture of your professional impact. And if they're all coming from one type of person (especially just bosses), you're missing a massive opportunity.

Recommendations: Generic Versus Strategic

Most people treat LinkedIn recommendations as nice-to-have testimonials. Thought leaders use them as strategic positioning tools.

Don't just collect random recommendations that say you're "a pleasure to work with" or "a team player." Strategically request recommendations that highlight the specific expertise you want to be known for.

When asking for a recommendation, try: "Would you be willing to write a brief recommendation focusing specifically on my work developing our customer retention strategy and the results it drove? That's an area I'm really looking to highlight in my profile."

This gives people clear direction and ensures the recommendations actually reinforce your personal brand, not just generic professional qualities.

The Recommendation Exchange That Actually Works

Let's be real: Asking for recommendations feels awkward. Like, really awkward. Nobody wants to be the person saying "please tell everyone I'm awesome."

Here's a recommendation exchange approach that doesn't feel sleazy:

1. Make a list of fifteen to twenty people across different relationship types.
2. Each month, write one or two *thoughtful, specific* recommendations for people on your list without asking for anything in return.
3. About 70 percent of people will reciprocate naturally.
4. For those who don't, follow up with a genuine note:

> "Hey Tasha! Hope that recommendation I wrote helped capture the amazing work you did on the Phoenix project. I'm currently building out my professional profile and would be grateful if you had time to share your perspective on our work

together—particularly that last-minute client pivot we handled. No pressure at all if you're swamped!"

This approach worked for my client Derek, who went from two recommendations to fourteen in just three months—without feeling like he was begging.

Getting Specific: The Anti-Generic Template
The death of a good recommendation is genericness. "Great team player, very professional" might as well be "has a pulse, shows up sometimes."

When asking for recommendations, provide context and specifics:

> "Hi Marcus! I've been reflecting on our work together on the Henderson acquisition, and I really valued your perspective on how I handled the due diligence process. If you have time, I'd love a LinkedIn recommendation that mentions that project—particularly the way we navigated the regulatory challenges. I'm hoping to build out my profile with specific examples rather than generic endorsements. Of course, happy to return the favor!"

This approach tells them why you're asking and gives them specifics: a project to reference, a skill to highlight, an impact to mention. The result? Detailed, meaningful recommendations that actually say something useful.

What If You're Just Starting Out?
If you're early in your career, you can still build a diverse recommendation portfolio from:

- professors
- classmates
- internship supervisors

- club/volunteer leaders
- project teammates
- mentors

My client Zoe was fresh out of grad school with zero full-time work experience, but she collected seven detailed recommendations from this exact mix of people. She landed a competitive role over candidates with more experience, and the hiring manager told her, "Your recommendations painted a clear picture of your capabilities, even without an extensive work history."

Your LinkedIn profile is a strategic marketing tool for your career, and recommendations are some of the most powerful content on it—if you use them correctly.

Now open your calendar, block thirty minutes this week, and get started on that list of people you're going to target for your recommendation strategy. Future you will be sending current you a thank-you gift basket.

Cheat Code #66
Turn Your Email Signature into a Mini-Résumé

I have this theory that most people are sleeping on the easiest personal branding hack in existence.

Literally right there, at the bottom of every email you send.

Your signature.

Last week I was helping my client Alexis update her résumé, and I noticed something weird. This woman had been featured in *Forbes*, led a viral TikTok campaign, and spoken at three industry events . . . but her email signature was just:

> Best,
> Alexis
> Marketing Manager, BlandCorp Inc.

Meanwhile, that same day I got an email from her coworker Tom with a signature that included "Host of the Marketing Mindset Podcast (84 listeners and growing!)" and everyone at their company treated him like he was Gary Vee's protégé.

This is the professional equivalent of having a billboard on Times Square but leaving it blank.

Think about it. How many emails do you send in a week? Fifty? A hundred? Two hundred? That's hundreds of opportunities to subtly remind people you're kind of a big deal without having to awkwardly bring it up in conversation.

From Basic to A Player in Five Minutes

Look at the difference between a basic signature and an A-Player signature:

Basic	A Player
Best regards, David Chen Software Engineer TechCorp Industries dchen@techcorp.com	Best regards, David Chen Senior Software Engineer | TechCorp Industries Creator of FastCache (10K+ GitHub stars) Latest: How We Cut AWS Costs by 72% [Link] Let's connect: [LinkedIn] | Book a coffee chat: [Calendly]
Regards, Marcus Johnson Financial Analyst Global Investments Inc. mjohnson@globalinv.com	To your financial success, Marcus Johnson, CFA Senior Financial Analyst | Global Investments Inc. Featured in *Bloomberg*: "Next-Gen Finance Leaders" Latest Analysis: 2025 Market Outlook [PDF] Free 15-min portfolio review: [Schedule Here]
Thank you, Dr. Sarah Patel Dermatologist Skin & Wellness Clinic dr.patel@skinwellness.org	To your health, Dr. Sarah Patel, MD, FAAD Dermatologist & Clinical Researcher | Skin & Wellness Clinic Published in *JAMA Dermatology*: "Advances in Eczema Treatment" New Patient Guide: What To Expect [Download] Book a consult: [Link] | Skincare tips: [Instagram]

Which person would you be more impressed by? Exactly. What should you include (without looking like a try-hard)? The key is to balance relevant flex with actual usefulness. Include:

- **One major credibility marker:** Awards, media features, speaking engagements
- **One recent win or content piece:** Latest article, project success, resource you created
- **One call-to-action:** Calendly link, portfolio, LinkedIn profile

People actually *expect* your email signature to sell you a little bit. It's one place where self-promotion is completely normalized.

So either use it to your advantage or keep sending emails that make you look like an intern.

Your move.

12

Becoming a Thought Leader

You've mastered your craft, built your reputation, and established yourself as someone who gets results. Now you're ready for the next level: being recognized as someone who not only executes well but shapes the conversation in your industry. Someone whose opinion actually matters when decisions get made in boardrooms you haven't even seen yet. And when it comes to the job market, you're no longer doing the chasing—*they're* hunting *you*.

You've likely already climbed several rungs of the career ladder. You've secured that position that seemed like a pipe dream when you first started. You've put in the years of solid work. You've established yourself as reliable and competent. Maybe you've been coasting comfortably for a while. But now you're eyeing that senior management role, that director title, or that partnership track—and you're wondering what separates those who plateau from those who continue to rise.

The answer: thought leadership.

I discovered this the hard way when I was passed over for a major industry panel in favor of someone with half my experience but ten times my online presence.

I was LIVID. I had put in the work! I had the expertise! I had the case studies and the client results!

But I had made one catastrophic career mistake: I had kept all of that brilliance locked away in my brain, project files, and email threads—where precisely nobody could see it.

Meanwhile, this other person had been writing publicly about our industry for years. They weren't just visible—they were perceived as a *thought leader*. Their insights, analyses, and forward-thinking perspectives were everywhere. When the conference organizers needed to fill a panel seat, guess whose name immediately popped into their heads?

Not mine.

This isn't a fluke. This is how human psychology works. We call it "top-of-mind awareness," and it's the single most powerful force in your professional trajectory—especially when you've reached that middle career stage where technical skills alone no longer differentiate you from your peers.

Let's play a game. Close your eyes and picture the top three to five leaders in your field. The ones keynoting the big conferences. The ones commanding obscene speaking fees. The ones whose research gets published everywhere. The ones fielding multiple job offers while everyone else is desperately refreshing their inbox.

Got them in mind? Great.

Reality check: These people are NOT the smartest in your industry. They're not the most talented. They're not the most experienced. I can absolutely guarantee it.

Think about it: When I say "chef," who pops into your head? Gordon Ramsay? Bobby Flay? That's top-of-mind awareness at work. They're not necessarily the best chefs in the world, but they're the ones who've positioned themselves as thought leaders.

The same principle applies in every industry. The developer who gets approached for the dream job. The designer who lands the speaking gigs. The marketer who commands premium rates. They've all done one critical thing: They've made themselves top-of-mind in their audience's consciousness. They've established themselves as thought leaders.

But why exactly does thought leadership matter at this stage in your career? The benefits are concrete and transformative:

Opportunities seek you out. When you're recognized as a thought leader, you stop chasing opportunities—they start chasing you.

Recruiters for senior positions don't want task completers; they want visionaries and industry shapers.

Accelerated promotions. When leadership is deciding who to elevate to the next level, they choose the person already demonstrating big-picture thinking and industry authority.

Negotiation leverage. Thought leaders command premium compensation because their personal brand adds value to their employer's brand.

Career mobility. If you're pigeonholed as "just" an analyst, programmer, or specialist, your options narrow as you advance. Thought leadership broadens your appeal across roles and even industries.

Internal influence. Being recognized externally translates to more respect and implementation of your ideas internally.

Your mission—if you want to break through the mid-career ceiling, if you want the opportunities, recognition, and compensation you deserve—is to build that same level of visibility in your professional ecosystem.

I know for certain that right now there are people with half your talent making twice your salary, simply because they've made themselves visible through thought leadership.

And the most infuriating part? This isn't some complex, mysterious process. It doesn't require special connections or a trust fund or a fancy degree.

It just requires you to start creating. Publicly. Consistently. About the things you already know and do.

That's it. That's the whole secret to elevating from "good at my job" to "thought leader who shapes the conversation."

So when I say this chapter might literally change your career trajectory, I'm not being hyperbolic. I've watched this exact strategy transform people from respected-but-overlooked mid-career professionals into sought-after industry authorities in less than a year.

Are you ready to stop being your industry's best-kept secret and step into thought leadership?

Cheat Code #67
Write Publicly and Often

The person who gets the opportunity isn't always the person who's most qualified. It's the person who's most visible.

I learned this the hard way when I watched my friend Jess—who was objectively less experienced than me—land her dream marketing role at Spotify. Did she have better technical skills? Nope. Better portfolio? Also no. What she had was fourteen months of consistent LinkedIn posts about music industry trends and marketing strategy that made her look like she lived and breathed the Spotify ecosystem.

This whole time, I was over here with my "better qualifications" sitting in complete digital silence, waiting to be discovered like some sad talent-show hopeful.

Spoiler alert: That's not how careers work.

The Simple Math of Visibility

You have thoughts, opinions, and expertise swimming around in your head that exactly ZERO people can see. What happens when you put those thoughts into public content? Let's break this down into embarrassingly simple math:

1 post = Maybe 500 people see it

52 posts (1x/week for a year) = Maybe 26,000+ people see some of your content

52 posts × multiple years = Exponential visibility and "Oh, I know you from [platform]!" moments

I had a client who committed to posting weekly LinkedIn updates about UX research for one year. By month eight, she was invited to speak at a conference. By month ten, a recruiter from Google reached out. None of this happened when her expertise was locked in her brain, only accessible to her immediate colleagues.

The Lazy Guide to Content Creation
"But I don't have time to become a content creator!" I hear this constantly, and it makes me want to throw things. I'm not asking you to become a full-time influencer. No ring lights required.

I'm asking you to spend thirty minutes a week documenting something you already think, know, or do. Don't worry about breaking the internet with industry-altering IP—your acquired knowledge is valuable to others (if you need a reminder, refer to the chapter on impostor syndrome, page 20).

Step 1: Choose Your Fighter (Platform)
- LinkedIn: For the corporate girlies
- X/Twitter: For the hot takes
- Medium/Substack: For the deep thoughts
- Instagram: For the visual queens
- TikTok: For the bold bestie

Step 2: Commit to Posting Once per Week for One Full Year
One platform, one post per week, one year. That's it. I'm serious. If you commit to one platform and post at least every week, your life will look completely different 365 days from now.

"But Courtney, I have nothing to post!" This is the number one excuse I hear, and it's complete bullshit. You absolutely have things to say—you're just not framing them as content (yet).

Every single day, you use tools, learn things, notice patterns, have opinions, make decisions, and solve problems.

That's literally all that content is. The game is just packaging those everyday professional experiences in a shareable format.

Let me prove it to you. Fill in these blanks right now:

Things I've Learned
Tools I use daily: _____
Mistakes I've made: _____
Processes I've improved: _____
Skills I've gained: _____
Books I've read: _____

Things I'm Learning
Current challenges: _____
New tools I'm trying: _____
Skills I'm developing: _____
Questions I'm asking: _____

Things I've Observed
Industry trends: _____
Common problems: _____
Team dynamics: _____
Market changes: _____

Boom. You now have thirteen content ideas. That's three months of weekly posts. You're one step closer to thought leader status.

For example, let's say under "Current challenges" you wrote "Balancing client work with internal projects." Here's how that becomes a LinkedIn post:

> 📊 **The Eternal Struggle: Client Work Versus Internal Projects**
>
> I've been wrestling with this challenge all month, and I know I'm not alone.
>
> When client deadlines loom, our own business development always takes a back seat. But without internal innovation, we're just treading water.
>
> My solution this quarter: "Internal Wednesdays"—one full day where client work is prohibited unless truly urgent.
>
> Three weeks in, and we've finally launched that email sequence we've been "planning" for six months.
>
> What systems have you put in place to protect your company's growth from the tyranny of the urgent?
>
> #AgencyLife #BusinessStrategy #TimeManagement

The Curation Hack (for When You're Really Lazy)

Here's a dirty little secret: You don't even have to create original content to build visibility. Curation is a legitimate strategy.

Ways to curate without creating:

- List your top five favorite books in your field, with one takeaway from each.
- Highlight a quote from a podcast and tag the host.
- Share a YouTube channel that helped you learn a certain skill.
- Round up three articles that changed your perspective on [topic].
- Create a "resource collection" for people in your role.

My client Amir built his entire professional brand by curating AI research papers with one-paragraph summaries in plain English. He didn't write the papers—he just made them accessible to nonresearchers. This led to a job offer from an AI ethics organization that doubled his previous salary.

The One-Year Visibility Timeline

Here's what typically happens when you commit to weekly content for one year:

Months 1–3	Crickets. You'll get minimal engagement as algorithms and humans figure out what you're about.
Months 4–6	Recognition within your network. Colleagues start mentioning your content in meetings or conversations.
Months 7–9	Strangers engage. People you don't know start commenting, connecting, and reaching out.
Months 10–12	Opportunities emerge. Speaking invitations, job offers, client inquiries, or collaboration requests start appearing.

This timeline varies, but the pattern is consistent: Visible expertise compounds over time.

Your Action Plan
1. Choose *one* platform where your target audience hangs out.
2. Block out thirty minutes on your calendar for the same time every week.
3. Use the content ideas worksheet above to list ten potential topics.
4. Start with a "zero-effort" post this week.
5. Set a twelve-month goal (fifty-two posts) and track your progress.

Your expertise deserves an audience larger than your immediate team. Start writing publicly this week, and watch how it transforms your career within a year.

Now close this book and go write your first post. Seriously. Do it now. I'll see you in the next cheat code. Your future self will thank you.

Remember: Nobody is waiting for your content, but everyone is looking for valuable insights. The only difference between those who build visibility and those who remain hidden is the willingness to put themselves out there consistently.

Cheat Code #68
Get Featured in the Press

I'll let you in on a little media secret: That person with "As featured in *Forbes*" in their bio? They probably didn't land that through some magical connection or PR team. They just knew how to play the game.

True thought leaders know this: Visibility in respected publications establishes your authoritative position in your industry. And honey, while your little LinkedIn posts are cute, media features are what separate the big kids from the toddlers.

Want to build credibility fast and cement your status as a thought leader? Start getting your name out there with industry press. It's the quickest way to go from "who?" to "oh, they're the expert on that topic" in your professional circle. While everyone else is begging for attention, you'll be turning down speaking requests.

When decision-makers see your insights featured in publications they respect, you inherit that publication's credibility. This third-party validation matters. Suddenly, your opinions aren't just opinions—they're published insights. That's thought leadership. And trust me, it looks way better on you than that impostor syndrome you've been wearing.

The Journalist-Expert Matchmaking Game

Here's how it actually works: Journalists are *constantly* scrambling to find sources for their stories. They need experts to quote, and they need them yesterday.

You know what you are? An expert in something. (Yes, you are. Stop with the impostor syndrome for a minute.)

Use a tool like Qwoted to connect with journalists looking for expert insights in your field. These platforms send you daily emails with journalist requests. See one that matches your expertise? Respond with a short, punchy quote. Do this consistently, and I guarantee you'll land in an article within three months.

My client Carter, a mid-level HR manager, responded to Qwoted requests every morning for fifteen minutes. Within two months, he was quoted in Business Insider. Within six months, he had press mentions on five different sites. Cost? Zero dollars. Just consistent effort.

The Niche Publication Strategy

Everyone wants to be in *Forbes* or Business Insider, but don't sleep on industry publications. Getting featured in the top publication in your specific field can actually be *more* valuable for your career.

My client Marcus couldn't land a quote in mainstream business press, so he targeted *Supply Chain Quarterly* instead—a publication read by literally everyone in his industry. That feature led to three speaking invitations and a job offer that increased his salary by 40 percent.

The people who matter in your world read your industry publications. Start there.

Cheat Code #69
Become a Podcast Guest

Podcast hosts are desperate for good guests. Like, genuinely DESPERATE. They need to fill fifty-two episodes a year, and there are over two million active podcasts out there all competing for guests. You don't need a book deal or a fancy title to get on podcasts. You just need to position yourself correctly and know where to look.

The Podcast Guest Application Hack

Start by searching "[Industry Keyword + Podcast Guest Application]" in Google. You'll find submission forms for dozens of podcasts actively looking for guests RIGHT NOW.

My client Jordan, a mid-level UX designer, used this exact search term and submitted ten podcast applications in a single afternoon. Within two weeks, she had booked three appearances. None of these were huge shows, but they all catered perfectly to her target audience of startup founders.

By month three, she was getting inbound requests from other podcasts who had heard her on the first round of shows. The snowball effect is real.

The Niche Podcast Strategy

Everyone wants to be on the big-name podcasts with millions of listeners. Forget that. Start with smaller, super-targeted shows where your specific expertise will genuinely help their audience.

Would you rather be the 437th guest on a mainstream show where your episode gets forgotten in a week, or a standout guest on a smaller podcast where listeners actually implement your advice?

My client Logan targeted podcasts specifically for real estate investors with fewer than ten thousand followers. After just five podcast appearances, he landed three new high-value clients who mentioned they'd heard him on those shows. The ROI on those forty-five-minute conversations was over $30,000.

Podcast guesting is one of the fastest ways to build credibility, expand your network, and position yourself as an authority in your field—all while simply having conversations about stuff you already know.

Cheat Code #70
Create and Publish a Digital Product

My client Thomas was a mid-level project manager who kept getting passed over for promotions. Meanwhile, his colleague Noah was being touted as the "project management expert" and getting all the high-visibility assignments.

The difference? Noah had created a simple project timeline template in Excel, slapped his name on it, and started selling it on the Gumroad e-commerce platform for $19.

That's it.

Except it's not, because that stupid little Excel file completely transformed how people perceived Noah. He wasn't just another project manager anymore; he was "the guy with the template." The expert. The authority. The thought leader.

Meanwhile, Thomas—who was actually *better* at project management—remained just another employee.

Creating a product—any product—automatically positions you as an authority.

It doesn't have to be complicated. Start with a simple spreadsheet, template, checklist, or resource roundup. When people see you've packaged your expertise into something tangible, it triggers an unconscious assumption: You know your shit.

Your product doesn't have to be revolutionary. It just needs to be *visible*. And visibility creates authority.

You Already Have Digital Products (You Just Don't Know It)

Let me guess: Right now you're thinking *But I don't have anything worth selling!*

That's complete bullshit.

You probably already *have* a digital product sitting on your computer. That budget tracker you made for yourself? The presentation template you created for your team? The checklist you send to your friends before they travel? The meal-planning spreadsheet you use every Sunday? Digital! Products!

The things you've created to make your own life easier are *exactly* what other people will pay for. Because we all want shortcuts to expertise.

The "How Did I Not Think of That?" Hall of Fame

Some of the most successful digital products I've seen my clients create are laughably simple:

- A project manager created a "client onboarding checklist" ($27).
- A graphic designer packaged her custom Canva templates ($39).
- A developer made a library of code snippets for common problems ($19).
- A fitness trainer created a workout tracker spreadsheet ($12).
- A marketer compiled a swipe file of high-converting email templates ($49).

None of these took more than a weekend to create. All of them sell while their creators sleep. And all of them transformed how these people were perceived in their industries.

Digital Product Ideas That Actually Sell

Want some inspiration? Here are digital products with proven track records:

- project timeline tracker
- budget planning spreadsheet
- branding template pack
- content calendar
- code snippet library
- automation workflow
- debug guides

- client questionnaire templates
- decision-making frameworks
- resource directory

Notice something? None of these require you to be on camera, create videos, or spend months developing. These are "weekend projects" that can establish your authority and create passive income for years.

> ✳ **The "Find Your Money-Making Idea" Exercise**
>
> Still stuck? Answer these questions:
>
> **What do people always ask about you?**
> 1. _____
> 2. _____
> 3. _____
>
> **What feels easy to you but hard to others?**
> 1. _____
> 2. _____
> 3. _____
>
> **What processes have you perfected?**
> 1. _____
> 2. _____
> 3. _____

See those answers? Each one is a potential digital product. The things that come naturally to you are exactly what others struggle with—and would pay to solve.

My client Jason was an account executive who thought he had nothing special to offer. When he did this exercise, he realized people always asked about his prospecting process. He created a simple cold email template pack with fifteen templates and examples, priced it at $29, and made over $2,000 in the first month.

The money is just an added bonus; the visibility is what matters.

You don't need to create the next master class. Start with something simple that solves one specific problem. The goal isn't to make millions (yet)—it's to establish authority and create a passive income stream that works while you sleep. Plus, nothing says "I know my shit" like having a product people actually pay for.

The "Just Good Enough" Product Strategy

The biggest mistake I see? People trying to create the perfect, comprehensive product right out of the gate.

Stop that. Seriously.

Your first digital product doesn't need to be the be-all-end-all resource. It needs to solve *one* specific problem for *one* specific audience.

My client Tasha kept delaying her "Ultimate UX Research Kit" because it wasn't "comprehensive enough." When she finally launched a much simpler "5-Minute User Interview Template," it sold better than she ever expected *and* gave her the confidence to create more products.

Start small. Solve one problem well. Build from there.

✻ How to Create Your First Digital Product in One Weekend

1. Friday evening (one to two hours):

Choose *one* specific problem you can solve.

Outline the solution in bullet points.

Decide on format (spreadsheet, template, guide, and so on).

2. Saturday (three to four hours):

Create the basic structure of your product.

Fill in the content.

Make it usable (not perfect, just usable).

> **3. Sunday (two to three hours):**
> Add some basic formatting to make it look professional.
> Create a simple cover image (Canva is your friend).
> Set up a Gumroad or Etsy account.
> Write a product description and set a price.
> LAUNCH.
>
> That's it. Spend about eight hours, spread over a weekend, and you've transformed yourself from "person with knowledge" to "person with a product."

The "But What If No One Buys It?" Fear

Here's the beautiful thing about creating a digital product: Even if it doesn't sell, you *still* win the authority game.

My client Priya created a resource guide that sold only twelve copies. Disappointing? On the surface, yes. But those twelve sales still gave her the ability to say "I'm the creator of a product." They also gave her something to link to her in her bio and profiles, a credential for speaking applications, and a tangible demonstration of her expertise.

The authority boost happens, whether you sell ten downloads or ten thousand.

Stop overthinking this. Take that spreadsheet you made, that template you use, or that process you've perfected, package it up this weekend, and put it out into the world.

Your future self—with enhanced authority, passive income, and new opportunities—will thank you.

Cheat Code #71
Volunteer to Lead a Presentation

Fun fact: The quickest way to position yourself as an expert isn't getting another degree or certification—it's volunteering to stand at the front of a room with a clicker in your hand. There's something about that forward-facing stance that rewires everyone's brain to think *Well, they must know what they're talking about.*

Want instant workplace credibility? Simple. Raise your hand when someone mentions "We should really do a session on . . ." You don't need to be the world's foremost authority on a topic. You just need to know slightly more than the people staring back at you.

The presentation sweet spot is finding that intersection between "things I actually know about" and "things my colleagues struggle with." Maybe it's those Excel shortcuts you use without thinking, that client management approach you've perfected, or that workflow trick that saves you two hours every week. The stuff that feels obvious to you is often revolutionary to others.

When you volunteer to present, you transform from "Alex from accounting" to "Alex, our Excel guru" or from "Jordan in marketing" to "Jordan, our social media strategist." One good presentation can rebrand you faster than a corporate makeover consultant charging $500 an hour.

Here's the secret weapon for making this happen without looking like you're desperately seeking attention:

The Presentation Pitch Template

> Subject: Quick Learning Session Proposal
>
> Hi [Name],
>
> I noticed the team has been [problem/question/need], and I'd love to share some insights about [topic] in a quick lunch and learn.
>
> I can cover:
>
> - [Key point 1]
> - [Key point 2]
> - [Key point 3]

> Time needed: [30–40] minutes
> Proposed date: [Next week]
>
> Would this be helpful?
>
> Best,
> [Your name]

Notice how you're not saying "I want to present because it would be good for my career." You're saying "I noticed a problem and I have a solution." You're not self-promoting—you're *helping*. (The career advancement is just a convenient side effect. Wink, wink.)

The beauty of this approach is that it works regardless of your position in the company hierarchy. Entry-level employee? You just demonstrated initiative. Mid-level manager? You're developing your team. Senior executive? You're sharing wisdom and staying connected to the troops.

So go forth and volunteer before someone else claims your spotlight. Your career will thank you, and so will that coworker who's been manually sorting spreadsheets for the past three years.

Pro Tip: People automatically see the person at the front of the room as the expert. It's like a weird corporate optical illusion—stand at the front, share some knowledge, and suddenly you're the authority. Even if you're sweating through your shirt and your voice cracks twice, the audience will still walk away thinking *Wow, they really know their stuff!*

Part 4

Staying Sane

Success without sustainability is just delayed burnout. You've probably reached a point in your career where you're juggling more responsibilities, managing more relationships, and fielding more demands on your time than ever before. The strategies that got you *here*—working harder, saying yes to everything, being the reliable one—might actually be holding you back from getting *there*.

This section isn't about work-life balance (that mythical concept). It's about work-life integration that actually works, boundaries that stick, and systems that protect your energy for what matters most.

Let's be real—modern work life is busy work disguised as productivity. Between the endless Slack notifications, "urgent" emails that somehow all require immediate attention, and meetings that could've been emails (that also could've been nothing), it's a miracle we get anything done at all.

By this point in your career, you've likely moved beyond entry-level scrambling. You're somewhere in the middle—perhaps a manager, a seasoned individual contributor, or climbing toward leadership territory. You've got some experience under your belt, enough to know the system isn't always designed for your success.

Your days have evolved from simple task completion to complex stakeholder management. The calendar that once had breathing room now resembles a game of Tetris, with meeting invites stacking up faster than you can clear them. You're juggling more responsibilities, more relationships, and definitely more notifications than ever before. Everyone wants a piece of you. And they all think their piece is the most important.

You're in a maintenance phase now. You've built something worth protecting: your reputation, your expertise, perhaps a team that depends on you. But that maintenance requires boundaries, especially when it comes to your time. And not just any boundaries—unapologetic ones.

This section is about reclaiming your time, energy, and mental space from the corporate machine that's designed to consume all three. Not tomorrow. Not when you get promoted. Today.

The secret? Creating nonnegotiable systems that protect you from other people's urgencies. Period. Starting with the biggest time thief of them all: your calendar.

13

Working Your Calendar

Your calendar is your life in visual form. If it's a disaster of back-to-back meetings with no breathing room, then your actual life probably feels like a disaster too. At this point in your career, you're important enough that everyone wants a piece of your time—but you desire more control over how that time gets allocated.

Time to stop letting other people's urgencies dictate your priorities.

One Tuesday afternoon, I stared blankly at my laptop screen, trying to remember what I'd actually accomplished that day. I had been "working" since 8 a.m., but my to-do list remained virtually untouched. Strange.

"I'll check my calendar," I muttered, scrolling through the day's events. Four back-to-back meetings, each bleeding into the next, with barely enough time to refill my coffee.

Curious, I zoomed out to view my entire week. The colorful blocks of scheduled time stared back at me like a game of corporate Tetris gone wrong. On a whim, I tallied up the hours.

Monday: 6 hours of meetings

Tuesday: 5.5 hours

Wednesday: 4 hours

Thursday: 7 hours

Friday: 2.5 hours

I blinked at the total. Twenty-five hours. TWENTY-FIVE? More than half my work week spent nodding, "contributing thoughts," and promising to "circle back" while my actual work piled up.

The revelation hit me all at once: I wasn't working forty hours a week with some meetings sprinkled in. I was attending twenty-five hours of meetings with some work sprinkled around them.

Something had to change. I wasn't being paid to be a professional meeting attendee. The following Monday, I blocked off entire chunks of my calendar with "focus time," declined nonessential meetings, and requested agendas for the rest.

I get it; it can be overwhelming to revamp your entire calendar. But this one boundary will at least set you in the right direction.

Cheat Code #72
Limit Meeting Durations

Change your default setting in your calendar app from "30 minutes" to "25 minutes," "60 minutes" to "50 minutes," and so on. Set it and forget it. Your future self—who no longer has to choose between being late or hitting the bathroom—will literally worship you for this.

Back-to-back meetings are basically corporate prison. Zero recovery time, zero brain space, zero chance to grab coffee before you're trapped in another hour of spreadsheet hell. And for what?

No more of that mess. With your tiny time heist, you can do the following:

- Process what just went down.
- Screenshot your action items before they vanish from memory.
- Vibe-check yourself before the next convo.
- Actually hydrate (revolutionary, I know).

When you drop that twenty-five-minute calendar invite, will your coworkers notice? Maybe. But they'll respect the boundary. For anyone who questions it, just hit them with "I find we accomplish the same work more efficiently this way" and watch them act like you've shared the secret to productivity. Which, tbh, you kind of have.

Cheat Code #73
Protect Your Focus Time with "DND" and Fake Calendar Blocks

Your coworkers will steal every minute of your day if you let them. That's not their fault—it's yours for leaving your calendar wide open like some goddamn 24/7 bodega.

Productivity is just a fancy word for boundary management. And boundaries are completely useless unless they're actually enforced.

Block your own calendar before others can. Set up recurring "Do Not Disturb" time slots that are nonnegotiable. Every day, same time, locked in.

When someone asks, "What's that meeting?" just look them dead in the eyes and say "Deep work." No further explanation needed. They'll assume you're doing something important because you're treating it as important.

Calendar Power Phrases

Practice these responses for when people question your calendar blocks:

When asked, "What's that meeting?"	• "It's my deep work block for [project]." • "That's my strategic planning time." • "It's a standing commitment I can't move."
When asked to move your block	• "I can't move that, but I'm free at [alternative time]." • "That time is allocated for critical deliverables, but I can help you at [time]." • "I've reserved that time for focused work to meet our team goals. Can we connect at [time] instead?"

Then take it further. I give you total permission to strategically place fake appointments throughout your week for your own sanity. "Doctor appointment" at 4 p.m. Friday? That's you at your favorite coffee shop catching up on emails. "Client call prep" at 11 a.m.? That's your mental break to avoid burnout. "Therapy" every Wednesday at noon? No one's going to question that, especially if you've set your calendar up to just appear as unnamed blocks of time to anyone other than you (as you absolutely should—no one needs to know your business).

Strategic Calendar Blocks

"Deep Focus Work"

"Strategic Planning"

"Project Development"

"Content Review"

"Research Block"

"Documentation Time"

"Process Optimization"

"Stakeholder Preparation"

People respect what looks official. A blank calendar says "I'm available for whatever nonsense you want to drag me into." A strategically blocked calendar says "My time is allocated to high-value activities."

The A Players aren't actually in meetings 70 percent of the day—they're just protecting themselves from other people's urgencies. The difference between reactive workers and strategic players is often just calendar management.

Some people will call this dishonest. Those people are probably the ones constantly booking pointless meetings. Remember: Your productivity is more important than their perception. You're not paid to attend redundant meetings—you're paid to deliver results.

So go block off ninety minutes tomorrow for "Project Planning." Whether you use it for actual work, a mental health break, or a gym session is nobody's business but yours. Nobody's checking whether that "Client Research" block actually involved clients or was just you finally having time to think clearly for once.

Caveat: If someone signs your paychecks, it's probably in your best interest not to tell them to piss off. I know you know that. Use your best judgment.

Cheat Code #74
Enforce a No-Meeting Day

Last summer, I hit breaking point. My calendar looked like a Rubik's cube being solved by someone with a caffeine addiction. I was in meetings to plan meetings about future meetings. My actual work? That happened between 9 p.m. and midnight, when normal humans were watching Netflix.

Then I stole a sneaky idea after getting a glimpse at my partner's calendar. Every Wednesday, his entire calendar shows as "Deep Work—Not Available." At first I thought this was some corporate-mandated thing, but nope. He just . . . decided to do it. And everyone respected it.

So I tried it. Blocked off every Thursday. Entire day. The first week, I felt like I was getting away with something illegal. The second week, I delivered two projects that had been stuck for months. By week three, I realized this wasn't a productivity hack—it was basic survival.

Having just one day a week without the constant context-switching of meetings is like hitting a reset button on your brain. It's the difference between frantically treading water and actually swimming somewhere.

I knowww you're rolling your eyes right now. "MY BOSS WOULD NEVER ALLOW THIS!" First, stop yelling. Second, you're probably right if you just block your calendar without explanation. The trick is how you position it. Try this script:

> Hey [Boss],
>
> I've noticed I'm struggling to make progress on [important project] with our current meeting schedule.
> Would you be open to me trying a "focus day" experiment for the next four weeks where I block off [Day] for deep work?
> I'd still be available for true emergencies, but this would let me concentrate on [specific deliverable they care about].
> I'm happy to track the results and report back on how it's working.
>
> Best,
> [Name]

The key is framing it as an experiment with a clear benefit to them. Four weeks is short enough that they won't feel like they're agreeing to forever, but long enough to prove it works. And once they see the results? Good luck trying to take it away from you.

If your workplace is too dysfunctional for even that approach, start smaller. Block out just one morning per week. Or two hours every other week. Or just immediately after big project deadlines when you need recovery time.

And if all else fails, create a recurring meeting called "project planning" or "strategic review" with yourself as the only attendee. It's technically a meeting—just one that actually produces something useful.

This isn't just for individual contributors either. Managers in my network who implement team-wide no-meeting days have cited higher team satisfaction and output. Turns out people like actually completing work instead of just talking about it. Revolutionary concept.

Give yourself permission to protect your focus. Your calendar belongs to you, not to every random coworker with access to Outlook. Claim your day, guard it fiercely, and watch your productivity (and sanity) transform.

Protect your focus time like it's sacred. Because without it, you're just in meetings about work instead of actually doing the work.

Now go block that calendar and practice saying "let me check my schedule" (even when you already know the answer is no).

14

Time Management and Boundaries

You've probably noticed that the higher you climb, the more people expect from you. More hours, more availability, more emotional labor. If you don't actively resist this expectation creep, you'll find yourself working around the clock while your personal life withers away.

The most successful people aren't those who work the most hours—they're those who protect their most important hours most fiercely.

Cheat Code #75
Never Finish Work *Too* Fast—Give Yourself a Buffer

It's 2 p.m. You just crushed that report your boss expected would take all day. Your first instinct? Run to their office like an eager puppy returning a ball, tail wagging: "Look what I did! So fast! Give me another!"

Stop. Right. There.

The fastest way to drown yourself in extra work? Let everyone know how fast you can swim.

That productivity high will fade real quick when they respond with, "Great! Here are three more just like it." Congrats: You just played yourself.

Forget productivity-maxing; what you really need is sustainable pacing. The corporate world runs on expectations. If you consistently deliver a task in half the estimated time, guess what happens? The time estimate shrinks, but the work doesn't get any easier.

Instead, finish at 2 p.m., then tell them at 4 p.m. Or even better, wait until the originally expected time. You can use that buffer to:

- Double-check your work (because rushing leads to mistakes).
- Take a mental breather (because burnout is real).
- Learn something new (because growth > grinding).
- Scroll mindlessly (tbh, you've earned it).

If you were raised on hustle culture, this feels wrong, I know. Like you're somehow cheating. But remember, companies set deadlines based on what they need, not on your maximum possible output. They need the report by Friday, not by Wednesday just because you can.

Your reward for digging ditches faster isn't a bonus—it's a bigger shovel.

This is the magic of managing perception. When you manage the perception of your time, you have more autonomy to manage your actual time, and you create expectations that are actually sustainable.

So next time you finish early, take a breath. Take a walk. Take a goddamn TikTok break. The work is done, the deadline will be met, and your secret superpower stays secret—ready to be deployed when it actually benefits you.

Discretion is key here. Don't be the person loudly announcing "I'm done!" at 2 p.m. while your colleagues are grinding through deadlines. Nothing burns goodwill faster than flaunting your efficiency while others are struggling. Keep your finished status to yourself. No victory laps around the office. No pestering colleagues with "anything I can help with?" when they're clearly in the zone.

And if you're someone who simply can't sit idle (I see you, overachievers), channel that energy strategically. Use those bonus hours to invest in your visibility. Clean up your LinkedIn profile (cheat code #64). Volunteer to lead that presentation everyone's avoiding (cheat code #71). Or better yet, use the time to learn something that puts your career on the fast track while everyone else is stuck in the day-to-day grind (cheat code #99).

The point is, finishing early isn't just about getting personal time back—it's an opportunity to get ahead while others are still catching up.

Cheat Code #76
Work-Life Balance Isn't Given—You Have to *Take* It

I'll be blunt: No one is coming to rescue your calendar.

That mythical moment when your boss says, "You know what? You seem stressed. Take more time off!" isn't happening. Not today, not next quarter, not ever.

Want work-life balance? Stop asking for permission and start setting boundaries.

I watched my former teammate Justine burn out spectacularly after six months of 9 p.m. emails and weekend "emergencies." Her breaking point? Realizing she'd missed three consecutive family birthdays for deadlines that nobody remembered a week later.

Meanwhile, my colleague Raj—doing the exact same job—never worked past 5:30. Ever. Same output, same quality, drastically different life. His secret wasn't extraordinary efficiency. It was simply deciding his time belonged to him.

Work-life balance isn't some corporate benefit that shows up after your ninety-day probation. It's a boundary you draw in permanent marker. Those boundaries look like:

- Setting your status to offline when you're done for the day (and actually being offline)
- Not apologizing when you decline 7 a.m. meetings because you go to the gym
- Letting after-hours calls go to voicemail without feeling guilty
- Setting up autoreplies that don't sound apologetic for being on vacation

"But my workplace culture—" Stop. The culture exists because everyone participates. Be the one who doesn't. Either others will follow, creating actual change, or they won't, and you'll still have your evenings back.

 Remember: Your company has unlimited work, but you have limited time. They will take as much as you give—not because they're evil, but because capitalism.

Boundary Scripts That Command Respect

When your manager texts on Saturday about a "quick task"

- "I'll handle this first thing Monday morning. Enjoy your weekend!"
- "I've blocked time on Monday to address this. Is there anything specific I should prioritize?"
- "I'm unavailable this weekend, but I've added this to my Monday priorities list."

When a client emails at 11 p.m. expecting an immediate response

- "Thank you for your email. I've scheduled this for my attention during business hours tomorrow."
- "I've received your request and will address it during our agreed service hours (9 a.m. through 5 p.m.). For true emergencies, please call our dedicated emergency line at [number]."
- "As per our service agreement, rush requests outside business hours incur a premium fee of $[X]. With this understanding, would you like me to proceed?"

When asked why you didn't respond to nonurgent messages after hours

- "I maintain focused work windows to ensure I deliver exceptional quality during business hours."

- "I've found that maintaining clear boundaries between work and personal time actually improves my performance and creativity when I'm on the clock."
- "My productivity system includes dedicated communication windows. I'm happy to discuss how this approach has improved my deliverables."

The Authority Paradox

People who bend over backward for every request are subtly communicating assistant-level energy, regardless of their actual title. Meanwhile, those who protect their time are perceived as authorities.

Think about it. Who's easier to get on the phone—the intern or the CEO? Who has more "rules" around their availability—the new hire or the executive? The more boundaries you set, the more others assume you have something important to protect.

Every time you enforce a boundary, you're training your colleagues, clients, and even your boss to value your time. And people value what they can't easily access.

Your boundaries aren't just self-care—they're career strategy. The most respected professionals aren't the ones working eighty-hour weeks; they're the ones who deliver tremendous value within clear, unapologetic limits.

Your work performance should speak for itself. If you deliver what's expected during work hours, how you spend your personal time isn't up for debate.

The next time your phone pings with a nonemergency work message at 8 p.m. on a Tuesday, ask yourself: *Would they pay for my therapy if I burn out?* If the answer is no (Spoiler: It's no.), then put the phone down and continue living your actual life.

You don't find balance. You create it, protect it, and enforce it. Every single day.

Cheat Code #77
You're Not Responsible for Your Company's Lack of Resourcing

Repeat after me: "It is not my responsibility to make up for the fact that my company didn't hire enough people to create the output they expect."

Okay, now repeat it again.

Let's clear something up: A staffing shortage is a management failure, not your personal emergency. That project needs three people but they only hired one (you)? Not your problem to solve. That deadline requires sixty hours of work but you're paid for only forty? Again, not a you problem.

When companies run lean, they're making a calculated business decision to save money. Then they turn around and frame it as a loyalty test for employees. "We're all making sacrifices," they say, while one sacrifice comes out of your personal life and the other comes out of their operating budget. Funny how that works.

I watched my friend Dani single-handedly cover for three vacant positions for six months. Her reward? Burnout, a mediocre performance review because she was "spreading herself too thin," and the crushing realization that those positions were still vacant when she quit. They had never intended to fill them—why would they, when she was doing it all?

When good companies are understaffed, they adjust expectations, extend deadlines, or hire more people.

When toxic companies are understaffed, they pretend nothing's changed and expect you to close the gap with your nights and weekends.

Don't fall for it. Your salary covers *your* job—not your job plus parts of two others. When they start piling on, you have options:

"I can take this on, but I'll need to put Project X on hold while I do."

"Given my current workload, I can start this in three weeks."

"I'd be happy to help with this. Which of my current priorities should I deprioritize?"

"Based on the scope, this needs more resources than just me. Can we discuss options?"

These aren't combative statements. You're not technically saying no. You're simply acknowledging the finite nature of time and human energy.

The A Player's most valuable career skill isn't working yourself to death; it's setting sustainable boundaries that allow consistent performance over time. Your mental health is not a renewable resource. So stop treating it like one.

 Remember: Your company wouldn't hesitate to lay you off if their financial situation required it. Apply the same business logic to your capacity. It's not personal; it's just resource management.

Cheat Code #78
Design Your Week (Don't Just Survive It) with Strategic Time Blocks

Nobody's handing out gold stars for martyring yourself at your desk until midnight. The "I worked eighty hours this week" flex is the corporate equivalent of peaking in high school—it impresses absolutely no one who matters.

Here's what actually counts: Did you move the needle? Did you deliver something valuable? Did you solve a problem that needed solving?

The difference between A Players and everyone else isn't just what they do—it's when they do it. Your brain isn't a 9-to-5 machine pumping out identical-quality work at all hours. It's more like a temperamental artist with very specific conditions for creating its best stuff.

The corporate world runs on results, not timesheets. Your boss doesn't care if it took you ten hours or two hours to finish that report—they care that it was thorough, on time, and solved the problem.

Here are some ways you can break free from the hours trap:

- Identify the 20 percent of your work that creates 80 percent of your impact.
- Ruthlessly eliminate or delegate low-value tasks.
- Track and communicate your wins based on outcomes, not effort.
- When you finish early, GO HOME (if you're remote, close the laptop).

Your brain is simply not designed to produce quality work for eight-plus consecutive hours.

Here's how to design your week instead of just reacting to it:

The Energy Map Strategy

1. Categorize your work into three buckets

- Deep Focus (strategy, complex problem-solving, creative work)
- Shallow Work (email, routine tasks, minor decisions)
- People Time (meetings, calls, collaborative sessions)

2. Align your work with your energy cycles

- morning hours (peak): Deep Focus work *only*
- midday (plateau): People Time
- afternoon (dip): Shallow Work
- late afternoon/evening (second wind): Learning, reflection, planning

3. Block your calendar accordingly

- nonnegotiable Deep Focus blocks (minimum ninety minutes, no interruptions)

- meeting blocks (contained to specific days/times)
- admin blocks (batched routine tasks)
- buffer blocks (thirty minutes between major transitions)

Either you design your week, or someone else will design it for you. And their design definitely doesn't prioritize your success.

 Remember: No one else is incentivized to help you use your time wisely. The calendar invites will keep coming. The meetings will multiply like rabbits. Your inbox will never announce, "That's enough for today!"

Cheat Code #79
Hard Work Is Only Rewarded with More Hard Work—So Work Smart

The fastest route to burnout? Being the hardest worker in the room.

Companies don't promote people for effort—they promote them for results. Yet somehow we've all bought into this fantasy that if we just grind harder, success will magically appear. (Spoiler: It won't.)

Hard work without strategy is just exhaustion with extra steps.

I watched my former colleague Rebecca pull seventy-hour weeks consistently for a year. Her reward? More work, a reputation as someone who "can handle anything," and eventually, a stress-induced health issue. Meanwhile, in the same department, Xavier automated half his tasks, focused solely on high-visibility projects, and got promoted twice in eighteen months while maintaining strict 9-to-5 boundaries.

The difference wasn't effort—it was strategy.

The Daily Swap: From Busy Work to Strategic Work

Don't Do This	Instead, Do This
Answering emails until 2 a.m.	Schedule fifteen minutes to call that potential client everyone's been chasing.
Taking meeting minutes and circulating them	Volunteer to present competitor analysis at the next team meeting.
Compiling reports that track vanity metrics nobody reads	Ask a VP to mentor you, and use that time to understand what metrics actually matter.
Organizing the office holiday party	Organize a lunch and learn where you present industry trends to leadership.
Being the go-to person for fixing the printer	Be the go-to person for explaining market shifts to your team.
Manually processing routine requests	Build a simple automation, then use the saved time to shadow someone in a role you want.
Responding to every Slack message immediately	Block focus time for projects that will be discussed in your performance review.

When you mindlessly power through mountains of work, leadership doesn't think *Wow, they deserve a promotion!* They think *Perfect, they've got everything handled down there.* Congratulations! You've become a reliable cog rather than a rising star.

Breaking the Hard Work Cycle

- Stop volunteering for everything. Be selective about what you take on.
- Ruthlessly prioritize tasks that decision-makers actually see and care about.
- Automate or simplify repetitive work instead of just doing it faster.
- Document your wins where people who matter will notice them.
- Deliberately create space in your schedule for strategic thinking.

Your boss doesn't care if you answered emails until 2 a.m. They care if you landed that client everyone wanted. They care if you solved that problem nobody else could crack. They care if you identified an opportunity that generated revenue.

"But I was taught to have a strong work ethic!" Great. Channel that work ethic into being strategic, not just busy. A strong work ethic applied to the wrong tasks is just wasted energy.

The corporate ladder isn't climbed by being the most tired person in the office. It's climbed by being the A Player who delivers disproportionate value compared to the time invested.

Stop wearing your exhaustion like a badge of honor—and start wearing your strategic impact like a crown. Anyone can be busy. Not everyone can be effective.

The system is designed to extract maximum value from your hard work while giving minimum rewards in return. The only way to win is to flip the equation: Extract maximum rewards from your company while giving valuable but sustainable effort. That's not cheating. That's MF survival.

15

Your Mental Health Matters

Work is inherently stressful. Deadlines, difficult people, uncertain outcomes, financial pressure—it's a lot. And the higher you climb, the more complex those stressors become. You're no longer responsible just for your own work; you might be responsible for other people's livelihoods, major business outcomes, or high-stakes decisions. Work will try to destroy you if you let it. Not in some dramatic, obvious way, but slowly, methodically, like water wearing down stone.

B Players think the solution is to just tough it out or work harder. They wear their stress like a badge of honor, as if burning out somehow proves their dedication. But here's what the most successful people figured out a long time ago: Taking care of your mental health isn't some fluffy self-care trend you can afford to ignore.

It's career maintenance—as essential as updating your skills or building your network. Because the executive who cracks under pressure doesn't get the next promotion. The leader who can't manage their own stress certainly can't manage a team through a crisis.

Your mental resilience isn't just about feeling better; it's about staying sharp when everyone else is falling apart.

Cheat Code #80
Use Your Sick Days for Mental Health Days

Your brain can be under the weather just like your body can. But somehow we've normalized taking sick days for the flu while powering through mental exhaustion.

Those sick days? They're for your whole health—brain included.

Corporate America loves a martyr. Someone who shows up with a 102-degree fever gets sent home, but showing up after crying in your car is somehow admirable. Make it make sense.

Taking a mental health day is basic maintenance. It's an oil change for your brain before the engine seizes up completely. One day off now beats two weeks of leave later.

However, even your supposedly progressive boss will file away the "emotional" days differently than the "physical" ones when review time comes around. Unconscious bias is real. So don't feed it. Keep your reasons vague. No one at work needs the details of your mental state any more than they need the details of your stomach flu. "I'm not feeling well today" works perfectly for both.

Mental Health Day Excuse Generator

"I'm under the weather" is valid and none of their business. Here are some useful variations to keep in mind.

Don't Say This	Instead, Say This
"I can't look at Slack without crying."	"I'm taking a wellness day tomorrow."
"I've been staring at the same email for three hours and need a goddamn break."	"I'll be OOO for personal matters this afternoon."
"If I see one more meeting invite, I'll scream."	"Offline for health matters."

Use the day properly. Don't check work messages. Don't feel guilty about the Netflix binge. Don't spend it doing housework. This is recovery time, not just different work.

My former coworker schedules a "sick day" every quarter whether she needs it or not. Pure prevention. She calls it her quarterly system update. Management thinks she has chronic migraines. Everyone wins.

Look, your company purchased your skills for certain hours, not your entire well-being. The corporate machine will run without you for a day.

Next time you feel the Sunday scaries lasting through Wednesday, send that vague "out sick" message and sleep until noon. Your job will be there tomorrow. Your mental health might not be if you ignore it.

Cheat Code #81
Take Advantage of Employee Assistance Programs (EAPs)

Your company has a secret menu of free shit you're probably not using.

Those EAP benefits buried in your onboarding paperwork? They're basically free therapy, financial advisors, and legal consultations that most people completely ignore.

I didn't touch my old EAP for two years because I thought it was just for people having a full-on crisis. Turns out I'd been paying hundreds for a therapist when I could've gotten six free sessions per issue through work. That's like having a gift card and never using it.

Typical EAP benefits include items in the list below.

- free counseling sessions
- financial advisors to help with budgeting or debt
- legal consultations for basic stuff like wills or tenant issues
- gym membership, subsidies, or discounts
- wellness coaching for everything from sleep to nutrition
- crisis support for when life really hits the fan

EAP education support can be extensive with benefits like the following.

- tuition assistance for degrees, certifications, or night classes
- professional development courses (leadership, project management)
- technical skills training (Adobe Creative Cloud, programming languages, data analysis)

- language learning programs
- trade certifications and specialized training
- hobby classes that relate to wellness (less common, but these exist)

Other hidden gems in many EAPs include a range of items:

- pet care resources
- elder care consultation
- home buying assistance
- identity theft protection
- travel planning services

Worried about your company snooping into (and judging) how you use your benefits? Relax. They have zero access to the details. They get a report saying "five employees used the EAP this quarter"—that's it. Your boss won't know if you're talking to someone about your anxiety, your credit card debt, or your annoying neighbor.

Why don't more people use these benefits? Because they're typically buried in benefits documentation nobody reads, mentioned once during orientation when you're overwhelmed, or marketed terribly with corporate jargon nobody understands.

Your EAP benefits are usually in your benefits portal, HR intranet, or that folder of papers they gave you on day one. Look for a phone number and access code. That's your ticket to services that would cost hundreds or thousands out of pocket.

My client who works at a FAANG company (a term for the five largest and best performing American technology companies) used her EAP to get three sessions with a financial advisor who helped her create a debt payoff plan. Another client used hers for legal advice during a nasty rental dispute. I used it when my anxiety was spiking during a stressful project. None of us had to tell our manager or get special approval.

These programs exist because burned-out, stressed employees cost companies money. They seem generous, but really, they're being practical. But who cares about their motivation if you get the benefits?

Corporations take enough from us. Take something back. Use every last benefit you're entitled to. The free counseling, the legal advice, the gym perks, the tuition reimbursement, all of it. It may feel like you're gaming the system, but you're using it exactly as designed. Your company is already paying for these services, whether you use them or not. Might as well be you instead of no one.

Cheat Code #82
Avoid "Hero Syndrome"—
You Don't Have to Save the Day Every Time

The thing that derails more careers than incompetence? Hero syndrome. That compulsive need to swoop in and fix every problem? It's a dysfunction.

My friend Daria worked as a pastry chef at a high-end restaurant in Chicago. During the James Beard Awards week, their kitchen was slammed with VIP reservations. The head chef was spiraling, and everyone was on edge.

The dessert supplier screwed up their order—sent the wrong chocolate couverture with a completely different melting point. Disaster for their signature dessert.

Daria's first instinct? Stay overnight reformulating the recipe, testing variations until 4 a.m., then coming in early to prep everything herself. Classic B-Player hero move.

Instead, she caught herself and tried something different. She called an emergency team meeting. Explained the situation. Asked for ideas.

The dishwasher's cousin worked at a specialty chocolate shop. The sous chef suggested a simpler alternative plating that wouldn't require the specific chocolate. The front-of-house manager identified which reservations could be offered a different special dessert with a comp.

In thirty minutes, they had three workable solutions that didn't require

Daria's all-nighter martyrdom. The restaurant got through the week, the reviews were stellar, and Daria didn't burn out.

"I realized I wasn't giving anyone else the chance to contribute," she told me later. "I was hoarding all the problem-solving because it made me feel important."

B Players with "hero syndrome" create three problems for every one they solve: They burn themselves out, prevent others from developing skills, and become the bottleneck for everything.

The alternative isn't slacking—it's collaboration. It's admitting you don't have to be the solution to every crisis. It's recognizing that sometimes your job is not to be the resource, but to coordinate resources.

Next time a problem lands on your desk, ask yourself *Does this actually need my specific expertise? Could someone else benefit from taking this on? Am I the one preventing a more sustainable solution?*

Sometimes the most valuable thing you can do is step back and let someone else be the hero. Your job security doesn't depend on being irreplaceable—it depends on building systems that work even when you're not there.

The A Players in any workplace aren't the ones working until midnight. They're the ones who build teams that don't need heroes in the first place.

And please, for the love of all that is sacred: Go no-contact on vacation. I know why. YOU know why. I promise, the world will keep spinning. Just do it. Deal? Deal.

Cheat Code #83
When You're Overloaded,
Ask Your Boss What to *Deprioritize*

Your boss isn't psychic. They have no idea of everything that's on your plate unless you tell them. When they drop another "urgent" project on your already maxed-out workload, your instinct is probably to nod, smile, and silently panic. Stop doing that.

Instead, use this simple reframe: "What should I deprioritize to make room for this?" This isn't saying no. It's saying physics exists and time is finite. You're simply acknowledging that adding something new means something else has to give.

I learned this from watching my good friend Marcus completely melt down at his commercial real estate job. He kept accepting new deadlines without pushing back, working nights and weekends until he eventually snapped in a meeting and went on stress leave for a month. The company didn't thank him for his sacrifice. They were annoyed at the disruption.

Meanwhile, his colleague Tara mastered the art of the deprioritization conversation. When given a new task, she'd calmly pull out her project list and ask which existing commitment should move. Her boss respected her for it.

The difference between Marcus and Tara? Tara made her boss an active participant in managing her workload instead of pretending she could bend time. An A-Player move.

Overwhelm Checklist

When you're feeling overwhelmed AF, try this formula for A-Player communication.

Steps	First Response	Ask Yourself	What You Could Say
Step 1	Express willingness to take on the project or task.	Did I acknowledge the importance of the new task? Did I show I'm a team player (without saying yes to everything blindly)?	"I'm happy to support this and want to make sure I have the tools/bandwidth to do it well."
Step 2	Voice concerns about your current workload.	Did I clearly lay out what I'm already working on? Did I avoid sounding like I'm complaining?	"Right now I'm focused on finishing [Project A] by [date] and managing [Task B], which has a client-facing deadline."

Steps	First Response	Ask Yourself	What You Could Say
Step 3	Mention your desire to deliver quality (this helps justify the need to deprioritize something).	Did I directly ask what should be deprioritized? Did I make it clear this is about maintaining quality and avoiding burnout?	"To give this new task the attention it deserves, what would you recommend I deprioritize?"

Following this formula puts the decision back on your boss by asking them to specify what should be deprioritized. It frames your response as wanting to "allocate time effectively" rather than just saying you can't do it all. Try this script:

> Hey [Boss],
>
> I'm happy to take on [task], but with my current workload, I'm concerned about being able to deliver quality work on everything.
>
> Could you let me know which of my existing priorities you'd like me to deprioritize or put on the back burner in order to focus on this new task?
>
> I want to make sure I'm allocating my time effectively and not dropping the ball anywhere.

Watch what happens when you use this approach. Often, your boss will realize they didn't know how much was already on your plate. They'll help you identify what can wait or be delegated, and/or even take the new task back entirely.

The beauty of this method is that you're not complaining or refusing. You're problem-solving collaboratively. You're treating your time like the limited resource it is and asking for strategic guidance.

Some managers will try to dodge the question with "everything's important." Don't let them off the hook. Respond with: "I understand everything's important, but given the limited hours in the day, what should I focus on first? What has the greatest impact?"

Force the prioritization conversation. Because if you don't, you're letting someone else overspend your time budget without your consent. And that's a cost you can't afford.

16

When Work Gets Messy

Toxic Work Environments

There's a difference between normal workplace stress and something being genuinely wrong. Maybe Sunday nights have started feeling like a vortex of dread. Maybe you find yourself walking on eggshells at work, second-guessing conversations that used to feel natural, or wondering if you're losing your mind when people deny things you clearly remember happening.

Sometimes the signs are obvious—screaming bosses, blatant discrimination, or harassment. But more often, toxicity creeps in slowly. It starts with small things that feel off but are easy to rationalize away. A comment that stings but gets brushed off as "just their sense of humor." Promises that never materialize but always come with reasonable explanations. Blame that somehow always rolls downhill to land at your feet. Gray area between microaggression and an aside spoken with no ill intent.

You might find yourself making excuses for behavior you'd never tolerate from friends or family. *They're just under a lot of pressure. That's just how this industry works. At least the pay is good.* These aren't insights—they're survival mechanisms. Your brain trying to make sense of an environment that doesn't actually make sense.

The tricky thing about a toxic workplace is that often it's really good at making you question your own reality. Those with power will tell you you're too sensitive—while creating situations that would make anyone feel unsteady. They'll promise things will get better while systematically making them worse. They'll claim to value you while treating you as disposable.

If you beelined for this chapter, then something probably doesn't feel right in your work environment. Trust that instinct. Your gut isn't overreacting—it's responding to information. And you deserve to work somewhere that doesn't require you to become smaller, quieter, or less like yourself to survive.

This chapter isn't about fixing toxic people or changing broken systems. It's not about fighting the odds to become an A Player, or fixing a bad situation through work ethic and a can-do attitude. It's about recognizing what you're dealing with, protecting yourself while you're in it, and finding your way out when you're ready. You're not stuck, even when it feels like you are. You have more options than they want you to believe.

"Courtney, what's a hummer?" my boss, Jace, asked me with a smirk.

I stood at the head of the conference room, frozen. Twelve men, all at least ten years my senior, giggled under their breaths.

"*Hummmerrrrr!*" one of them shouted, fueling the laughter.

I was a twenty-one-year-old social media manager who had just presented a knockout proposal I'd worked tirelessly over for three weeks. I'd opened the floor for Q and A, and they were asking me about . . . cars?

"Ummm. A Hummer is . . . a type of car . . . ?" I answered, confusion written all over my face. "But what does that have to do with—"

The room erupted.

"No, Courtney," Jace said, the smirk never leaving his face. "It's when you vibrate your lips on my cock." Then he demonstrated, pursing his lips and blowing, "*Pfffffft.*"

The men around him burst into laughter, joining in. "*Hummmmm!*" "*Pfffft, pfffft!*"

My face felt like it was on fire. My throat tightened, and my vision started to blur. I could feel tears welling up, but I swallowed hard and forced myself to play along. I laughed nervously. "Oh . . . ha! Yeah, you really got me."

The room kept buzzing with jokes, like a pack of wolves with a scent for weakness. My head was spinning. I wish I could say I walked out of that conference room, quit on the spot, or slapped the damn smile off his face. But I didn't.

I told myself to "pull it together." I tried to convince myself it wasn't a big deal. But deep down, I knew—*this was not okay.*

This wasn't an isolated incident. It was part of a pattern. The inappropriate comments, the sexual innuendos—they'd started subtly, then built up over time. It got to the point where I was on guard every single day, just bracing myself for what was next. And whenever I tried to address it, I'd be met with gaslighting and excuses.

"You need to learn to hang with the boys," Jace would say.

Sometimes the threats would come out. "I know everyone in this industry. You wouldn't want to get on my bad side, would you?"

I felt trapped. I was young, new to the industry, and terrified. What if he really could ruin my career? What if speaking up only made things worse?

The breaking point came during a work trip to NYC. Jace requested to switch hotels to stay closer to me and demanded I meet him at the hotel bar that night. The dread I felt was so intense it permeated every cell in my body. That was when I finally listened to the voice inside screaming *Enough*. I didn't get on the plane. I quit on the spot.

That night, I made two promises to myself. One, I would *never, ever* let myself end up in a situation like that again. And two, I would do everything I could to help others recognize the warning signs of toxic environments and escape before they were trapped.

We spend 70 percent of our lives at work. If your workplace isn't safe, supportive, or empowering, it's all too easy to get stuck in a cycle of abuse. But here's the thing: Recognizing workplace abuse isn't always straightforward, especially when you're new to the corporate game. Abuse doesn't always show up as the overt harassment I've described—it can creep in slowly, subtle, disorienting, until you start to doubt whether it's even happening at all.

In this section, we're going to discuss the *most* important aspect of your career—your mental health and safety. Let's start by helping you identify the warning signs.

> ### ✳ Am I Being Gaslit? Scorecard
>
> Rate how often you experience these (1 = rarely, 5 = constantly):
>
> They say you're "too sensitive": _____
> They make you question your memory of events: _____
> They blame you for others' mistakes: _____
> You're told "That's just how it is here": _____
> Your achievements are minimized: _____
> Their feedback is vague and unhelpful: _____
> Your boundaries are called "attitude": _____
> They make promises they never keep: _____
> You're isolated from teammates: _____
> Comments are made about your identity (gender, race, religion): _____
> When you address discrimination, you hear you're "being too political": _____
> Neurodivergence or disability are mocked or minimized: _____
> They say you're "imagining things": _____
> Your concerns are dismissed as "overreacting": _____
> History is rewritten ("I never said that"): _____
> Your reality is denied ("That never happened"): _____

Total Score:

0–20: Probably normal workplace stress

21–40: Some toxic elements—stay alert

41–60: Major red flags—time to plan your exit

61+: Get out ASAP

It took me years to recognize what had happened to me—as not just "a bad experience" but workplace harassment and abuse. I'd normalized it, blamed myself for not being tough enough, and convinced myself it was just part of "paying my dues."

But here's what I know now: No career advancement is worth losing your dignity. No job is worth damaging your mental health. And no workplace has the right to make you feel unsafe or small.

If you feel like your workplace is toxic, you're not imagining it, you're not exaggerating, and you're not alone. Trust your instincts. Document everything. And most importantly, know that there are people and resources ready to help you fight back or find your way out.

The next few cheat codes are all about recognizing toxic environments, protecting yourself when you're in one, and finding the courage to leave when that's your best option. Your career should be challenging, not traumatizing.

Cheat Code #84
HR Works for the Company, Not for You

Let's get one thing straight: HR isn't there to be your bestie. They're there to protect the company, not you.

I know, I know, they love to give you that warm and fuzzy "we're here to support you, we're family!" speech, but don't get it twisted. When things get messy at work, don't expect HR to have your back. Their job is to minimize risk for the business, not to advocate for your well-being. If push comes to shove, they'll always put the company's interests first.

My friend got pushed out of her job as a personal trainer after reporting her boss to HR for crossing boundaries with clients. She went in thinking she was doing the right thing. The HR rep nodded sympathetically, took notes, and promised to handle it "confidentially." Three months later, her previously stellar reviews tanked. She was mysteriously excluded from contributing her creative ideas, after being creatively involved in the studio for years. Her old boss? Still there, still problematic.

HR's priority is making sure the company doesn't get sued. It's *not* making sure you feel valued and safe. Now, I'm not saying don't go to HR if you're in a bad situation—sometimes it's necessary. But go in knowing that they're there to protect the company's interests, not necessarily yours. If you expect them to be your ride-or-die, you're setting yourself up for disappointment.

When you do talk to HR, remember to take these steps:

- Bring receipts (emails, texts, dates, witnesses).
- Frame problems as business risks.
- Know which company policies were violated.
- Keep your emotions in check.
- Never reveal your next move.

The fastest way to get HR's attention? Mention terms like "hostile work environment," "discrimination," or "retaliation." Watch how quickly that meeting gets scheduled when they hear lawsuit language.

Last year, at the pharmacy where my friend worked, employees complained for months about a director's inappropriate behavior. HR did absolutely nothing until someone dropped the phrase "I believe this violates Title VII" in an email. Suddenly, action happened.

Most HR folks are just decent humans caught between employees and executives. But their paychecks come from protecting the company, not you. Keep your real talk for your friends, your therapist, your attorney. Those are your actual allies. HR is just another department with its own agenda, and that agenda isn't you.

Cheat Code #85
Document Everything

If you find yourself in a toxic situation, you need to be strategic. Document *everything*—keep records of inappropriate comments, uncomfortable situations, and sketchy emails. Have receipts, and I mean *all* the receipts, because when you go to HR (or a lawyer), you want to come prepared with facts, not just feelings.

Your memory against a manager's selective amnesia? Please. You'll lose that fight every time.

My friend Kira's boss was a master gaslighter—constantly moving deadlines, then acting shocked when she "missed" them. After one particularly brutal meeting where he claimed she had never delivered something (she had, twice), she started a dedicated "cover my ass" folder. Every email. Every Slack. Every changed requirement, with time stamps.

Three months later, when he tried pulling the same stunt in front of the executive team, she pulled up an entire timeline of his contradictory instructions. The look on his face was worth the price of admission.

Don't wait until you're actively being screwed over to start collecting evidence. By then, it's too late to capture the pattern.

Your Documentation Arsenal

Documentation Tool	How to Execute	How It Saves Your Ass
The Follow-Up	"Just confirming our conversation where you said XYZ..."	Forces them to correct the record or accept your version.
The Witness	"Thanks @Sam and @Taylor for the input during today's meeting where we decided to push back the launch."	Tag witnesses so your boss can't pretend things never happened.
The Paper Trail Forward	BCC your personal email on anything sketchy.	The company can take away access to work accounts in a heartbeat.

Documentation Tool	How to Execute	How It Saves Your Ass
The Sneaky Screenshot	Grab screenshots of passive-aggressive comments or contradictory instructions immediately.	Message history can be deleted... unless you have a backup.
The Voice Memo	Record the details during or right after verbally abusive meetings. Date, time, quotes, witnesses. (Check recording consent laws in your state first.)	You'll have a record of the abuse when you need it.
The Praise Portfolio	Save every bit of positive feedback you receive during this period.	It will show you're not trying to cover up shabby work by getting messy; YOU showed up to work, THEY showed up toxic.

The gaslighting in corporate America is next-level. "We have no record of you raising these concerns before" really means "We were hoping you weren't smart enough to document this."

When my old coworker got put on a bullshit performance improvement plan, he walked into the meeting with a folder labeled "Receipts" containing every glowing email about his work from the past year—including from the very manager now claiming he was underperforming. Performance Improvement Plan mysteriously disappeared.

Trust me, nothing shuts down BS faster than replying, "Actually, I have the receipts right here. Should I forward those to you, or would you prefer I share them with [person above them]?"

Cheat Code #86
Know When to Leave a Toxic Work Environment—Don't Sacrifice Your Sanity

If you're waking up every day *dreading* work, it's time to get real about your situation. A toxic work environment will suck the absolute soul out of you if you let it. If you're constantly feeling undervalued, stressed to the max, or like you're just surviving every workday, that's your cue. Absolutely no job is worth sacrificing your peace of mind.

Early in my career, I stayed at a soul-crushing agency job for ten months longer than I should have. *It'll get better after this client leaves. Things will improve once we hire more staff. Maybe I'm the problem.* (Spoiler alert: It didn't, they didn't, and I wasn't.)

The day I finally quit, my chronic migraines disappeared. My insomnia? Gone. That weird eye twitch that had become my personal trademark? Vanished. My body had been screaming what my brain refused to admit: This job was literally making me sick.

The most expensive career mistake isn't leaving too soon—it's staying too long. Every month in a toxic workplace is a month of your potential wasted, your confidence eroded, and your standards for how you deserve to be treated getting lower.

Set a deadline for yourself to see if things change. If they don't, start planning your exit. You deserve better than being stuck in a place that drains you—so protect your energy and make your move when it's time. Your mental health just isn't up for negotiation.

The "Get Out Right TF Now" Checklist

Gaslighting Red Flags	• You're constantly questioning your own memory of events. • "That's not what I said" is a regular response to your recollections. • Your genuine concerns are dismissed as "overreacting." • You apologize for things that aren't your fault. • You find yourself documenting everything just to prove you're not crazy. • Promises are made and then denied later. • Your achievements are minimized while mistakes are magnified.

Narcissistic Leadership Warning Signs	• Your ideas mysteriously become your boss's, and they get the credit. • Feedback is one-way: They critique you, but can't handle any criticism. • Rules apply to everyone except certain people. • Loyalty is valued over competence. • The workplace hero-worships certain executives despite toxic behavior. • Failures are always someone else's fault. • Empathy is seen as weakness.
General Toxic Environment Signals	• You filter yourself in meetings out of fear. • High turnover is normalized ("people just can't handle it here"). • Working nights/weekends is expected, not exceptional. • You feel physically sick on Sunday nights. • Your friends have commented on negative changes in your personality. • You're constantly exhausted but can't sleep. • You no longer talk about your work with pride or interest.
Workplace Discrimination GTFO Signals	• The only diverse employees are in entry-level or support roles. • Coded language is used to describe colleagues ("aggressive" for assertive women, "not a culture fit" for minorities). • Your accent, appearance, or cultural practices become regular topics of "jokes." • Accommodations for disabilities are treated as special favors rather than rights. • Concerns about bias are met with defensive reactions instead of reflection. • People from marginalized groups leave at significantly higher rates.

Still confused? If you're three hours and two glasses of wine into the depths of Reddit trying to determine whether you're in a toxic work environment—you're in a toxic environment.

Stop normalizing your addiction to stress. Stop hoping toxic people will magically become decent humans. Start respecting yourself enough to walk away from environments that dim your light.

The best career move I ever made was quitting my job without having another job lined up. The harassment became too much to bear, and I had no other option. Financially terrifying? Absolutely. But it created the space and personal safety to find myself again. And I do recognize having the freedom to leave a toxic situation is a privilege, but I hope the cheat codes covered so far have set you up to always have a pivot in your back pocket.

Your resignation letter doesn't need to explain every factor that went into your decision. "I've decided to pursue other opportunities" works just fine. Save your real exit interview for your therapist and that group chat where your friends have been begging you to quit your toxic AF job for months.

Cheat Code #87
Know the Line Between "Paying Dues" and Abuse

It's one thing to "pay your dues" early in your career—putting in extra hours, taking on grunt work, or handling a heavy workload is normal at times. But there's a line, and if you don't know when it's crossed, you could end up stuck in a toxic situation.

So how can you tell the difference? Paying dues is about growth and career progression—it should feel challenging, not dehumanizing. Abuse, on the other hand, will leave you drained, demoralized, and questioning your self-worth. Know your value, set boundaries, and don't let anyone convince you that tolerating mistreatment is just part of the process. It's not.

I once had a boss who'd say, "I slept under my desk for three years to get where I am, and you should too." But when I looked closer, I realized he wasn't successful because he slept under his desk—he was successful in spite of it. That toxic grind culture was just the baggage he carried, not the rocket fuel that launched his career.

Every industry has its version of "paying dues." In kitchens, it's working the worst station. In law, it's doc review. In entertainment, it's fetching coffee. There's nothing wrong with starting at the bottom. The problem is when people use "dues paying" as a cover for exploitation.

Paying Dues	Abuse
Hard work with clear purpose	Pointless work to prove obedience
Occasional long hours during crunch times	Constant expectation of 24/7 availability and zero boundaries
Constructive feedback to help you improve	Criticism designed to undermine confidence
Everyone doing their fair share of grunt work	Only certain people getting stuck with thankless tasks
Challenging assignments that build skills	Impossible assignments designed to make you fail
Recognition for extra effort	Extra effort treated as the minimum expectation
Learning opportunities built into tough tasks	Tough tasks with no learning value or support
Clear path to advancement	Perpetually moving goalposts

The "pay your dues" lie is most dangerous when it normalizes abuse across an entire industry. "That's just how it is in finance/fashion/law/tech." No, that's how some people with power have decided it should be, and enough people believed them to make it stick.

My friend Elena worked at a prestigious design firm where eighty-hour weeks were considered normal. "It's competitive—this is how you prove yourself," they told her. After two years of no advancement, despite burning out, she realized they had no incentive to promote someone willing to do senior-level work at an entry-level salary.

The moment she set boundaries, suddenly she wasn't "committed enough." Classic abuse disguised as "paying dues."

Here's your gut check: If senior people in your industry glorify their trauma rather than try to prevent you from experiencing the same, they're more hazing coordinators than mentors.

Real mentors say: "I had to struggle through this, but I'm going to help you find a better way," or "This is a struggle, but you got this; here are some resources to support." Toxic leaders say: "I suffered, so you should too."

Paying dues should be temporary, purposeful, and lead to advancement. If the goalposts keep moving and the rewards never materialize, you're not paying dues—you're being exploited.

Your career will have plenty of legitimate challenges. Don't waste your resilience on people who confuse subordination with dedication.

Cheat Code #88
When in Doubt, Lawyer Up

If you're dealing with some shady stuff at work—whether it's harassment, unfair treatment, or straight-up illegal behavior—don't sit around hoping HR will swoop in and save the day. Lawyer up. Get someone in your corner who actually knows the game and has *your* interests in mind, because the company's legal team is there to protect *them,* not you. When you exist in the workplace as part of a minority, you're often made to feel like you should be grateful just to be there. I hope the materials we've covered in this book so far have shown you not only that you deserve to be there, but that you have just as much right to advocate for yourself as anyone if you're not being treated fairly.

An employment lawyer can help you understand your rights, look at your situation from a legal perspective, and guide you on how to approach HR or management without jeopardizing your job.

I'll be real—I didn't hire a lawyer when I was being sexually harassed at work because I *thought* I didn't have the resources. HR led me to believe I was powerless, and I didn't get a second opinion. Turns out, they were wrong. There are *thousands* of free resources, pro bono lawyers, nonprofits, and organizations that can help you. You don't need a ton of money to get legal advice—just the willingness to protect yourself and find the support you deserve. Don't let anyone make you feel powerless. You do have options, even if you're being gaslit to think you don't.

My friend Zoe put up with a manager who kept "accidentally" touching her during meetings for six months before finally calling an employment attorney. After one consultation, she learned she had way more options than HR had led her to believe. The attorney helped her draft an email that mentioned specific legal protections—and suddenly the company found a way to fire her harasser instead of suggesting she "work it out" with him.

The magic words "I've consulted with an attorney" can transform how quickly your complaints get addressed. Companies fear lawsuits more than they fear unhappy employees.

But when should you actually call a lawyer? Earlier than you think, especially if you've run into any of these issues:

- When behavior persists after you've reported it.
- When you're facing retaliation for speaking up.
- When you're being asked to sign something you don't understand.
- When you're suddenly terminated after raising concerns.
- When your employer is violating wage, overtime, or safety laws.
- When discrimination based on protected characteristics is happening.
- When you're questioning abuse (it's always safer to get a second opinion).

Don't wait until you're fired or forced to quit. By then, you've lost leverage. Take advantage of the abundant resources that have your back. Make sure to do some research into the workplace protections in your territory and the resources available to help you (many of which will be free). The organizations listed below are available if you're in the US. If you're elsewhere, government websites, NGOs, or trade unions are a good place to start. For example, in the UK, you could contact ACAS (Advisory, Conciliation and Arbitration Service), Citizens Advice, or check out gov.uk for how to receive legal aid.

General Support

Equal Employment Opportunity Commission (EEOC): Files workplace discrimination claims at no cost. eeoc.gov

Legal Aid at Work: Free clinics and helplines for workplace issues. legalaidatwork.org

National Employment Lawyers Association: Find employment attorneys who offer free consultations. nela.org

American Bar Association Free Legal Answers: Online platform for legal questions. abafreelegalanswers.org

Sexual Harassment Support

Time's Up Legal Defense Fund: Connects sexual harassment victims with legal help. nwlc.org/times-up-legal-defense-fund

RAINN: Resources for sexual assault and harassment. rainn.org

9to5: Support for women facing workplace harassment. 9to5.org

Discrimination Resources

National Action Network: Civil rights organization with legal resources. nationalactionnetwork.net

Lambda Legal: Support for LGBTQ+ workplace discrimination. lambdalegal.org

Asian Americans Advancing Justice: Resources for Asian American discrimination cases. advancingjustice-aajc.org

Wage Theft and Labor Violations

Department of Labor's Wage and Hour Division: Handles wage theft complaints. dol.gov/agencies/whd

Workplace Fairness: Information on workplace rights. workplacefairness.org

Workers' Rights Clinics: Many law schools run free clinics for employment issues.

Unfortunately, the corporate system is designed to make you feel powerless and alone. That's how companies avoid accountability. But you're not alone, and you're not powerless. Pick up the phone. Make the call. Your future self will thank you for standing up now rather than living with "I should have" regrets later. In all truthfulness, I live with regret every day for not confronting my abuser. I genuinely hope this chapter has inspired you to take action if you're facing a similar situation as I did. You have rights, you have power, and you have a voice. Please don't be afraid to use them.

Pro Tip: Most of the organizations I've listed offer services in multiple languages and don't require citizenship documentation. Many employment lawyers work on contingency—meaning they get paid only if you win—so don't assume you can't afford help.

Part 5

Leveling Up

You've put in the work. You've learned the game, built the relationships, and proven you can deliver. You're no longer the person frantically googling "how to write a professional email" or wondering if you belong in important meetings. You've earned your seat at various tables, and people actually listen when you speak.

But now you're facing a different kind of challenge: What comes next?

Maybe you're eyeing that next promotion but realizing it requires a completely different skill set than what got you here. Maybe you're considering starting your own thing but aren't sure if you're ready to bet on yourself. Maybe you're comfortable where you are but know that comfortable can quickly become stagnant in today's economy.

This is the phase where your moves need to be more strategic, not just tactical. Where the risks are higher but so are the potential rewards. Where you're not just trying to advance your career—you're trying to shape it into something that actually excites you.

The strategies that worked when you were climbing the ladder don't necessarily work when you're trying to build your own. The skills that made you successful as an individual contributor might hold you back as a leader. And if you're not careful about what you do next, the safety of being really good at what you do can become a prison.

This part is about making those bigger moves—the ones that feel scary because they matter—whether that means finally going after that promotion you've been circling for months, building something on the side that could become your main thing, or positioning yourself as the expert everyone turns to when shit hits the fan.

You're not starting from zero anymore. You have credibility, experience, and hopefully some financial cushion to take calculated risks. The question isn't whether you're qualified for the next level—it's whether you're brave enough to claim it.

17

Promotions

Climbing the Career Ladder

Let me guess. You're watching some mediocre asshole get promoted again while you're still sitting in the same chair, perfecting spreadsheets that nobody reads and wondering what cosmic injustice landed you in this parallel universe where merit apparently doesn't matter.

You've been the model employee. You arrive early, stay late, volunteer for the shit projects nobody else wants, and deliver work so polished it could be framed. Yet you see your coworker—who spends half the day gossiping by the coffee machine and the other half recycling last year's ideas— getting the recognition, the stretch assignments, and the fast track to leadership.

What the actual hell is happening here?

Well, being amazing at your current job is not a promotion strategy. It's a retention strategy. The promotion game isn't about who deserves it most—it's about who plays it best. The A Players getting ahead aren't necessarily the smartest or hardest working. They're the ones who figured out that competence is table stakes, and everything else is theater.

You can keep perfecting your craft while others climb over you, or you can learn the actual rules of advancement—which have nothing to do with how well you execute tasks and everything to do with how well you position yourself for bigger ones.

There's a dirty little secret that HR is keeping from you: That fairy tale about talent rising and hard work being rewarded is pure corporate propaganda designed to keep you grinding away in your sad little cubicle while others with half your talent claim the corner offices.

These are the brutal truths you need to accept sooner rather than later.

- Corporate America doesn't promote the most qualified person—it promotes the one who makes sure EVERYONE KNOWS they're qualified.
- Corporate America doesn't give a damn about your eighty-hour workweeks—it rewards the person who documents their wins and broadcasts them to decision-makers.
- Corporate America doesn't reward team players—it rewards those who build a powerful network of advocates who fight for them when promotion conversations happen.
- Corporate America couldn't care less about your innovative thinking—it promotes the person who knows how to sell those ideas up the chain with confidence that borders on audacity.

Your perfect execution and permission-seeking behavior have kept you exactly where you started. But strategic audacity and territorial claim staking? *That's* what gets you the title, the office, and the compensation package you deserve.

Close those forty-seven tabs of someone else's priorities right TF now. Put down that report nobody will actually use. What you're about to learn are the career cheat codes that the A Players have been using all along—while you've been too busy being "excellent" to even notice you're playing the wrong game entirely.

Cheat Code #89
Ask for It—Closed Mouths Don't Get Promotions

Every single day you don't ask for a promotion is a day you're donating thousands of dollars back to your company. That's a fucking financial crime against yourself.

I'm not here to coddle you with corporate fairy tales about how "your work speaks for itself." We both know that's the BS that keeps the A Players wealthy and the B Players waiting. Your company will do everything in its power to not pay you a cent more than what think they can get away with.

I've worked with thousands of professionals who were exactly where you are—crushing the work but watching promotions pass them by like Ubers in the rain. My client Naomi was working herself to burnout creating award-winning campaigns while watching mediocre Vivian get promoted above her. When I asked if she'd explicitly told her boss she wanted advancement, she looked at me like I'd suggested she rob a bank. "Shouldn't it be obvious from my work?" GIRL. NO.

The minute—THE MINUTE—she started having regular check-ins specifically about her career path using my exact scripts that follow, everything shifted. Three months later? Senior marketing manager with a $27K raise. That title had been available the whole damn time.

Your Ask-for-It Promotion Scripts

The Initial Conversation	"I've been thinking about my growth here, and I'd really love to move toward [specific role/title] in the next six months. Based on what you've seen in my work, what skills or projects should I focus on to get there?"
The Follow-Up (2 to 3 months later)	"I wanted to check in about our conversation regarding my path to [role]. I've been working on [specific things they mentioned], and I'm wondering if there's anything else I could be doing to prepare for that next step?"
The Direct Ask (when you've been crushing it)	"Given the success of [specific project/achievement] and the additional responsibilities I've taken on with [name other examples], I believe I'm operating at the level of [next title]. I'd like to discuss formalizing this with a promotion. When would be a good time to talk about this?"

Your boss isn't losing sleep wondering how to advance your career. They're focused on *their* promotions, *their* bonuses, *their* problems. If you don't explicitly put your advancement on their agenda, it simply won't make the list.

And that discomfort you feel about asking? That's the patriarchal, corporate conditioning designed to keep workers quietly producing while the owners extract value. Break free from it.

When you ask powerfully for what you deserve, one of two things happens: You get it (win!) or you discover this company will never value you properly (also a win—because now you can stop wasting your genius there).

Your Emergency Confidence Boost

I know you're probably staring at this book right now, thinking *But what if they think I'm not ready?* or *What if I AM not ready?* or my personal favorite, *What if they laugh at me?* (They won't. You're fine.) Keep this list handy for when impostor syndrome hits before asking for that promotion.

Remember all of these facts:

- You were hired for a reason.
- Everyone successful had to ask at some point.
- The worst they can say is "not yet."
- If you don't ask, the answer is always no.
- The world belongs to the people who ask.

The A Players aren't waiting for permission. They're busy creating leverage, visibility, and demand for themselves while you're still color-coding that report nobody asked for.

So take a deep breath. Do a power pose in the bathroom like the badass you are. And go get what's already yours. Your bank account will thank you. And so will future you.

Cheat Code #90
The Excellence Paradox:
Stop Being Too Good at Your Current Role

Let's play a little game.

What do you think is stopping you from getting that promotion you've been eyeing?

- Not working hard enough? No.
- Not smart enough? Definitely not that.
- Not dedicated enough? Please.

The real answer: You're too damn good at your current job.

Yes, you read that right. Your exceptional performance—the late nights, the crisis management, the "I'll handle it" attitude—has become your career prison. While you've been perfecting your execution, the system has found its perfect cog. And guess what? Perfect cogs don't get promoted. They get exploited.

Your boss isn't thinking *Wow, we should totally promote this rock star!* They're thinking *Yay! Thank god we found someone who'll do the work of three people without complaining or demanding more money.*

The corporate math is simple: Why would they move their MVP player to a new position when they're crushing it exactly where they are? That would create two problems—finding your replacement *and* training you for something new. Meanwhile, your mediocre colleague who does just enough to not get fired? He's getting that promotion because he's REPLACEABLE.

I know this feels backward. But after coaching thousands of professionals through career transitions, I see a clear pattern: The more irreplaceable you are in your current role, the more invisible you become for promotion.

Once more, with emphasis: The more *irreplaceable* you are in your current role, the more *invisible* you become for promotion.

Please put down that extra project you volunteered for. Stop being everyone's emergency contact. Your excellence should be strategic, not a life sentence.

The SCALE Method

Derek was the ultimate customer support hero at a fast-growing SaaS (software as a service) company. We're talking 98 percent satisfaction scores; the company average was 76 percent. VIP customers would request him by name. The CEO literally mentioned him in quarterly all-hands meetings as "the gold standard."

But after three years of watching junior colleagues climb past him, Derek was still stuck in the same role with measly 3 percent annual raises. When he applied for the team lead position, he got passed over—THREE SEPARATE TIMES.

After our first coaching session, Derek realized he'd built himself the most beautiful career prison. His boss finally admitted the truth: "Derek, you're our best agent. If we promote you, who would handle our VIP customers?"

Translation: "Your excellence is too valuable exactly where you are."

So how do you work yourself out of a job? Derek used the SCALE method, a strategy I created for all of the rock stars that want to unstuck themselves from their task prison.

The SCALE Method

1. Spot your golden handcuffs.
2. Capture your genius.
3. Assign your replacements.
4. Level up to next-tier problems.
5. Escape with strategic incompetence.

Here's how Derek systematically broke free using each step of the SCALE method:

1. SPOT Your Golden Handcuffs

Derek mapped out every "only Derek can do this" task. The list was shocking—handling escalated VIP complaints, troubleshooting certain technical issues, and writing responses for sensitive situations. He realized these "special skills" were actually keeping him trapped.

2. CAPTURE Your Genius

Over six weeks, Derek created what he called his "support bible"—detailed step-by-step guides for handling every type of customer interaction, including templates for those "Derek magic" responses that customers loved. Instead of keeping his techniques secret, he turned them into blueprints anyone could follow.

3. ASSIGN Your Replacements

Derek approached his boss: "I've noticed I'm the bottleneck for VIP support. I'd like to train Maria and Jason on these accounts to improve our team's resilience." Notice he framed it as solving a company problem, not his personal career advancement. By month three, Maria and Jason were handling 70 percent of what used to be "Derek-only" tasks.

4. LEVEL UP to Next-Tier Problems

While making himself replaceable at his current job, Derek simultaneously started solving team-level problems: analyzing patterns in customer complaints, creating team dashboards that highlighted improvement opportunities, and proposing a new onboarding system that reduced training time by 40 percent. He was demonstrating team lead skills while still in his support role.

5. ESCAPE with Strategic Incompetence

Derek started practicing "strategic incompetence" on low-value tasks. Not with critical work, but with the energy-draining busywork that kept him stuck. When asked to create the monthly metrics report (again), he responded: "I've documented how I do it here, but I think this would be a great development opportunity for Taylor. I can guide her through it while I focus on the new knowledge base system I mentioned last week."

The results were transformative. Within four months, his boss saw him differently—not as an irreplaceable individual contributor, but as someone who could elevate the entire team. When a Team Lead position opened up again, Derek was the obvious choice.

The biggest mindset shift? Understanding that A Players don't hoard their expertise—they systematize it, share it, and then move up to solve bigger problems. Your technical excellence should be a stepping stone, not your final destination.

Derek's advice: "I spent three years trying to be irreplaceable, wondering why I wasn't moving up. Once I deliberately made myself replaceable while demonstrating higher-level impact, everything changed in less than six months."

Your excellence is an asset only when you deploy it strategically. Otherwise, it's the very chain keeping you captive where you are, unable to reach the corner office and compensation you deserve.

Cheat Code #91
Get out of Task Mode and into Strategy Mode ASAP

So you're great at checking off your to-do list? Congratulations! You've mastered the skill set of a $12 smartphone app. That gold star you're giving yourself for inbox zero? It's worth exactly zero dollars in your bank account.

While you're over there color-coding spreadsheets and responding to emails within three minutes, the A Players aren't managing tasks—they're creating *leverage*. They're not asking *How do I finish this faster?* They're pondering *Does this even deserve my energy?* and *What's the high-leverage move here instead?*

I can hear you now: "But Courtney, my to-do list is never-ending! My calendar looks like a 3D jigsaw puzzle! When am I supposed to find time to be strategic when I'm drowning in deadlines?"

Let me be crystal clear: That drowning feeling? It's by design. The system WANTS you busy. Busy people don't disrupt industries. Busy people don't demand raises. Busy people don't start competing businesses.

Being the "taskmaster" is the perfect setup to keep you exactly where you are—forever. Period. You get to feel productive. Your boss gets to call you "reliable." Everyone's happy except your bank account and your future self who's still going to be answering emails at 10 p.m. five years from now.

It's time to stop confusing motion with progress. It's time to stop mistaking busyness for business. And it's definitely time to stop playing small just because you're good at it.

The question isn't how to get more done. The question is: Are you ready to play a completely different game?

Managers don't get promoted for checking off tasks—they get promoted for their thinking. For seeing problems nobody else sees. For connecting dots that change the game. For asking "Why are we doing this?" when everyone else is asking "How quickly can we do this?"

Ten Questions to Dig Deeper on a Task and Get Strategic

1. What's the larger objective we're trying to achieve with this task, and how does it fit into the bigger picture?
2. Is this task addressing a high-priority problem, or could we be focusing on something with a bigger impact?
3. Is this task solving the actual problem, or just treating a symptom?
4. Are there any gaps in the process, tools, or resources that could make this task easier or more effective?
5. Who are the stakeholders or end users impacted by this task, and how can we best meet their needs?

6. Is there a way to simplify, automate, or eliminate steps to make this process more efficient?
7. How will we know if this task has been executed successfully? Are there metrics or benchmarks we should define?
8. Beyond completing the task, is there an opportunity to innovate, improve, or add extra value?
9. Are there other teams, departments, or individuals who should be looped in for input or collaboration?
10. What potential challenges or unintended consequences should we consider before moving forward?

Print out these questions and keep them on your desk. Seriously. Or rip them out of this book, I don't care. They're your ticket out of task-robot mode and into the strategic thinker zone where promotions actually happen.

Showing off your ability to think bigger than your to-do list? That's just the beginning. When you step up and start asking the questions nobody else has the courage to ask, people don't just notice—they *scramble* to keep you.

Cheat Code #92
Act Like a Peer, Never a Subordinate

When you walk into a meeting with those "important people" and suddenly forget your own name, that's not just you being awkward. That's literally your primitive brain firing off ancient survival signals. Your amygdala—that prehistoric part of your brain—is SCREAMING "Don't challenge the alpha! You'll get kicked out of the tribe and die alone!"

Science doesn't lie, people. Anthropologists have tracked this pattern across every single human culture. The moment someone with a fancy title walks in, your brain chemistry starts flooding your system with submission signals.

A Players know that this fear response is just biological noise. Not truth. Not reality. Just leftover caveman wiring that has zero place in your journey to career stardom.

The C-suite executives you're intimidated by? They get nervous before big presentations too. The difference? They've trained themselves to override their amygdala's outdated programming.

This isn't personal development fluff. This is neuroscience. And understanding it is worth more than any MBA program you could waste money on. Just ask Dr. David Rock, a leading expert in workplace neuroscience and author of *Your Brain at Work*. His research reveals how the brain reacts to authority, stress, and hierarchy—key factors in how we navigate workplace dynamics—and offers strategies for overriding our primitive brain's hardwiring to better perform in high-stakes environments.

When you recognize that your deference is just biology, not destiny, you can finally show up with the energy of someone who belongs in the room where decisions get made. And when you show up differently? You get paid differently.

But let's be real—for women and minorities, this isn't just about overriding primitive-brain wiring. You're also fighting centuries of messaging that you don't belong in these spaces to begin with. While everyone's amygdala freaks out at least a little around authority figures, yours might be screaming extra loud because society spent generations telling people who look like you that boardrooms weren't meant for you. That's not personal weakness—that's historical baggage. The difference is, now you know the game is rigged and you can choose to play it anyway. Your brain might be carrying extra weight from systemic bullshit, but the solution is the same: Recognize it's programming, not truth, and override it anyway.

My client Anna showed classic subordinate behaviors: voice elevation or upspeak, excessive apologizing, minimizing language ("This might be stupid, but . . . "), and retreating to the corners and sidelines in any group situation. Her ideas, although amazing, were consistently overlooked because they were delivered with what I call "permission energy." She was unconsciously signaling *I don't really belong here.*

This happened not because she lacked competence, but because of how her brain processed hierarchical cues.

The good news is, organizational hierarchy is a shared fiction. It's fake. Not real. Totally, completely made TF up.

Look, I'm not saying higher-ups don't know things—fine, they do. But that whole "oh my god, it's the VP" worship thing you've got going on? That's just you psyching yourself out because you've bought into their marketing campaign.

Most of how people perceive your status comes down to how you carry yourself, not what brilliant things you're saying. Your posture, your voice, your eye contact. It's literally a performance, and baby, if you recognize yourself in Anna and the others I describe, you're bombing your audition.

That director who has you shaking in your boots? She puts on SpongeBob pajamas and drunk-orders from Amazon at 1 a.m. That VP who makes you stutter? He's not genetically superior—he just decided he's hot shit, and everyone believed him. And that terrifying C-suite exec? She's just as full of doubt as you are—she's just better at faking it while crying in the bathroom stall instead of at her desk like an amateur.

Stop. Treating. These. People. Like. They're. Special. They put their designer pants on one leg at a time just like you do. They're just humans with better haircuts and more expensive therapy.

But here's the thing—and listen up, Gen Z—there's a Grand Canyon–sized difference between not being intimidated and being disrespectful. You want to humanize them in your head, not treat them like your college roommate. Acting like you belong doesn't mean acting like you own the place.

Never quiver when they walk into a room, but also don't slouch in like you're grabbing snacks from the kitchen. Don't go all fangirl when they mention their Harvard MBA, but don't roll your eyes either. Don't nod at everything they say like they're handing down commandments from corporate Mount Sinai, but do acknowledge their experience and expertise. Respect what they know—and show that respect through your professionalism, not your fear.

Think of it this way: You're not their subordinate, but you're also not their buddy. You're their colleague who happens to be newer to the game. Act accordingly.

The second you put someone on a pedestal, you're basically handing them a ladder to climb above you. Congrats—you just played yourself.

Cheat Code #93
Title-Hack Your Way up by Going Small

Pause your doomscrolling for a hot second and check your LinkedIn feed. See all those randos with "VP of Whatever" and "Chief Something Officer" titles? Notice how half of them work at companies that sound like they were named by throwing darts at a tech buzzword board? That's not an accident. That's *strategy*.

The Small Company Express Lane

If you're trying to climb the corporate ladder at some Fortune 500 behemoth, you might as well be wearing cement shoes. Those places have more red tape than a Christmas gift-wrapping station.

At MegaCorp, you'll waste your prime years waiting for that pathetic promotion from "Associate" to "Senior Associate" (ooh, *senior*). But at smaller companies? Baby, you could go from coordinator to director faster than your corporate friends can get approval for a new stapler.

My client Miles spent *four years* kissing ass at a Fortune 500 organization, constantly being told he was "on track" for promotion (translation: "We're stringing you along until you burn out"). His former cubicle buddy Vincent bounced to some random fintech startup and went from analyst to director in eighteen months. When Miles finally got his big promotion? "Senior Analyst." Congrats on the extra $2K and zero additional authority, bro.

Big companies have entire *systems* designed specifically to slow your ass down. Promotion committees. Calibration meetings. "Career progression frameworks." It's all corporate theater to make you feel like there's a reason Chad got promoted instead of you.

Meanwhile, at smaller companies, if the CEO notices you in the kitchen not screwing up the coffee order, you could literally get promoted in a random Tuesday meeting because someone said, "Hey, isn't Remy the only one who understands how our database works? Let's make her director of technology."

Think about basic math (I know, painful): At MegaCorp with thirty thousand employees, you're competing against hundreds of equally desperate souls for that next-level role. At startups with fifty employees? You might be the *only* one in your department. Who else are they going to promote? The office plant?

But Is This Cheat Code for Everyone?
I'll be real—this strategy is NOT for everyone. If you're the type who needs the security of corporate benefits and can't handle some chaos, maybe stick with a big company. Some situations where you might want to ignore everything I just said:

- If you're in an industry where the company name matters more than your title (like certain law firms, investment banks, or if you're trying to eventually be a C-suite at a Fortune 100)
- If corporate benefits like dependable healthcare are not "nice to have," but essential to your survival
- If you genuinely have no idea what you're doing and need years of hand-holding while you figure it out (no shame, but know yourself)

For everyone else? Small company express lane all the way.

Your Fast-Track Game Plan

The impatient and ambitious (a.k.a. you) need their own strategy.

1. Get your fundamentals at a respectable company for one or two years, max (any longer and you're just drinking corporate Kool-Aid).
2. Jump to a smaller, growing company where you can level up twice as fast.
3. Use that inflated title to leap to an even better role elsewhere.
4. Rinse and repeat until you're exactly where you want to be.

The best part? At smaller companies, chances are you won't be siloed into one tiny specialization. You'll actually *learn* things instead of just formatting PowerPoints, because these smaller companies need their employees to be multifaceted. You'll make real decisions, build real skills, and have multiple areas of expertise to brag about. So when you do leverage that director title elsewhere, you'll actually know what the hell you're doing, unlike half the "seasoned leaders" out there.

And before you ask—yes, this is exactly how I became a marketing director at twenty-two while my classmates were still "marketing coordinators" drawing up Instagram calendars for approval by six different managers.

I started at companies so small the CEO was still answering customer service emails. My first "director" title came when I was basically running marketing by myself at a fifteen-person startup. When I interviewed at bigger companies later? They didn't care that my "director" role was at a company with the budget of a lemonade stand—they just saw "director of marketing" and started foaming at the mouth.

By the time my college friends finally clawed their way to manager level at their prestigious companies, I'd already been a "director" for three years and was interviewing for VP roles. Same graduation year, same degree, wildly different trajectories.

The bigger company wants to hire you eventually? Great—but let them hire the "already been a director for years" version of you, not the "please, sir, may I have a promotion?" version.

 Remember: There's a time and place for the big-name companies, and there's a time for title acceleration. Evaluate your own goals and choose wisely.

Cheat Code #94
Network Within the Company

You know what's cute? Having one work friend who saves you a donut at the monthly all-hands. You know what's *powerful*? Having a strategic network of allies planted across every department who can back-door an approval, an internal transfer, or whatever else your little A-Player heart desires.

Here's what they're not telling you at those useless orientation sessions: The official org chart is just some executive's fantasy about how work *should* flow. The *actual* company runs on invisible networks of gossip, favors, and alliances. Those shadow networks determine everything, from who gets the plum assignments to who gets promoted when no one's qualified. We already discussed using office buddies to get shit done (see cheat code #36). Now we're going to use them to get ahead.

The Department Buddy System: Your Career Secret Weapon
You need to identify and cultivate one key ally in *every* major department. Not the random quiet person who never talks in meetings—I'm talking about the respected insiders who know where all the bodies are buried and aren't afraid to spill that tea.

Think of your department buddies as your personal intelligence network, feeding you the information HR would rather die than tell you:

- Which departments are secretly getting budget increases (translation: job opportunities)

- Who's about to quit, before they update their LinkedIn (translation: replacement opportunities)
- What projects are coming that need someone with your skills (translation: promotion opportunities)
- Which managers are actually psychopaths (translation: dodge-that-bullet opportunities)
- Who holds power in each department (translation: backdoor approvals and shortcuts)

Let me be crystal clear: The Department Buddy System works only if it's mutual. You need to be equally valuable to them, or they'll see through your fake friendship faster than you can say "synergy." Share your department's updates, invite department buddies to your meetings when relevant, connect them with your other buddies. The stronger your relationship, the more they'll think of you when the good shit comes their way.

The Backdoor Approval Machine

Let's talk about the *most important* reason you need department buddies: getting shit done in a company that's designed to say no.

Your department buddies are a back door to every locked system in the company. Here's how it really works:

> **Need finance approval?** Your finance buddy tells you exactly what language to use in the request form and which budget codes won't raise red flags.
>
> **Need IT to prioritize your ticket?** Your IT buddy moves you to the top of the queue while everyone else waits two weeks.
>
> **Need legal to review something quickly?** Your legal buddy tells you their team's specific concerns so you can address them before submitting.

Need HR to make an exception? Your HR buddy tells you which policy points are actually flexible and which are set in stone.

The official channels are designed to slow you down and say no. Your department buddy network is your personal fast track to yes.

Cheat Code #95
Use External Offers as Leverage (Carefully!)

If things are really stagnant at your company—if you've had the promotion conversation multiple times, and they keep feeding you "next quarter" bullshit—sometimes you need a little outside nudge to remind them how in-demand you actually are. An external offer isn't just about potentially leaving; it's about getting real data on your market value and giving your current employer a wake-up call about what they're about to lose.

Getting an offer from another company is a power play, but it's not a card you should throw down just for fun. If you're gonna use that external offer to push for a promotion or raise where you are, you *better* be ready to walk if they don't match it. This isn't just a cute little bluff—you've gotta be willing to follow through.

James—a smart guy, killer at his job—gets a juicy offer from a competitor: 25 percent more than his current salary. He marches into his boss's office with his chest puffed out and drops the news. His boss says, "We'll miss you, but congratulations!" James panics because he never actually wanted to leave, he just wanted a raise. Two uncomfortable weeks later, he's at a new company he hates, wondering what the hell happened.

Here's a breakdown of possible outcomes when you present your counteroffer to your current employer, and things to consider before you proceed.

Scenarios	What the Employer Does	What the Employer Says	Points to Consider
Scenario 1	They let you walk.	"Thanks for your contributions. We wish you all the best."	Are you ready to clean out your desk TODAY? Is that other offer actually something you want? Have you practiced saying "Yes, I accept" to the other company?
Scenario 2	They counter, but now you're marked.	"We'd hate to lose you! Here's a 15% raise."	But your loyalty card is now permanently punched. You're first on the chopping block when cuts come. Your boss knows you've got one foot out the door.
Scenario 3	They give you what you want.	"We can't afford to lose you! Here's that promotion and 25% raise."	You proved your market value and got rewarded for it. You've established yourself as someone who knows their worth. You can use this momentum to negotiate future opportunities from a position of strength.

Be strategic about it. Let your current company know you're committed to your role but also that other opportunities are knocking. If you decide to drop the "I've got another offer" bomb, just remember: They could say "Congrats, good luck!" and let you walk, or they could give you what you want but keep an eye on you, knowing you were ready to bail.

The smartest use of an external offer is to not have to use it at all. Build your value, document your wins, and ask for what you deserve before you ever have to go looking elsewhere. The external offer should be your backup plan, not your primary strategy.

And if you do decide to leverage an offer, do it with extreme care. Have the conversation in person, emphasize how much you value your current role, and frame it as "I've received this opportunity, but I'd prefer to stay here if possible." Never make it an ultimatum unless you're 100 percent ready to follow through.

Because trust me, few work situations are more awkward than that two-week notice period after your bluff has been called and you're stuck leaving a job you actually wanted to keep.

Cheat Code #96
Job Hop When You Have Nothing Left to Learn

That company badge around your neck? It's not a wedding ring, bestie. Corporations talk about "family" while running spreadsheets on how to replace you with someone cheaper. So why are you still playing the loyalty game they invented?

The modern career path isn't a ladder—it's a jungle gym. The moment you stop growing, start packing.

The Three Signs You've Outgrown Your Role
When you're bored enough to count ceiling tiles during meetings, that's not "job security"—that's career death. Your skills are literally atrophying while you collect mediocre paychecks.

Sign #1: You're No Longer the Student
Remember when you first started and everything felt slightly overwhelming? That beautiful discomfort meant you were stretching. Now? You're the one explaining things to everyone else. You've become the office Wikipedia. Flattering? Sure. Career advancing? Absolutely not.

When was the last time you learned something that excited you enough to tell someone about it?

Sign #2: The "New" Projects Feel Recycled

Your boss unveils the "innovative new initiative" and you can predict every slide of the presentation because you've done this dance three times already—run. You're not experiencing déjà vu; you're experiencing career stagnation.

Does your job challenge you weekly, or just annoy you daily?

Sign #3: Comfort Has Become Your Captor

"But I like my team." "The commute is so convenient." "They let me work from home on Fridays."

Stop confusing a comfortable job with a good one; humans need challenges in order to feel fulfilled. Your salary might pay your bills, but these small perks are the golden handcuffs keeping you from your actual potential. Your work besties will forgive you when they see the light in your eyes comes back.

When was the last time you learned a new skill at your job?

Execute the Pivot Like a Pro

Don't wait until you're completely checked out to start looking. The best time to job hunt is when you don't desperately need to.

Update that LinkedIn profile (cheat code #64). Take those coffee meetings (cheat code #43). Get curious about what other companies are building. Interview even when you're not sure (cheat code #19); practice makes perfect, and sometimes the role you didn't think you wanted becomes your next obsession.

Your growth is *your* responsibility. Not your manager's. Not HR's. Yours. The job market rewards the brave, not the comfortable.

Pro Tip: The biggest salary jumps happen between companies, not within them. That "promotion" with the fancy new title and 5 percent bump? Please. Job hoppers average a 15 to 30 percent increase with each strategic move.

✱ Your Promotion Action Plan

When you finally embrace these strategies, something shifts. That knot in your stomach before asking for what you deserve? It loosens. That seething resentment as you watch mediocre colleagues advance? It fades. Because you're no longer the sucker playing a rigged game—you're the one who finally learned the actual rules.

So stock up on shameless self-promotion. Build your internal network like your career depends on it (because it does). Stop being so damn good at a job you're trying to leave. And for the love of god, start acting like you belong at the table, because nobody's sending out formal invitations.

Immediate Moves:
1. Schedule that promotion conversation THIS WEEK (script it, practice it, do it).
2. Identify one high-visibility project to volunteer for in the next thirty days.
3. Make your strategic shift from task robot to problem solver.
4. Connect with one person from another department every week.

Ninety-Day Strategy:
- Train someone else to do your "irreplaceable" tasks.
- Get one external offer, to understand your market value.
- Build your internal personal brand around a specific expertise.

- Move at least one strategic idea up the chain.
- Start showing up as a peer, not a subordinate.

 Remember: The promotion you're vying for doesn't go to the most deserving—it goes to the most strategic. Stop waiting to be discovered and start demanding to be seen.

18

Delegate Like a Pro

Your biggest career obstacle isn't incompetent colleagues or impossible deadlines. It's you, clutching your work like a security blanket and refusing to let anyone else touch your precious projects.

You've probably spent years becoming the person everyone turns to when something needs to be done right. The fixer. The reliable one. The human safety net who catches every dropped ball. And let's be real. You're addicted to being needed. There's a sick satisfaction in being the only one who knows how the magic happens.

But here's the plot twist nobody tells you: Being irreplaceable isn't job security—it's career quicksand. While you're busy being the hero who saves every deadline, you're also the person who can never take a real vacation, never get promoted—because "who would handle all your stuff?"—and never scale beyond what you can personally micromanage.

Every task you refuse to delegate is a vote against your own advancement. Every time you think *It's faster if I just do it myself,* you're choosing short-term efficiency over long-term growth. You're not being helpful—you're being a bottleneck with a hero complex.

The most successful people you know aren't doing everything themselves. They figured out how to clone their expertise, multiply their impact, and sleep soundly knowing their projects won't implode if they're unreachable for twenty-four hours. They learned the dark art of getting shit done through other people—and making it look effortless.

Time to stop hoarding tasks like a productivity dragon and start building systems that work without you. Your control-freak tendencies aren't protecting your career—they're suffocating it.

Cheat Code #97
Stop Being a Control Freak and Start Delegating

Delegation is a muscle, and yours is probably atrophied—especially if you're new to managing or used to being the catch-all assistant, or you came from a small company where each employee had to be their own individual problem-solving task force. Like with any muscle, you don't start by deadlifting three hundred pounds. You start small, where it feels less terrifying.

Micro-Delegation: Your New Religion

Those "it'll only take five minutes" tasks? Like scheduling appointments, answering "quick question" emails, formatting slides, ordering office crap, or finding the cheapest flight to Chicago? These are the silent killers of your productivity.

Before you say "I'll just do it myself" (the mating call of the perpetually overwhelmed), ask instead: "Who else could do this while I advance my actual career?"

My friend Gideon insisted he was "terrible at delegation" until I pointed out he was using that as an excuse to keep doing everything himself. So we started small—I made him micro-delegate—that is, delegate one tiny thing per day.

Day 1: Ask his partner to pick up the dry cleaning.

Day 5: Let his kid pack her own lunch (even though he "did it better").

Day 10: Have his assistant schedule meetings without triple-checking.

Day 30: Let his junior teammate handle an entire client presentation.

By day 30, his delegation muscle had gone from sad little noodle arm to respectable bicep. And guess what? He got promoted that quarter because suddenly he had time for strategic work.

> ✳ **The Twenty-Four-Hour Delegation Challenge**
>
> 1. Write down every single task you plan to do tomorrow.
> 2. Put a "D" next to anything that could potentially be delegated.
> 3. Pick the three easiest "D" tasks.
> 4. Find someone to delegate to *within twenty-four hours*.
> 5. Feel the sweet relief as your to-do list shrinks and your impact grows.

 Remember: Your inability to delegate isn't a quirky personality trait—it's a career-limiting behavior keeping you in the weeds instead of rising to the strategic level where you belong.

Cheat Code #98
Use Delegation to Think Like a Leader

I watched my colleague Nandita spend three hours updating client contact lists while her quarterly strategic review sat untouched on her desk. When I asked about her business development goals, she sighed: "I'll get to strategy once I catch up on admin work."

Sad to say, Nandita will never "catch up," because she's thinking like an employee, not a leader. Leaders don't do everything—they ensure everything gets done while they focus on what drives results.

Every hour you spend on tasks someone else could handle is an hour stolen from leadership activities that actually grow your career and impact. You're choosing to stay operational when you should be going strategic.

Every minute you spend on tasks below your pay grade is career suicide. Your brain space is valuable real estate, and you're using it to store the equivalent of a Dollar General.

Which leader do you want to be? The burned-out control freak who's still formatting their own slides while their employees anxiously try to invent tasks for themselves outside their job description, or the strategic thinker who's built a support system that lets them operate at their highest level?

The Delegation Mindset Shift

Delegating isn't about finding someone to do things exactly as you would (sorry, but that's impossible). It's about finding someone to get the job done to an acceptable standard while freeing you up for more important things.

Most of us create our own delegation paralysis—that frustrating middle ground where we think a task is too important to hand off but not important enough to justify the time it takes to properly train someone else. We end up hoarding tasks that we could absolutely delegate if we just got over our perfectionist bullshit.

The key is recognizing that this "dead zone" is where your career goes to die. You're literally choosing to stay busy with lower-level work instead of investing a little upfront time to free yourself for bigger things.

Ask yourself: *Does this task truly require MY unique skills and talents?* If the answer is no, it's a candidate for delegation.

"But I Don't Have Anyone to Delegate to"—Stop Lying

You have more options than excuses:

> **Team Members:** Your peers are capable of helping you out. They can step in while you're on vacation, on set for the day with a client, and so on. Use these as opportunities for delegation.

Skill-Swap: Find a peer who hates what you love and vice versa. You love creating spreadsheets, but hate the creative stuff? Swap responsibilities with your more creative coworker.

Hire a VA: For the price of your daily coffee habit, you can get a virtual assistant. My VA handles my inbox for $15 an hour, and she's better at it than I ever was.

Automate: If you're manually doing what software could do, you're the problem. Are you still paying bills one by one instead of setting up autopay? Still manually posting to social media instead of batch scheduling? Time to join this century.

Delegate to Future You: Setting up batch emails on Sundays is delegating to future you. Setting up auto-responses is delegating to robot you. Work smarter.

Remember: The most valuable people aren't those who can do everything; they're those who do only what matters while someone else handles the rest. And if you're still taking notes for your own meetings while complaining about career stagnation, I really can't help you.

19

Skills That Pay the Bills

Your college degree used to be a lifetime subscription to career stability. Now it's more like a free trial that expires faster than you can figure out what you're actually good at.

At this point, the skills that got you your first promotion might be becoming obsolete. That Excel wizardry you're so proud of? AI can do it faster. That industry knowledge you spent years accumulating? That shit is shifting faster than TikTok trends. The half-life of professional skills is shrinking so rapidly that by the time you master something, it's already time to learn what's next.

In today's economy, going back to school for another degree sounds about as feasible as becoming a professional athlete at thirty. You need skills that pay off immediately, not academic theory that might be relevant someday.

But here's where most people screw up: They panic-learn whatever's trending on LinkedIn, or they chase certifications that sound impressive but don't actually make them more valuable. They end up with a random collection of half-learned skills that don't connect to anything meaningful.

A Players take a different approach. They figure out which skills actually multiply their value instead of just add to their résumé. They learn things that make everything else they do more effective, more efficient, or more profitable.

You don't need to become a lifelong student. You need to become strategically skilled.

So we're diving into how to upskill, learn, and outsmart your way to becoming the person everyone wants to hire—without going broke or burning out in the process.

Cheat Code #99
Make Your Company's Budget Your Self-Development Sugar Daddy

Let me tell you about my friend Iris. This poor, sweet, naive little lamb was about to drop TWO THOUSAND DOLLARS of her own money on a UX design course. Her own money!

"Stop right there," I told her. "Have you even asked about your company's L&D budget?"

She looked at me like I was speaking Klingon. "My what now?"

Turns out her company—you know, the one making millions—had a $3,500 annual learning budget *per employee* that almost nobody used. It was just sitting there, collecting digital dust, begging to be spent.

Not only did Iris get her fancy UX course fully funded, but her boss actually had the audacity to act THRILLED about it, like he was doing her a favor instead of, you know, giving her what was literally already earmarked for her. He probably went home and told his wife what an amazing, supportive boss he was.

Your Company Is Hoarding Money with YOUR Name on It

Your company has most likely *already* set aside money for your professional development. It's literally in the budget with little invisible sticky notes that say "For Felix's brain upgrades" or "To make Gemma less useless at Excel."

But they're counting on you being too scared, too uninformed, or too "I don't want to be a bother" to actually ask for it.

It's the corporate equivalent of your parents setting up a college fund but never telling you about it, then being surprised when you take out crippling student loans. Don't be the schmuck leaving free money on the table.

Why This Is More Strategic Than Your Sad Little Five-Year Plan
This isn't just about scoring free stuff (though let's be honest, that part is delicious). It's actually the smartest career move you're not making:

> **You get upgraded skills that follow you everywhere.** Unlike that sad little desk plant they gave you for your work anniversary, these skills don't stay with the company when you inevitably leave for a better offer.
>
> **Your market value increases while someone else foots the bill.** It's like having a rich asshole boyfriend who pays for your plastic surgery right before you dump him.
>
> **You give off "growth mindset" vibes without working nights and weekends.** Unlike volunteering for that cross-functional project that's stealing your soul, this professional development actually makes your life *better*.
>
> **Your boss gets to feel like a talent-nurturing genius.** Every time a manager's direct report develops new skills, they get to take partial credit, like they personally poured knowledge into your brain. Let them have this delusion—it works in your favor.

When you're ready to make your move, you need to sound like you're doing the company a favor by becoming more valuable. Here's how:

Subject: Professional Development Investment Opportunity

Hi [Person Who Controls the Money],

I've identified a [course/certification/conference] that would directly enhance my contribution to [specific thing that makes the company money].

The program costs [$X] and would equip me with [specific skill] that would allow me to [specific way this helps the team/company].

Key benefits to the team include:

- I can take ownership of [specific responsibility/project type] that currently requires external resources.
- We can reduce our reliance on [contractors/consultants/other departments] for [specific task].
- I'll be able to [specific new capability that saves time/money/improves results].

Timeline and logistics:

- The program runs [dates/duration].
- I can complete this while maintaining all my current responsibilities.
- I'll share key learnings with the team upon completion.

This investment would benefit both my professional development and our team's capabilities. I'm happy to discuss how this aligns with our department goals and answer any questions you might have.

Best regards,
[Your Name]

Don't *Just* Ask for Courses

Your company's budget can pay for way more than just online classes taught by monotone instructors. Get creative with your requests:

Industry Conferences: These are essentially paid vacations where you learn a few things, collect free pens, and network with people who might hire you away someday. And yes, companies will often cover flights and hotels too.

Books and Subscriptions: That stack of business books you keep meaning to buy? Company card. That premium app subscription? Company card.

Professional Memberships: Those fancy industry associations with the abbreviations everyone tosses around? Get your company to pay the dues.

Coaching and Mentorship: One-on-one guidance from someone who's already figured out what you're struggling with. Way more effective than your boss's vague "feedback."

The Sugar Daddy Action Plan

Today	Find out exactly how much L&D budget your company has with your name on it.
This week	Identify one valuable skill that would make you either: a) more effective at your current job, b) more attractive to future employers, or ideally c) both.
This month	Submit a formal request for development funding. Use the template I gave you, customize it, and hit send before your impostor syndrome talks you out of it.
Next quarter	Flaunt your new knowledge like the intellectual peacock you are. Then casually mention in your performance review how this company-sponsored development directly contributed to [impressive business outcome].

Go find that budget and make it rain on your career before your co-workers figure out this cheat code and drain the fund.

 Remember: These funds exist for this purpose. Not using them is like having dental insurance but never getting your teeth cleaned because you're worried the dentist will judge your flossing habits.

Cheat Code #100
Follow the Top 10 Percent Rule

The whole "be the best at one thing" advice your boomer uncle gave you at your college graduation? Complete bullshit. Sure, getting into the top 1 percent at anything sounds impressive, but it's a high-stakes game where only a handful win, and everyone else burns out trying. It's the professional equivalent of playing the lottery with your career.

Let me introduce you to something that actually works: the top 10 percent rule.

The top 10 percent rule says: Don't aim to be the best at one skill. Instead, aim to be in the top 10 percent at two to four complementary skills.

Why? Because when you combine multiple skills at which you're very good (but not necessarily the best), you create a unique skill set that *no one else has*.

Suddenly, you're in your own category. You're not competing with everyone anymore—you're competing with no one. You're not just "another designer" or "another marketer"—you're the designer who also crushes content strategy and knows how to sell like a pro.

Real-World Money-Making Skill Stacks

Let's say you're in marketing. Instead of killing yourself trying to be the world's best social media strategist (competing with literally millions of others), you also become a talented copywriter, learn to speak conversational French, and develop a knack for understanding data analytics.

Now you're not just a marketer—you're a triple threat. When a global company needs someone who can create scroll-stopping content in French *and* track its ROI, guess who's getting paid premium rates? YOU.

Or, let's say you're an engineer. Cool, but so are thousands of others with the exact same degree and technical skills. Instead of trying to out-code everyone (good luck with that), you learn project management to keep teams organized, develop public speaking skills to pitch technical concepts, and get comfortable with business strategy and finance basics.

Now you're not just the engineer building tech—you're the one who can communicate its value, manage the team building it, and align it with business goals. That's not just an engineer—that's executive material, with a salary to match.

Stop Leaving Money on the Table

The market pays a premium for unique combinations. Being in the top 10 percent of multiple skills is *way* more achievable than being in the top 1 percent of one skill, and the payoff is often bigger.

Think about it. There are thousands of great designers. There are thousands of solid marketers. But how many great designers also really understand marketing psychology *and* can write killer copy? A handful. And they're getting *paid*.

> **Step 1: Identify Your Core Skill.** What's the one thing you're already great at or passionate about? This is your anchor—the foundation everything else builds on.
>
> **Step 2: Identify Two to Three Complementary Skills.** Think of two to three skills that align with or enhance your core skill. These should be adjacent enough to make sense together, but different enough to create contrast.

Step 3: Uncover Your Hidden Superpower. What's that thing you think is obvious or that "everyone knows"? That language you speak? Your knowledge of sports, beauty, or fishing? Your obsession with psychology? This is often something completely different from your career path—and that's EXACTLY what makes it valuable. This is your secret weapon in creating a truly unique stack.

Most people make the mistake of trying to compete head-on with everyone else in their field. They're playing a game they can't win, burning themselves out for mediocre pay.

Smart people—A Players—create their own categories that make them the only viable option. They don't compete on price or even skill level—they compete on uniqueness.

When you're the only one who can offer a specific combination of skills, you don't have to compete at all. The work comes to you.

Cheat Code #101
Always Have a Side Hoe

Like most of America, I was laid off. That random Tuesday all-hands turned into me and *everyone* on my team losing our jobs. Instead of panicking, I just switched my side gig from five hours a week to fifteen while I job hunted. My boss didn't know that I'd secretly been cheating on my full-time job with my side hoe—ghostwriting LinkedIn posts for tech bros at $100 per post.

Job security doesn't exist. What does exist? Your ability to make money from literally any skill you have.

Always, always, always have a side hoe (a.k.a. a side hustle). Start with finding a way to use your skills to make an extra $100 per month, then build from there. This way, if anything happens to your main income source, you won't be 100 percent reliant on that income.

The Side Hoe Starter Pack: For the Corporate Girlies

If You're Good at ...	You Can Make Money by ...
Presentations	Creating pitch decks ($100 to $500/deck)
Spreadsheets	Building financial models ($50 to $200/hour)
Project Management	Virtual assistant or DBA work ($25 to $75/hour)
Writing	Email copywriting ($50 to $250/email)
Coding	Website updates ($50 to $150/hour)
Social Media	Account management ($300 to $1000/month)
Analytics	Data reporting ($75 to $150/hour)

How to Start Without Looking Desperate

Don't Post	Do Post
Looking for side work!	Really enjoyed helping a client with [skill]. Love using my [expertise] to solve [problem]. Happy to connect if anyone needs similar support!
Don't Say	**Do Say**
I need extra money.	I'm taking on a few select clients for [service] in my spare time. Thought of you since you mentioned needing help with [problem].

 Remember: Your 9-to-5 is not your only option. It's not even your best option—it's just your most reliable option right now. Build your side hoe into your backup plan, your fun money, or your future empire. Start small. Start now. Start before you need it. Because the best time to start a side hustle was last year. The second-best time is right TF now.

Corporate Wants You to Find the Difference Between "Loyal" and "Stupid"

Corporations will drop you faster than your ex after that disastrous family dinner. That company you're giving fifty-plus hours a week to? They've already calculated how much your severance package would cost. They've already discussed which parts of your job could be automated or outsourced.

You think Patty in HR is your friend? Patty has a spreadsheet with your name on a list somewhere, just waiting for the quarterly review where they decide whose desk gets cleared out. So why the hell are you putting all your financial eggs in that basket?

You need leverage. When you have a side hustle bringing in even a modest $500 a month, you're suddenly operating from a position of power. You're not taking shit from that micromanager, because you know you've got options. You're negotiating your salary increase with confidence, because you're not desperate.

What My Side Hoe Taught Me About Value

When I started charging $100 per LinkedIn post, I was terrified. Who was I to charge that much? Then I realized those tech bros were making $5K to $10K in client deals from *my words*. I wasn't charging enough.

Your side hustle will teach you your actual market value better than your job ever will. At work, they'll call that 3 percent annual raise "generous." Meanwhile, your side clients happily pay you $150 an hour for the exact same skills.

How to Keep Your Side Hoe on the Low

I'm not telling you to neglect your day job. That steady paycheck is funding your career-building. But there are ways to manage both without burning out or getting caught:

> **Batch your tasks.** Two hours of focused side hustle work beats five hours of distracted effort. Set specific time blocks and stick to them.

Automate and template everything. I have canned responses, proposal templates, and pricing sheets ready to go. I can onboard a new client in under fifteen minutes.

Set boundaries from day one. Train your side clients that you respond to messages between 7 and 9 p.m. on weekdays, not during your 9-to-5. They'll respect what you teach them.

Raise your rates regularly. As your skills improve and demand increases, your price should too. This naturally limits your client load while increasing your income.

Keep your mouth shut. Your coworkers don't need to know. Your boss definitely doesn't need to know. Social media doesn't need to know. Success moves in silence until you're ready to make noise.

The Only Real Security Is What You Build Yourself

Corporate America promised security in exchange for our most productive years. Then they started mass layoffs via Zoom.

Your side hustle is the only real security you have. It's the only thing you truly control. It's your personal insurance policy against economic uncertainty, toxic workplaces, and the whims of executives who've never even met you.

So start now. Not tomorrow, not next week, not when you "have more time." The world doesn't reward people who wait for perfect conditions. It rewards those brave enough to start messy, learn quickly, and build something that belongs entirely to them.

Your side hoe might just save your life one day. Treat her accordingly.

Cheat Code #102
Build a "Pick My Brain" Consultation

You've spent years mastering your craft. Thousands of hours learning the ins and outs. Countless mistakes and hard-won victories. And yet somehow, your cousin's friend's sister's boyfriend's bestie thinks your expertise should be FREE with their shitty coffee.

"Hey girl, can I pick your brain about [insert your ENTIRE CAREER here]?"

HELL TO THE NO.

Your knowledge isn't community property. It's your intellectual property—the asset you've built with blood, sweat, and tears that these brain-pickers want to access for the price of nothing.

Set up a paid consultation link using Calendly. Add it to your LinkedIn bio, Instagram profile, and email signature with zero apologies.

The next time someone slides into your DMs wanting to "pick your brain," send them directly to your booking page. $150 for thirty minutes. $450 for an hour. Whatever your expertise is worth. And watch how quickly their "quick question" disappears when there's a price tag attached. MAGIC. Those who value your expertise will pay. Those who don't? They were never your clients anyway.

The Consultation Setup That Actually Books

Setting up a consultation offer isn't complicated, but most people mess it up. They create vague "coaching calls" nobody wants.

Your consultation needs one (or all) of the following:

- a specific, tangible outcome
- clear time boundaries
- a price that reflects your expertise
- payment required to book

Weak Consultation Examples	Strong Consultation Examples
Social Media Strategy Session	30-Minute TikTok Algorithm Audit: I'll review your last ten videos and identify exactly why they're not hitting the FYP. ($149)
Business Coaching Call	45-Minute Launch Strategy Call: We'll map out your next digital product launch with an exact timeline and promotional strategy. ($249)
Marketing Consultation	60-Minute Content Calendar Build: We'll create your next thirty days of social content with hooks, topics, and CTAs. ($299)

See the difference? The first column promises theoretical rainbows and hypothetical butterflies. The second column promises specific outcomes in specific time frames.

How to Transition from Free to Paid Advice
The next time someone slides into your DMs asking for "quick advice" or wants to "grab coffee and pick your brain," respond along these lines:

> Thanks for thinking of me! I've actually started offering dedicated consultation calls for exactly this type of advice. I'd love to help you with [specific problem they mentioned]. You can book a time here: [link]. Let me know if you have any questions about the process.

Some will disappear. Good. They wanted freebies. Some will book. Better. They value your expertise.

Let's be real—the cash is nice, but the power shift is everything. When you have a paid booking link, you instantly transform how people perceive you. You're no longer the helpful friend—you're the *authority*. The *expert*. The person whose time is valuable enough to command actual dollars.

Watch how executives suddenly respond to your emails faster. Notice how your opinions carry more weight in meetings. See how recruiters start approaching *you* instead of the other way around.

Your paid link isn't just a payment processor. It's your credibility badge. It's your authority marker. It's your A-Player signal. The money is just a bonus.

20

Sneaky Networking

Traditional networking advice assumes you're starting from zero—that you need to collect business cards at mixers and make small talk with strangers about what they do for work. But you're past that phase. You've established relationships, accumulated some social capital, and developed enough expertise to be genuinely valuable to others.

Now it's time to network like the professional you've become: strategically, authentically, and with the confidence that comes from having something real to offer.

Cheat Code #103
Connect Others—and Become the Web

When you connect two people, they both owe you. It's simple fucking math. Person A owes you because you gave them access to Person B. Person B owes you because you gave them access to Person A. And who's the web that shares the connection? YOU.

Now multiply that by twenty connections a month. That's forty people who owe you favors. By the end of the year, that's 480 people who feel indebted to your ass.

The A Players don't play by the same networking rules as everyone else. They don't waste time at shitty networking events collecting business cards. They build private networks where they broker introductions and take a cut of the value—whether that's in actual cash, equity, or future opportunities.

The Sneaky Psychology of Social Triangulation

When you introduce two people who subsequently create value together, something fascinating happens in the human brain. Both parties experience what psychologists call "triangulated gratitude"—a heightened form of appreciation directed not just at their new connection but at the person who facilitated it.

This creates a unique psychological bond where both parties now feel a sense of indebtedness to you that far exceeds what you'd gain from a direct transaction. Congrats! You've positioned yourself as the catalyst for value creation rather than as merely a participant.

Research from social network theory shows that individuals who occupy these "structural holes" between otherwise disconnected groups wield disproportionate influence. In his landmark studies, sociologist Ronald Burt discovered that people who bridge different social circles consistently generate better ideas, advance faster in their careers, and create more value for their organizations.

Let me tell you why you'll absolutely run the world when you become a connector.

> **Your social capital goes through the damn roof.** When you connect people who end up doing business together or becoming friends, both parties subconsciously credit you for that value. It's like earning relationship interest without lifting a finger.

> **People feel weirdly obligated to you.** It's basic reciprocity psychology—humans are hardwired to feel indebted to those who help them. By connecting others, you're collecting social IOUs without explicitly asking for anything.

> **You get access to all the juicy information first.** While everyone else is stuck in their little bubble, you're hearing about opportunities from six different networks. The psychological term is "information asymmetry," and it's a massive advantage.

You literally create opportunities out of thin air. When you understand what different people need, you can see connections that nobody else can—that's "associative thinking" at work—the same cognitive skill behind most creative breakthroughs.

Eventually, you'll transcend from being in the network to being *the* network. You're no longer asking for access—you're granting it. Every connection you make is a brick in the foundation of your future influence.

So open your contacts right now. Who should know one another but doesn't? Make that introduction today. Then do it again tomorrow.

Cheat Code #104
The Dream Question: The Single Most Powerful Tool in Your Connection Arsenal

Forget small talk. Forget industry gossip. Forget asking what people "do" (boring as hell—see cheat code #24). Ask people about their DREAMS instead.

"What's your dream?" is infinitely more powerful than "What do you do?" Snooze.

This simple pivot changes everything about the interaction. Here's why it's pure social dynamite: When you ask someone about their dreams, you trigger the triple-win. Three things happen immediately.

1. You Become Instantly Memorable

While everyone else at the event is having the same mind-numbing conversations about traffic and weather, you're the one person who made them light up by talking about what actually matters to them. They'll remember you as "the person who got me."

2. You Activate the Puzzle Piece Principle

Once they share their goal, you'll instantly recognize one of two opportunities. **You have a piece they need.** Maybe it's a connection, a resource, or specific knowledge. When you can immediately provide value, you've just created an instant ally. **You know who has their missing piece.** Even better, you become the connector. "You're trying to break into tech sales? My friend Taylor just hired three sales development reps at her company. Can I introduce you?"

The connector always wins, because you've just created two grateful connections instead of one (see cheat code #103).

3. You Build Authentic Social Capital

People instinctively trust those who show genuine interest in their ambitions. By focusing on their future (not just their present), you've positioned yourself as someone who sees their potential.

People guard their dreams closely. When someone shares theirs with you, they're revealing something vulnerable. This creates instant intimacy that shallow networking could never achieve.

Plus, when someone articulates their goals out loud to an interested listener, it actually strengthens their commitment to those goals. You've just done them a favor without lifting a finger.

The magic happens in the follow-up: "That sounds amazing. What's the biggest challenge you're facing with that right now?" Now you've given them the chance to problem-solve out loud *and* positioned yourself to be helpful.

Don't Ask	Do Ask
"What do you do for work?"	"What dream are you actively pursuing right now?"
"How long have you been at your company?"	"What future are you trying to bring into existence?"
"Are you working on anything interesting lately?"	"What change are you most passionate about making in your field or community?"

Your Assignment

At the next event, meeting, or even casual gathering, skip the "what do you do?" bullshit. Instead, lean in slightly and ask, "So what are you excited about building these days?"

Then shut up and actually listen.

Watch how quickly the conversation transforms from transactional to meaningful. Watch how quickly people warm to you. Watch how easily you identify ways to add value.

Cheat Code #105
The Two-Minute Cold Outreach Method

Ever notice how some people seem to "magically" connect with industry titans while you're still waiting for a reply from that assistant manager? The hack is not magic. It's math.

My good friend Avni Barman has created a wildly successful network of empire-builders using a ridiculously simple tactic that most people are too lazy or intimidated to try: the two-minute morning outreach. In the amount of time it takes her coffee to brew, Avni sends daily cold messages to people she admires.

As she brilliantly explains, the secret is just in the consistency of the habit itself. Here's how the math works in your favor:

- Every morning, take two minutes to research one recipient and send them a message they can read in thirty seconds.
- Most people will ignore you (this is expected).
- By year's end, you'll have sent 365 messages.
- The probability of *zero* responses approaches zero.
- Just *one* meaningful response can change everything.

Most people mistake this strategy for luck, but according to Avni, it's actually "a guaranteed outcome of a habit you worked hard to come into."

The genius is in the counterintuitive approach:

1. **Volume trumps perfection:** A good-enough message sent consistently beats a perfect message sent rarely.
2. **The bar is incredibly low:** Most people never reach out at all.
3. **Timing is everything:** Eventually, you'll catch someone at exactly the right moment.
4. **Asymmetric returns:** One yes from the right person outweighs hundreds of nonresponses.

This simple habit has delivered Avni life-changing outcomes: six-figure job offers, investment capital, meetings with self-made billionaires, and even meaningful friendships.

The Two-Minute Message Template
The key is keeping your message brief, specific, and easy to respond to.

> "[Name], your [specific work] on [specific topic] made me think differently about [specific impact]. I particularly appreciated [one detail that shows you actually paid attention]. Quick question: [something they can answer in under thirty seconds]."

Your Action Plan
1. **Create your list:** Identify a hundred-plus people who could meaningfully impact your career/business.
2. **Set your daily alarm:** Block two minutes every morning for this ritual.
3. **Track your outreach:** A simple spreadsheet works.
4. **Play the long game:** Commit to 365 days minimum.
5. **Expect nothing:** The magic is in the math, not the individual message.

Are you going to spend two minutes each morning creating your own "luck," or keep waiting for opportunities to find you? The choice is yours.

 Remember: What looks like "luck" to others is actually a predictable outcome of consistent action over time.

Part 6

The Ultimate, Game-Winning Cheat Code

Congratulations! You've made it. You crushed that corporate ladder and became everyone's favorite colleague. You have your bosses eating out of your hands and recruiters knocking on your LinkedIn. But there's one final piece of wisdom for me, your Career Fairy Godmother, to impart upon you. So stick with me here, because this is arguably the most important cheat code in the book.

Everyone wants to love their work—not just tolerate it, not just survive it—and actually look forward to Monday mornings and feel energized by what they do all day. Yet career advice often falls into two camps. There's the privilege-blind "follow your passion" crowd who've never worried about rent, and there's the soul-crushing "work is work" fatalists who've completely given up on the idea that Monday mornings don't have to feel like a death sentence. The truth is somewhere in between. Whether you're just starting out, are mid-career and restless, or are looking to make a major change, there's a strategic way to identify what actually fulfills you—and then build toward it.

Cheat Code #106
Find a Career That Makes You Look Forward to Monday

A lot of career advice focuses on the external: job boards, résumés, certifications, referrals, networking. All useful, yes—and I hope you've picked up some tips throughout this book. But now it's time to focus on the most important career element: your dream.

You can't strategize your way into a fulfilling career without decoding your own inner wisdom. Because the biggest career mistake people make isn't lack of ambition—it's aiming for the wrong thing.

They choose what's visible instead of what's *vital*.

They ask "What job will hire me?" instead of "What life do I actually want?" A dream career isn't reserved for the privileged few, or those who had their choice of entry-level jobs. By this point, I hope I've convinced you that you're deserving of (and more than capable of getting) whatever you want. Let's just make sure that what you "want" is truly what you *want*.

The Hamster Wheel I Couldn't Escape

I spent years trapped in the cycle myself. Résumé polishing. Certification chasing. Networking until my face hurt from fake smiling. Each new job or promotion brought a temporary high, followed by the same hollow feeling within months.

My days blurred together into a series of unfulfilling tasks and deadlines. I was the poster child for "doing" culture—always productive, always moving, always checking boxes. On paper, my career progression looked impressive. But inside, I felt like an impostor running on a treadmill that was getting faster, not closer to anything meaningful.

The breaking point arrived like a face slap of irony during my performance review. I was about to reach what I thought was my career dream—getting an opportunity to step into executive leadership as a CMO, chief marketing officer. As the CEO heaped praise on my "exceptional contributions" and slid the promotion letter across the conference table, something inside me flatlined. My goal had been accomplished, but I felt empty. I nodded and smiled mechanically, a perfect corporate puppet going through the motions.

That night, I sat alone on my apartment balcony, still in my wrinkled Theory suit pants, nursing a celebration champagne that tasted like nothing. I finally confronted the question that had been stalking me for years: *If this trophy of success feels like an empty cup, am I playing the wrong game altogether?*

The Pause That Changed Everything

What I needed wasn't another certification or connection. I needed stillness. Space to hear myself think beyond the noise of shoulds and coulds.

I took a two-week sabbatical—nothing dramatic, just enough time to break the pattern. Instead of filling every hour with productivity, I allowed myself to wander. To read books outside my field. To have conversations without agenda. To remember what naturally captured my attention before I learned to prioritize practicality over passion.

The clarity didn't come as a lightning bolt. It emerged gradually, like a photograph developing in solution. I realized I'd been optimizing for external validation rather than internal resonance. Climbing a ladder leaned against the wrong wall.

You might not have the luxury of a sabbatical, but I bet you do have time to do some journaling, research, or reflection. The rest of this cheat code is filled with more exercises to help you start considering what lights you up and how you can turn that into your dream career.

Consider this your permission to dream audaciously, remember what lights you up, and dismantle the mental blocks keeping you small. You're not missing credentials. You're missing *clarity*. And that clarity is buried under old programming, watered-down desires, and career advice from people who secretly hate their jobs.

Let's fix that.

The Dangers of Perpetual Motion

We live in a culture that worships action. "Hustle harder." "Rise and grind." "Sleep when you're dead." The underlying message is that constant movement equals progress. But motion without direction is just burnout with a vision board.

I was the queen of busy. My calendar was color-coded perfection. My to-do lists had sub-lists. I attended every workshop, joined every committee, volunteered for every stretch assignment. Colleagues called me "ambitious," but in retrospect, I was just anxious—filling every moment to avoid the harder work of asking what I actually wanted.

True ambition doesn't require doing everything. It requires doing the right things. And finding what's right requires stillness—the courage to stop, look inward, and listen to the quiet voice that's been drowned out by everyone else's expectations.

Reclaiming Your Original Vision

Remember when you were young and someone asked what you wanted to be when you grew up? Your answer wasn't based on market trends or salary ranges. It came from something purer—curiosity, joy, natural inclination.

Somewhere between childhood dreams and starting your career, practicality smothered possibility. Well-meaning advice narrowed your vision. Responsibilities piled up. And that original spark—the one that doesn't care about job titles or LinkedIn profiles—got buried under adult concerns.

But that spark is still there. And reconnecting with it doesn't require quitting your job tomorrow or making dramatic life changes. It starts with permission—permission to want what you genuinely want, not what you've been conditioned to want.

The Path Forward

In the following pages, we'll explore practical exercises to excavate your true desires from beneath years of conditioning. You'll learn to distinguish between external pressures and internal wisdom. You'll develop tools to hear your own voice amidst the noise.

Because here's the truth I wish someone had told me years earlier: Your dream career isn't as far away as you think. Often, it's not about making massive external changes, but about removing internal barriers—the "I'm not qualified" stories, the "but what will people think" fears, the "I should be grateful for what I have" guilt.

You don't need more credentials. You need more courage—courage to admit what you really want, and to take the first small step toward it today.

Own Your Genius

The thing you're most meant to do could be a thing you barely notice. It's so second nature, you're bored by it. You may assume everyone thinks like that, solves problems like that, sees the world like that.

They don't.

You could be numb to your own genius.

Many of us have something that comes so naturally to us that we discount it. *That's just common sense,* we think. *Anyone could do that.* But that's where we're wrong. Dead wrong.

The Curse of Competence

There's a psychological principle at work here—the better you get at something, the less remarkable it seems to you. Psychologists call it the "curse of knowledge" or "expert blindness." I call it the curse of competence.

It's why top photographers can't understand why you're impressed with their work. It's why brilliant strategists brush off compliments with "It's just connecting the dots." It's why the friend everyone turns to for advice doesn't see their own wisdom.

Your genius feels ordinary because you live with it every day.

But what's ordinary to you is extraordinary to others. And there's a market for that extraordinary.

The Hidden Clues

Look for these signals that you might be numb to your own genius:

- People repeatedly ask for your help with the same types of problems.
- When explaining something, you find yourself saying, "It's not that complicated."
- You're confused when people are impressed by something you did.
- You have a skill you learned so long ago you can't remember not knowing it.
- You've had the thought *I can't charge for this—it's too easy.*

These are all flashing neon signs pointing toward your hidden superpowers.

Borrow Someone Else's Eyes

Here's where the real work begins. When you can't see your own genius clearly, you need to borrow someone else's perspective.

Ask your friends:

- "When do you come to me for advice?"
- "What do you think I'm freakishly good at?"
- "What do I do that seems effortless to me, but impressive to you?"

Then shut up and take notes. Because your dream job might not be hiding in a job board—it might be hiding in your group chat.

When I tried this exercise myself, I was shocked. People kept mentioning how I was so good at giving direct and honest career advice and making it dead simple to understand. To me, that wasn't special—it was just how I thought. But to them, it was valuable enough that they'd pay for it.

That revelation became the foundation of my business.

Turn Ordinary into Income: Find Your Financial Twin
Once you identify your hidden genius, the next step is to recognize its market value. Ask yourself, *Who needs exactly this skill? Who's struggling with the same problems that this solves? Who would pay to avoid the pain of not having this expertise?*

Now look around and ask yourself, *Who's already getting paid for something like this? How are they doing it? What do they know that I haven't let myself believe yet?*

I call this finding your "financial twin"—someone who's monetized the same pull you feel.

And before your brain tries to talk you out of it, remember this: Someone less qualified, with fewer ideas and more audacity, is already doing it.

They're out there right now, getting paid for the thing you think is "unrealistic." The difference isn't talent. It's belief and action. Let them inspire you!

Unleash Delusional Imagination to Unlock Your Dream Job
Most people settle for jobs that make them feel safe. Very few ask what would make them feel *alive*.

If your dream feels "delusional," that's a sign you're getting closer.

The Size of Your Dream Is the Size of Your Life
We've been conditioned to be reasonable. To set "realistic" goals. To have "practical" expectations. But when was the last time you felt truly alive pursuing something practical?

The most fulfilled people I know aren't the ones with the most sensible careers. They're the ones who dared to want something that made others uncomfortable. Something that made them sound a little crazy at dinner parties. Something that made them question themselves.

Here's what most career coaches get wrong: They treat your wildest dreams as distractions to be tamed rather than data to be studied.

The vision is the intel. Your desires are not distractions—they're GPS signals from your future self.

So here's your assignment:

If I locked you in a room with no expectations, no judgment, and no bills—what would you spend your days doing?

Now take it one step further.

The Expansion Prompt

If you had unlimited money, unlimited access, all the power and support in the world—and the laws of physics didn't exist—what would you *actually* be doing?

Don't water it down. Don't make it reasonable. Let the vision be wild. Let it be excessive. Let it be *you* before the world taught you to be smaller.

The first time I did this expansion prompt exercise myself, I wrote: "I'd build a massive, genre-bending career empire where I un-gatekeep everything I've learned and lead people into the most high-expression, soul-aligned versions of their work lives."

At the time, I was answering emails for someone else's dream and trying not to cry during lunch breaks.

And yet—look where we are. You're holding the book. I wrote it.

The vision wasn't just a fantasy. It was a compass.

At the time, I was working at a marketing agency, taking meeting notes and scheduling social media posts. My vision sounded absolutely ridiculous. But a decade later, I see that elements of that vision have materialized in ways I couldn't have planned if I'd been "practical."

The point isn't to replicate your wildest dream exactly. The point is to extract the essence of what makes you come alive and find ways to infuse it into your reality.

Your Action Plan: Dream Deliberately
This week, I want you to:

1. Spend thirty uninterrupted minutes with the expansion prompt. Write with zero filters. Be completely audacious.
2. With your dream articulated, identify the three most persistent limiting beliefs holding you back. Write them down verbatim, the way they speak to you in your head.
3. For each limiting belief, create a power reframe that flips the script. (Example: "I'm too old to start over" becomes "My experience gives me advantages that others don't have.")
4. Find one small action that your reframed belief would inspire, and do it this week. No matter how small. Just push a tiny domino.

Your dream isn't waiting on the perfect conditions. It's waiting on you to believe something different about what's possible.

The "delusional" imagination you've been taught to suppress? That's your most powerful asset. It shows you where you're meant to go before you have any logical reason to believe you can get there.

Trust it. It knows more than your fear does.

✷ Translating Desire into Direction

Dreaming is not a detour—it's a data collection mission. Now that your desires are on the table, let's turn them into next steps:

1. Write Down That One Vision That Lights You Up the Most
Maybe your brainstorm produced multiple potential dream careers. Pick the *one* that creates the strongest emotional response when you imagine it. The one that feels like it's already been trying to get your attention.

- Circle it. Star it. Make it sticky.
- Write it down in present tense: "I am a…"
- Visualize it in vivid detail. What are you wearing? Who's around you? What does the space feel like?

2. Research Your Road Map

Find the breadcrumbs others have left for you.

- List three people who are doing something similar.
- Stalk them (respectfully). What can you learn from their paths?
- Notice: Did they make a direct leap or use bridge roles?
- What skills, connections, or credentials enabled their transition?

3. Identify and Flip Your Limiting Beliefs

Your biggest obstacles aren't external—they're internal. Remember step 3 of your action plan? It's time to dig deeper.

- Identify your top three limiting beliefs about making this change.
- Then flip each one into an empowering belief.
- Example: "I'm not experienced enough." → "I bring a fresh perspective."
- Example: "It's too late to start." → "My life experience gives me unique advantages."
- Example: "I can't afford to change." → "I can't afford to stay stuck in work that drains me."

4. Design Your Bridge Strategy

Thinking about the steps between where you want to be and where you are now, create your transition plan.

- What one element of your dream could you move toward right now?

- What role or transition could put you in closer proximity to your goal?
- What specific skill would make you more qualified for your target position?
- What arrangement (financial, physical, time-related) would give you more time to build toward your vision?

5. Take One Micro-Action Within Forty-Eight Hours

Momentum starts with tiny movements.

- DM a creator. Post about your idea. Block off an hour to write. Buy the domain.
- Email someone doing work you admire and ask for a fifteen-minute call.
- Update your LinkedIn to reflect the identity you're moving toward.
- Apply for one role that could serve as your bridge.

6. Make It Real Through Declaration

Internal commitment isn't enough. External accountability creates momentum.

- Say it out loud to someone you trust: Speaking the dream makes it real.
- Ask them specifically: "Would you check in with me about this in two weeks?"
- Set a calendar reminder to assess your progress in thirty days.

7. Create Your Timeline Milestones

Determine how you'll know when it's time to cross from your bridge to your destination.

- What specific achievements would indicate you're ready for the next step?
- What financial benchmarks need to be in place?
- What skills do you need to develop and demonstrate?
- How will you measure your progress?

The cheat codes throughout this book are set up to help you get a foot in the door and move up in a career of your choosing. Now, whether you are just starting out or already in an office with a door you can close, you can use these same cheat codes to make the move to the job of your dreams. I believe in you.

You've done the inner excavation, you know the rules, and you have the tools to make the system work for you. Now take one brave, tiny step.

You're not building a career. You're building a life.

And it starts now.

Conclusion

An Invitation to Break the Rules

So here we are. You made it through over one hundred cheat codes. You've learned the unspoken rules, the strategic moves, and the uncomfortable truths about how success actually works in the modern workplace.

But knowing the cheat codes isn't enough. You have to use them.

Right now, as you're reading this, there are two versions of your future playing out in parallel universes.

Timeline A: You close this book, nod thoughtfully, and go back to doing exactly what you were doing before. You keep your head down, work hard, and hope someone notices. You stay in your lane, apologize for taking up space, and wonder why you're still waiting for your big break while complaining about how unfair the system is.

Timeline B: You close this book and immediately implement one cheat code. Just one. Maybe you finally ask for that promotion. Maybe you take steps toward your side hustle. You make one strategic move, then another, then another. Five years from now, you're the one that other people are calling "lucky" while you're secretly laughing because you know exactly which cheat codes got you there.

The choice is yours. But let me reiterate: The system you've been taught to respect? It doesn't respect you back.

The Rules Were Never Designed for You

That "work hard and wait your turn" philosophy your parents taught you? It was designed to create compliant workers, not thriving leaders. The "don't rock the boat" mentality? Perfect for keeping you exactly where you are while others sail past you to better opportunities.

The corporate world has spent decades convincing you of these old cautions:

- Self-promotion is bragging.
- Asking for what you want is pushy.
- Changing jobs too often shows disloyalty.
- Success should come naturally if you're "deserving."
- Playing politics is beneath you.

These aren't moral guidelines. They're control mechanisms designed to keep you small, grateful, and manageable.

A Players have been ignoring these manufactured rules from day one. They've been playing by the real rules: Visibility matters more than perfection, relationships open more doors than credentials, and audacity beats modesty every single time.

Your Permission Slip to Play Differently

Consider this your official permission slip to break every "rule" that's been holding you back:

> **Permission to be visible.** Stop hiding your accomplishments like they're embarrassing secrets. Your work doesn't speak for itself—you have to speak for it. Loudly. Repeatedly. Without apology.

Permission to be strategic. Stop confusing working hard with working smart. The corporate world rewards strategic impact, not exhausted martyrdom.

Permission to be audacious. Stop asking for permission to want what you want. The corner office, the six-figure salary, the flexible schedule, the recognition—you're allowed to want it all. And you're allowed to go get it.

Permission to be selfish with your energy. Stop giving away your most valuable resource—your time and mental bandwidth—to everyone who asks. Your career is not a charity. Your expertise is not free community property.

Permission to be embrace the discomfort. Stop avoiding conversations, situations, and opportunities that make you squirm. Growth lives in discomfort. If you're comfortable all the time, you're not growing. You're stagnating.

Permission to be unapologetic. Stop apologizing for taking up space, having opinions, or wanting more. You belong in every room you enter. You deserve every opportunity you pursue. You are worthy of every success you achieve.

The Compound Effect of Small Acts of Rebellion

You don't need to torch your entire career to start playing by the real rules. You just need to start making small, strategic rebellions against the systems designed to keep you small.

Send that follow-up email asserting your value. Book that call with a potential client. Ask for that promotion using the exact words that command respect. Set that boundary with your boss. Delegate that task you've been hoarding. Negotiate that salary like your rent depends on it.

Each small act of rebellion compounds. Each time you choose strategy over struggle, visibility over invisibility, audacity over apology, you're not just advancing your career—you're rewiring your own neural pathways. You're teaching yourself that you're the kind of person who gets what they want because you ask for it, work for it, and refuse to accept less than you deserve.

The Ripple Effect

When you start playing by the real rules, something magical happens: You give other people permission to do the same.

When you negotiate your salary, you're setting a new standard for what people in your role should be paid. When you set boundaries around your time, you're showing others that it's possible to have a life outside of work. When you promote yourself shamelessly, you're demonstrating that competence combined with visibility is unstoppable.

Every time you use these cheat codes, you're not just changing your own trajectory—you're changing the game for everyone who comes after you, especially those who look like you, sound like you, or share your background.

The gatekeepers want to keep the cheat codes secret because their power depends on information scarcity. But information wants to be free. I'm handing you a bit of that freedom here; it's up to you to use it well and pay it forward.

Your Next Move

Don't let this book grow dusty on your shelf. Don't let it become another "great advice" conversation topic that you never actually implement.

The cheat codes in this book work. They've worked for me. They've worked for thousands of professionals I've coached. They'll work for you—but only if you actually use them.

These cheat codes aren't just one-and-done. You'll come back to them every time you hit a new level. The real challenge is figuring out which codes unlock something for you—whether it's today, next week, next month, or even a year from now. Here's your assignment:

> **Today:** Pick one cheat code that made you uncomfortable and implement it before you go to bed. The discomfort is the point—it means you're doing something different.
>
> **This week:** Have one conversation you've been avoiding. Ask for one thing you've been scared to request. Send one message to someone you've been wanting to connect with.
>
> **This month:** Make one strategic move that your old, permission-seeking self would never have attempted. Apply for that stretch role. Start that side hustle. Set that boundary. Ask for that promotion.
>
> **This year:** Become unrecognizable to your former self. Not because you've changed who you are, but because you've finally started acting like who you've always been: someone who deserves success and isn't afraid to claim it.

The Revolution Starts with You

The corporate world is changing, whether the old guard likes it or not. Remote work is normalizing flexibility. Social media is democratizing personal branding. The gig economy is proving that loyalty to companies who don't return it is financial suicide. Younger generations are refusing to accept "that's just how it is" as an answer to systemic inequities.

But change is slow. And you can't wait for the entire system to evolve before you start thriving within it.

So start your own revolution. Break the rules that were designed to keep you small. Use the cheat codes that the A Players have been hiding. Play the game better than the people who wrote it.

And when you're sitting in that corner office, cashing those bigger paychecks, setting those unapologetic boundaries, remember: None of this happened by accident. It happened because you decided that you deserved more than what you were being offered, and you had the audacity to go get it.

The career you want is waiting for you. But it's not going to come to you. You have to go claim it.

So what are you waiting for? An engraved invitation? A perfect moment? More preparation? The invitation is this book. The moment is now. You're already prepared.

The only question left is, are you ready to break the rules and finally start winning the game?

Your empire is waiting. Go build it.

Acknowledgments

Lucas, words will always fall short of what you've given me. You saw my potential when I couldn't see it myself and never let me settle for less than I was capable of. You are the most extraordinary partner I could ever dream of. I am endlessly grateful to walk this crazy journey with you. Gracias, mi amor.

Thea, you were the first to recognize the book waiting to be born, and you saw the diamond in the rough before it had taken shape. Thank you for your guidance—it has been a compass through every step of this process. And thank you to Lizzie, Sohayla, Kristin S., Kristin C., Dan, Allison, and the entire Ten Speed Press team for supporting this journey.

Jan and Lauren, your creativity, wisdom, and big-sister energy turned this journey into something that felt less like work and more like magic. You stood for me and poured your vision into shaping this book in ways I could never have dreamed of on my own. Quite simply, this book would not exist without you. Thank you.

Bailey, Kelsey, Naajidah, and all of Team CJ, this book was only possible because of your unwavering support behind the scenes. Thank you for being the force that kept everything moving. I couldn't have asked for a better team and I'm so lucky to have you all in my corner.

Ellen, thank you for reminding me of the stories I'd almost forgotten. Your generosity in connecting the dots helped shape the very outline of this book, and I'm endlessly grateful.

Thank you to Alexandria, Christa, Kaylin, Bari, the Fully Focused Community, and all of my other coworking and brainstorming partners for keeping me on task and accountable. Thank you, Simone, for holding space for conversations around deeper layers of this book. Thank you to my ALA family for facilitating the transformations that allowed me to be the person this book needed.

And to my clients, followers, listeners, and community, I'm so grateful for you. Your support has been the foundation beneath every word I've written. You've reminded me, over and over, that knowledge is meant to be shared, not gatekept. None of this would exist without you. I am endlessly grateful for the community we've built, the vision we've shared, and the world we're creating together.

Notes

1. Gettysburg College, "One Third of Your Life Is Spent at Work," www.gettysburg.edu/news/stories?id=79db7b34-630c-4f49-ad32-4ab9ea48e72b.
2. Carmine Gallo, "70% of Your Employees Hate Their Jobs," *Forbes*, November 11, 2011, www.forbes.com/sites/carminegallo/2011/11/11/your-emotionally-disconnected-employees/.
3. Chartered Management Institute, "Socio-Economic Background Is Seen as a Major Factor in Career Progression, Research Shows," press release, February 7, 2022, www.managers.org.uk/about-cmi/media-centre/press-releases/socio-economic-background-is-seen-as-a-major-factor-in-career-progression-research-shows/.
4. Steve Burns, "How Social Class Affects the Career Ladder," New Trader U, August 20, 2024, www.newtraderu.com/2024/08/20/how-social-class-affects-the-career-ladder/.
5. Daniel Laurison and Sam Friedman, "The Class Ceiling: Social Mobility and Why It Pays to Be Privileged," *Social Forces* 99, no. 1 (March 2020): e5, doi.org/10.1093/sf/soz170. See also UK Data Service, ukdataservice.ac.uk/case-study/the-class-ceiling-social-mobility-and-why-it-pays-to-be-privileged/.
6. Marianne Bertrand and Sendhil Mullainathan, "Are Emily and Greg More Employable than Lakisha and Jamal? A Field Experiment on Labor Market Discrimination," *The American Economic Review* 94, no. 4 (2004): 991–1013, www.jstor.org/stable/3592802. See also Alice G. Walton, "Think You're Not Racist? Research Uncovers Our Secret Prejudices, and Ways to Overcome Them," *Chicago Booth Review*, December 16, 2014, www.chicagobooth.edu/review/think-youre-not-racist.
7. Ernesto Reuben, Paola Sapienza, and Luigi Zingales, "How Stereotypes Impair Women's Careers in Science," *Proceedings of the National Academy of Sciences of the United States of America* 111, no. 12 (March 2014): 4403–8, doi.org/10.1073/pnas.1314788111. See also "Study Shows Strong Gender Bias in Hiring for Jobs Involving Basic Match," Kastner Kim LLP, www.kastnerkim.com/articles/study-shows-strong-gender-bias-in-hiring-for-jobs-involving-basic-math/.

8. Jacques Buffett, "170+ Must-Know Resume Statistics for Job Seekers in 2025," Enhancv, November 27, 2023, www.enhancv.com/blog/resume-statistics/.
9. Emily Gersema, "The Quality of Audio Influences Whether You Believe What You Hear," USC Today, April 17, 2018, today.usc.edu/why-we-believe-something-audio-sound-quality/.
10. Elena Bild, Annabel Redman, Eryn Newman, Bethany Muir, David Tait, and Norbert Schwarz, "Sound and Credibility in the Virtual Court: Low Audio Quality Leads to Less Favorable Evaluations of Witnesses and Lower Weighting of Evidence," *Law and Human Behavior* 45, no. 5 (October 2021): 481–95, doi.org/10.1037/lhb0000466.